Visions of the Merkabah Riders

The Chariot of Fire

By Mark F. Dennis

יהוה

שירה

A Golden Iris LLC
Publications   2014

*On the first day of the seventh
month, Ezra the priest
brought the law before the
assembly of men, women, and
all who could listen with
understanding... and they
read from the book of the
Law of God, distinctly
communicating its meaning,
so they could understand the
reading.*

Nehemiah 8

And it shall come to pass in the last days, God says,

"I will pour out my Spirit upon all flesh; and your sons and your young men shall see visions, and your old men shall dream dreams.

And on my servants and on my handmaidens I will pour out in those days of my Spirit; and they shall prophesy."

Joel 2:28-29

Table of Contents

Introduction ....**xxix**

    In the Beginning xxix

    Creation xxx

    Ancient Jewish Mysticism xxxi

    Four Worlds xxxii

    Fifth World..xxxiv

    Ten Sefiroth...xxxiv

    Sefiroth in Scripture xl

    Knowing God...xli

    Merkabah Riders...xliii

    Names of God xliv

    Bible Code - ELS xlvi

    Word Alignment xlvii

    Gematria...xlviii

    Temurah xlix

    What we Believe xlix

Jewish Mysticism **1**

Roots ***1***

Jewish Mystic Thought.....................................***1***

    The Almighty 1

The Creator...2

The Ten Sefiroth...2

Schools of Thought.......................................*3*

Practical Mysticism.......................................3

Speculative Mysticism 4

The Prophetic Prayer......................................5

Ten Sefiroth...**7**

Tree of Life..8

Three Pillars 8

Positive and Negative Attributes.........................10

The Four Worlds...*11*

Spiritual World of Atziluth 11

Sefiroth Kether...*11*

Sefiroth Hokhmah *12*

Sefiroth Binah *13*

The Trinity of Atziluth.................................*14*

Da'at...*16*

Moral World of Beri'ah 17

The Abyss...*17*

Sefiroth Hesed..*17*

Sefiroth Gevurah..*18*

Sefiroth Tifereth *18*

Throne of God *20*

Babel *21*

Metatron *22*

Seven Heavens *22*

Two Kingdoms *23*

Material and Sensual World of Yetzirah 24

Sefiroth Netsah. *24*

Sefiroth Hod. *24*

Sefiroth Yesod *24*

Earthly Kingdom of Assiah and Malkuth 25

The Greater and Lesser Countenance **26**

Macroprosopus 27

Microprosopus 27

The Light 29

Shekinah 30

Second Temple Mysticism 32

Chariot Mysticism **35**

Jewish Literature **35**

Chariot of Fire 35

Great Assembly 36

Babylonian Influences 37

Magi 37

Melchizedek 38

The Dead Sea Scrolls Translated 39

Moses 41

Names of God....................**43**

The 22 letter name of God....................43

The 42 letter name of God....................43

The 72 letter name of God....................44

72 Names of God/ Angels 45

The First Merkabah Riders **47**

Enoch Taken....................47

Enoch's Throne Vision....................48

Melchizedek 49

Abraham's Throne Vision 51

Moses Vision....................52

Elijah Taken 53

Isaiah's Throne Vision 54

Daniel's Throne Vision 56

Ezekiel's Throne Vision 57

John's Throne Vision 58

Solomon's Temple......................................**61**

    Sea of Glass....................................63

    Wheels of King Solomon's Throne...............64

    Enoch's Temple Visions 66

    Ezekiel's Temple Visions.....................68

    Zechariah's Seven Candlesticks...............70

    Throne of Zeus 72

    Intoxicants, Religion and Visions 73

Mystical Visions **75**

    Mansions of the Elect........................75

    Ezekiel's Wheel in a Wheel 76

    Four Living Creatures 77

    The Four Presences 79

    Shamash 79

    Twenty-four Elders of Revelation.............80

    Priestly Lineage............................82

    Daniel's Image 84

    John's Vision...............................85

    Daniel's Vision.............................85

    The Image of Adam...........................86

    Daniel's Last Vision........................86

The Book of Zechariah **89**

    Seven Candlesticks 90

    The Two Anointed Ones 90

    Seven Horns and Seven Eyes 92

    Four Horses 92

The Book of Isaiah **95**

    Holy, Holy, Holy 95

    Babylon has Fallen, has Fallen 96

The Books of Enoch **99**

Enoch I, II and III *99*

    History 99

    Son of Man 100

    Holy, Holy, Holy 102

Influences of Enoch *103*

    Enoch and Revelation 103

    Book of Hebrews 104

    Paul's Writings 105

    Teachings of Jesus 105

    Enoch and the Old Testament 107

    Enoch Lifespan 108

    Who was Enoch 109

Metatron, Melchizedek and Michael............111

Hermes and Enoch 113

Atenism 114

Ten heavens of Enoch 116

Jewish Priesthood **121**

History of the Priesthood.............121

Was Jesus a Levite?....................122

Jesus and John in Qumran 125

Cult of Aten...............................128

The Word Amen..........................129

Amara Hymn to Aten 130

Semitic Hyksos...........................132

Freemasonry 133

Mormonism 134

Names of God **135**

Jewish Writings 135

Ancient Hebrew Names of God 135

El 136

El Shaddai 136

El-Elyon 137

Elohim 138

YHWH (Jehovah)..139

Mount Sinai 140

El Replaced by YHWH:...........................143

Divine Light..**145**

First and Second Adam 145

Divine Light 145

Light of the World.................................147

Wisdom 147

Wisdom – The Firstborn of Creation 148

What is Salvation?.................................151

Essenes – Sons of Light 152

The Jewish Calendar 153

Jewish Magic **155**

Prohibition 155

White Magic 157

Miracles or Magic 159

Semantics 160

Origins of Magic 161

Torah Code **163**

Jewish Numerology 163

Gematria Code..164

ELS Code 165

Temurah Code 167

Jewish Numerology 169

The Magic Cube 170

Value of Bible Code 171

History of Israel **173**

Israel's Captivity 173

Battle of Carchemish 173

Megiddo 174

Temple Destroyed 174

Cyrus the Great.............................175

Alexander the Great 176

Seleucid Empire 177

Antiochus IV Epiphanes...............177

The Temple Desecrated.................178

Second Temple Destroyed 178

Masada 179

The Rise of Gnosticism **181**

Gnosticism.....................................181

Gnostic Symbolism 181

Fountains of Wisdom *182*

xix

The Elect One *183*

Gnostic Mysteries in the Gospel of John 183

Logos 184

Son of God 189

A Knowable God 190

Gnostic Mysticism in Paul's Epistles 192

Paul's Visions 193

Other Mystic Attributes 193

Extended and Lesser Countenance 195

The Mediator 197

Redemption 198

Fruit of the Spirit 199

Christianity **201**

Who Really Was Jesus? 201

Birth of Christianity 201

Synoptic Gospels 203

Gnostic Gospels 203

Orthodox Christian Doctrine 206

Mysticism in Jesus' Teachings **209**

Jesus and the Law of Moses 209

Knowing God 210

Gnostic Doctrine 211

The Word..213

Questions...214

One With God 215

Jewish Mysticism 216

Light of the World...218

Salvation..220

Bridegroom and Bride.....................................221

By Their Fruits 222

Other Mystic Similarities 223

Jesus and the Ten Sefiroth...............................224

Patience 231

Jesus as a Merkabah Rider 232

Mysticism in the Book of Hebrews...............233

Veil of the Temple...234

The Death of Christ 235

The Suffering Servant 237

Biblical Extra...238

Kingdom of Heaven **239**

Historical Jewish View....................................239

Freedom from Rome 240

Beatitudes Matthew 5:3-10 242

Message of Hope 242

Salvation in this Life or After? 243

What is the Kingdom of God? 244

History of Israel 244

King of the Jews 248

The Messiah 249

Perspectives 250

The Last Merkabah Rider **253**

Mohammed's Night Journey 253

Knowing God 254

Teachings 255

Who was Jesus? 256

Docetism 257

Creation **259**

Spiritual Kingdom *259*

Wisdom, Knowledge and Understanding.....260

Gaining Wisdom and Knowledge: 261

Earthly Kingdom 262

Redemption 263

Wisdom's Rebuke: 264

Mysticism and the Fall 267

    Fall of Man 267

    Fall of Lucifer 269

    Fall of Man 270

Conclusion **273**

    In the Beginning 273

    The Bride 275

    The Merkabah Riders 275

    The Messiah 276

    Son of God 277

    Ten Sefiroth 278

    Knowledge of Good and Evil 278

    Tree of Life 278

    Mother and Father 279

    The Message 281

    Salvation 282

    Role of Religions 287

    Personal Salvation 288

    A Universal Truth 293

References *299*

Index *307*

For my children, Analise
and Jared, who have
grown up so fast.

Be a Light to those
around you!

Have vision, have faith
and belief in yourself.

You can accomplish what
you set out do!

Dream big!

Visions of the Merkabah Riders

The Chariot of Fire

Introduction

In the Beginning

In the beginning there was only God. This is the Almighty God, the Alpha and Omega, God without beginning or end. In Hebrew, God is called, *She-en lo tiklah*, the "Endless One," *Ein-Sof*, סוף אין, the "Infinite God" and "nothingness" (Ponce' pg. 73).

In ancient Jewish teachings, before God created anything at all, He was alone, without any form and without resemblance to anything else because there was nothing else (Bulgakov, pg. 141). This God could have no desire, no thought, no word, or action that could be attributed to Him by man. He was incomprehensible, unknowable and without name. Just in the nature of having a name, God in fact would have limitations applied to Him. To the ancient Jews, it was forbidden to create an image of Him or to even say or write a sacred name ascribed to Him. Even in conservative Jewish writings today, the word God is often spelled as G-d and called the ineffable or indescribable one.

*Revelation 19:12 ...His eyes were as a flame of fire, and on his head were many crowns; and he **had a name** written, **that no man knew**, but he himself.*

Creation

After God created the first of His creations, God could be revealed in a "limited" way through the creation of His hands. After He created the form of the "Heavenly Man," *Adam Kadmon*, a form created in His own image, God could walk and talk with him in the Garden (Ponce' pg. 70). Here in the Garden, Adam could relate to God and "know" Him in a "limited" way, having a relationship and the ability to "spend time" with God. This spiritual Adam was created in the very beginning; *for from the beginning to the end you have formed me* (Psalm 139:5), and was a "companion" of God; within Adam's sinless human form existed all of God's divine elements and attributes.

Jewish theology taught that this Adam was the Spirit of the "Messiah" that *"moved upon the face of the waters"* in Genesis chapter 1. In Isaiah 11:2, this is the Spirit of the Lord (Kether and Netsah), that will rest on the earthly (Malkuth) Messiah with the Spirit of Wisdom (Hokhmah) and Understanding (Binah), the Spirit of Advice (Hesed and Yesod) and Power (Gevurah), the Spirit of Knowledge (Da'at) and the Awe (Tifereth and Hod) of the God. This is the form of the spiritual Adam which was the "chariot" in which the light of God would descend; this "knowable" form of God is called the sacred name 'YHWH' in the Zohar (Smetham, pg. 376).

Ancient Jewish Mysticism

The word mystic to most conservatives or orthodox of any faith many times is troubling. Paganism, witchcraft, black magic, the occult and even Satan worship are often mistakenly associated with mysticism. The fundamentals of Jewish or Judaic mysticism are relatively basic and in many ways mirror many faiths in existence today. This faith was based on the belief that there is only one God, the Almighty God who is indescribable. However, through creation and through God's revealed Word, these early believers taught that God could be "known" in a personal way through ten "human like" characteristics or attributes. These devout believers taught that God was knowable and that anyone could develop a personal relationship with him outside of the pious structure of established religion.

It was during the Reformation in Europe, at the turn of the Middle Ages, that reformers like Martin Luther and John Calvin began to teach a very similar theology, that salvation was through faith and by the grace of God, not through the Church nor the works of man. This teaching caused a split in the Roman Catholic Church and the Protestant era began.

This ancient Jewish mysticism goes back beyond the time of David and even before the days of Abraham. The foundation of the mystic teachings was in the Ten Sefiroth and the Four Worlds – the Tree of Life, the source of God's Light that gives life to man.

Four Worlds

These divine elements are expressed in ten different "divine attributes" or Sefiroth that were visualized within the original image of man before the "fall." These attributes are simply anthropomorphic personifications or characteristics of human nature that are attributed to God in an effort to "know" and "understand" Him. These personifications of God are expressed in feminine, masculine and neutral characteristics, the three pillars to Jewish mysticism. Horizontally, these attributes are separated into the Four World's or Realms; Spiritual, Moral, Sensual and Physical (Ponce' pg. 68).

In the Jewish mystic pictorial representation of the **Tree of Life**, the **Ten Sefiroth** are divided up into these four worlds; *Atziluth, Beri'ah, Yetzirah* and *Assiah*. The source of these four worlds comes from the book of Isaiah chapter 43 and from these four words, "Glory," "Created," "Formed" and "Made."

Isaiah says this:

Isaiah 43:7 ...Every one that is called by My name and for My glory (Atziluth), I have created (Beri'ah), I have formed (Yetzirah), even I have made (Assiah).

These four worlds are parallel to the four elements of air, (Aquarius), Fire (Leo), Earth (Taurus) and Water (Scorpio). In Ezekiel the four faces of a man, lion, ox, and eagle are closely related (Ezekiel 1:10 & Rev. 4:7).

Atziluth is the first world, the Spiritual realm of God, <u>hidden</u> from mankind. This is the world that emanates the Light of God down to man, the source of Life, the **Glory** of God. Here resides the first and highest triad of Sefiroth or attributes of God; *Crown,* which represents Ein-Sof, *Wisdom* and *Understanding.*

Beri'ah is the second world, the Moral world, the world of the throne of judgment. This moral world is a world that can discern right from wrong and good from evil. Here the light of God in the Spiritual world emanates down into the **Created** world, the Higher Garden of Eden, giving light for the path of righteousness and is the habitation of righteous. Wisdom and Understanding in the upper triad together create Knowledge or Da'at which feed down to this next triad of *Loving-kindness, Beauty* and *Strength.*

Yetzirah is third world, the **Formed** world, the world of the senses, desire and of emotion; also called the Lower Garden of Eden. It is here that the desire to "Know" God arises. The triad of *Eternity, Foundation* and *Splendor* reside here.

Assiah is the fourth world, the **Made** world, the earthly kingdom of man, the **Bride**. The three upper worlds each contain three triads of God's attributes. This last and lowest world only has one attribute called *Malkuth.*

> *Isaiah 62:4-5 …Your new name will be "The City of God's Delight" … for the Lord delights in you and will claim you as his **bride**.*

Fifth World

A fifth world is sometimes visualized; the world of the first creation before the fall, the world of *Adam Kadmon* where only good existed and where man walked with God. This first Adam is united with God as seen in the attribute symbol of the crown, Kether of the hidden Spiritual World. At this point the ten Sefiroth were expressed as vessels that contained the light of God. It was in the shattering (*Shevirah*) of these vessels that creation occurred and the Knowledge of both good and evil was revealed; the act of disobedience was the cause, the fall of man. These Sefiroth are the powers that serve to bind the structure of the world together. The fifth world also can represent the Messianic Age when mankind is renewed through *Tikkun*, where the shattered vessels that held God's Light and Glory are reconstructed, restored and reunited with God (Leet, pg. 25).

Ten Sefiroth

In the First World of **Atziluth** is the first triad.

Kether - רֶתֶּכ - "Crown" or "Authority" is the topmost of the Sefiroth of the Tree of Life and is the source of endless light, the light that gives life to mankind. This is the Bridegroom of the earthly Bride Malkuth. The crown also represents Ein-Sof, the Almighty unknowable God and spiritual Abba, the **Father** of creation. This is the highest level where the Throne of God resides and is above comprehension.

As you will see throughout this text, these ten Sefiroth or attributes of the "one" God can be seen throughout the Scriptures.

> *1 Timothy 1:17 Now unto the **King eternal, immortal, invisible,** the only **wise God,** be **honor** and **glory forever** and ever. Amen.*

Hokhmah - חכמה - "Wisdom" is the masculine Sefiroth in the Spiritual World; as Job says, "Wisdom comes from nothingness." Proverbs says that Wisdom was from the beginning before anything was made, as the *"first of His works."* Wisdom is the first manifestation of awareness and intellect. Wisdom with Understanding is Knowledge.

> *Jude 1:25 ...To the only **wise** God our Savior, be **glory** and **majesty, authority** and **power,** both now and **forever.** Amen.*

Binah - בינה - "Understanding" or "Discernment" is the feminine Sefiroth of the Spiritual World. Understanding is processed Wisdom that creates Knowledge. She is also considered the Spiritual **Mother,** Imma, from her womb creation was formed.

Da'at – דעת – "Knowledge" or "Reason" is not a true Sefiroth but represents the upper triad of Kether, Hokhmah and Binah as the "revealed" light of God. If Da'at is shown in the Tree of Life as a Sefiroth, then Kether is not normally shown; one or the other.

The definition of knowledge is having "*awareness*," and "*understanding gained through experience*." This is the Divine Light of God revealed to the World, Malkuth. It can be said that all ten Sefiroth are united as one and seen as Da'at, the "*Light of the World.*"

> *Exodus 31:3 ...I've filled him with the **Spirit of God**, with **wisdom**, **understanding** and **knowledge**.*

In the Second World of **Beri'ah** is the second triad.

Hesed – חֶסֶד - "Kindness" or "Loving Kindness" is the source of restoration called *Tikkun olam*. Grace, Mercy and Compassion are components of this attribute. The Greek word *Agape* referenced in I Corinthians chapter 13 is a major principle in Paul's writings and Jesus refers to Hesed in Matthew 22:36 as the most important commandment in the law of Moses, to 'love the Lord your God with all your heart, all your soul, and all your mind.' This is a steadfast love, the love of God expressed in His Covenant to mankind, God's love for his people Israel.

> *1 John 4:16 ...**God is love**. Whoever lives in love lives in God, and God in them.*

Gevurah – גבורה - "Power," "Strength" or "Justice." This is the power of God seen in creation and in His judgment of evil in the world.

Psalm 71:16 ...Lord GOD, I will come in the **power** *of your mighty acts. I will proclaim your* **justice***.*

Tifereth – "Beauty," "Compassion" or "Glory" mediates between Hesed and Gevurah; also a balance of Justice and Mercy. This also represents Ze`ir Anpin, the **Son** of Kether or Abba, the **Father** of **creation** and Binah the **Mother**, Imma, from her womb **creation** was formed. The **Son** is the Lesser Countenance, the revealed image of God as the **bridegroom**, the Messiah with Shekinah and Malkuth as the bride.

Hebrews 1:3 ... His **Son** *is the reflection of God's* **glory** *and the exact* **likeness of God's being***.** *He holds everything together through his powerful words. After he had cleansed people from their sins, he received the highest position, the one next to* **the Father** *in heaven.*

The Third World of Yetzirah has the third triad.

Netsah – "Eternity," "Firmness," "Sincerity" "Victory" a means to an end, making choices in one's day-to-day life. It also implies Truth, Patience and Confidence.

Psalm 86:15 ...But you, Lord, are a **compassionate** *God,* **merciful** *and* **_patient_***, with* **_unending_ gracious love** *and* **faithfulness***.*

Hod – "Splendor," "Majesty," "Humility," "Gratitude." An acknowledgment of the Divine splendor; recognizing God's presence and influence in the world.

*Psalm 104:1 ...Lord my God, you are very great; you are clothed with **splendor** and **majesty**.*

Yesod – "Foundation," the channel in which God and the Shekinah strive to reunited with each other. Mankind reaching up to God and God down to man. This Sefiroth directly connects man with the three upper worlds, the world of the senses, moral and spiritual worlds. This is the foundation on which all the other Sefiroth rest. This is the foundation of relationships, both with God and man.

*Luke 6:48 ...They are like a man building a house, who dug down deep and laid the **foundation** on rock.*

The Fourth World of **Assiah** has on attribute.

Malkuth – "Earthly Kingdom" is not an attribute of God but a reflection of God through His creation.

Revelation 11:15 ...The kingdom of the world has become the kingdom of our Lord...

Jewish mysticism symbolized this attribute as the **Bride** which is sometimes called Shekinah, the glory of God and the **Bridegroom** is God. This bride is often visualized as a forlorn bride that is separated from her husband, longing for the day of his return.

*Matthew 25:1-6 ...At that time the kingdom of heaven will be like ten virgins who took their **lamps** and went out to meet the **bridegroom**.*

*Five of them were foolish and five were wise. The foolish ones took their **lamps** but did not take any oil with them.*

*The wise ones, however, took oil in jars along with their lamps. The **bridegroom** was a long time in coming, and they all became drowsy and fell asleep.*

At midnight the cry rang out: 'Here's the bridegroom! Come out to meet him!'

Isaiah portrays the Bride as Jerusalem and Israel awaiting the coming of the Messiah. Judaic mystics saw the Sabbath as a time when the Bride and Bridegroom reunite for twenty-five hours. The book of Revelation envisions the Bride of the "Lamb" as the 'Church" but also in reference to the "New Jerusalem."

Sefiroth in Scripture

*Isaiah 11:2 ...This is the Spirit of the Lord that will rest on the **earthly** Messiah with the Spirit of **Wisdom** and **Understanding**, the Spirit of **Mercy** and **Power**, the Spirit of **Knowledge** in **Awe** of God Almighty.*

David's Prayer:

*1 Chronicles 29:11 ...Yours, Lord, is the **greatness** and the **power** and the **glory** and the **majesty** and the **splendor**, for everything in heaven and earth is yours. Yours, Lord, is the **kingdom**; you are exalted as head over all.*

The Lord's Prayer:

*Matthew 6:13 ...For yours is the **kingdom**, and the **power**, and the **glory**, forever. Amen*

Solomon's Wisdom:

*2 Chronicles 2:12 ...And Hiram said, "Blessed is Jehovah, God of Israel, who made the heavens and the earth, who hath given to David the king a wise son, **knowing wisdom** and **understanding**, who doth build a house for Jehovah, and a house for his **kingdom.**"*

God's Power and Loving-kindness:

*Psalm 59:16 ...But I will sing of your **strength**, in the morning I will sing of your **love**; for you are my **fortress**, my refuge in times of trouble.*

The word *sefer* means "scroll," or "book" in Hebrew:

*Revelation 20:12 ...And I saw the dead, great and small, standing before the throne, and **books were opened**.*

*Another book was opened, which is the **book of life**. The dead were judged according to what they had done as recorded in the **books**.*

Knowing God

Jewish mysticism seeks to understand that which is not said, to read between the words of Scripture and gain knowledge and understand what is not understood. It is an esoteric **doctrine**, defined as understood by only a few, a secret **doctrine** if you will. Deep within these believers is a strong desire to unify with the divine, to know God; this is accomplished only through deep meditation and reflection.

In order to know God, mankind had to pray and meditate, dwelling on Him. Jewish mystics believed that this was a "personal relationship" based on devotion, without the need for priests or religious rituals. It was rooted in the fervent belief that the

Torah, the five books of Moses, were the revelation of God and the "Word of God." The Torah in fact was the story of the "life of God" revealed to Moses; it was inspired by God and could not be changed not even by one "jot or tittle." These are the little strokes over the Hebrew letters called crowns and spikes providing pronunciation.

Since the Torah was the "secret life of God," the "story of God," it contained His names; in fact the Torah is one long name of God. This story of God existed with Him long before creation and by definition, was God. Before creation, the words of the Torah had always existed with God but were jumbled up and without form; the Torah was the blueprint for **creation** (Ponce' pg. 27). At the point of creation, as **creation** came into being, the words, phrases and sentences of the "life of God" began to take form; changing the words of the Torah was an impossibility as this would in fact change creation and change God. This "Word of God" was viewed as a "living organism" to these believers and in it was contained the "Spirit of God" that gives mankind life. The mystic believed that in meditating on the Word of God, God reveals Himself personally in a way that is reserved specifically for those who desire "knowing" Him (Ponce' pg. 28-29). There was an attempt by Ezra as seen in Nehemiah chapter 8 with the use of the "Oral Torah," to expound on the meaning of the Word to the common people.

This could not be "written" as that would change the Word of God.

*Nehemiah 8:8 ...and they read from the book of the Law of God, distinctly **communicating its meaning**, so they could **understand** the reading.*

To the mystic, this was blasphemous, because God's revelation was personal; this Oral Torah was replacing the 'spoken' words of God. This interpretation of the Law would continue and was memorized at first; eventually however it was written down in the Mishna and the Talmud.

In an attempt to satisfy a deep desire to know God and become one with God, the Jewish mystic ventured beyond the traditional rituals of Judaism and focused on a personal journey. Rather than "doing" what was required of the Law to "appease" God in hope of His "approval," the Jewish mystic emulated the traits of the ten Sefiroth, refining one's self as gold in a fire and "being" more "godly" or "God like". In this way, they became a light to the world and able in a way to become one with God. Developing one's self with the spirit of loving kindness along with these other traits was considered the best way to "know" God.

Merkabah Riders

The journey to experience the divine nature of God for many of these devoted, began with isolating one's self in prayer. Through fasting, prayer, the burning of Frankincense and the repetitious recitation of hymns, they would come to the point of entering a trance. In knowing the Torah and meditating on the names of God in the Torah, these mystics would enter into visionary experiences that brought them into what they perceived to be the dwelling place of God. These were expressed as visions of palaces or temples with great hallways and passageways, leading to various levels known as heavens, up to the highest heaven, to the throne of God (Ponce' pg. 55).

These were the visions of the Merkabah Riders, (Ponce' pg. 57) those who were able to achieve a state of "ascension," and ascend to the throne-chariot of God. To many, these Merkabah Riders were the likes of Enoch, Moses, Elijah, Ezekiel, Isaiah, Daniel, John, Peter, Paul and even Jesus. Most of the writings of these types of visions were written during the periods immediately after the destruction of the First Jewish Temple of Solomon in 586 BC and the Second Temple in 70 AD.

Names of God

It was through the knowledge of the Torah and the **names of God** that these visions were revealed. The **names of God** have been interpreted in various ways throughout the centuries; many of these names of God were revealed in His attributes which were expressed in the ten Sefiroth reviewed previously. Through these names, the mystic was also able to invoke "good" powers which some refer to as "white" magic (Ponce' pg. 15).

For this purpose, the name of God was holy.

Exodus 20:7...You shall not take the name of the Lord your God in vain, for the Lord will not hold him guiltless who takes his name in vain.

Since the ancient Hebrew is an *Abjad* language, a language that did not use vowels when written, the correct pronunciation of the names of God has been lost to time, unless secretly kept known within certain secret societies. An example in English would be like this: "*mk sntnc wtht vwls.*" Only those who know English and are familiar with the words and context being written could know what the sentence above says. Likewise, only with the knowledge of Hebrew and specific "secret" knowledge, could the correct pronunciation of God's names be known. Only with the correct pronunciation could the powers of God be called upon to work "miracles" or "magic" for good (Ponce' pg. 15).

The greatest name of God was considered to be the Torah itself when made into one long word. The forty-two letter name of God comes from the first forty-two letters of the Torah (Ponce' pg. 183). Another **name** most familiar to Jews and Christians alike is the **name** YHWH, known as the Tetragrammaton or Yahweh, also interpreted as Jehovah; this is the "I am that I am" of Exodus 3 :14. YHWH is spelled without vowels and the word Yahweh using an "a" and an "e" is only an assumption; the name may have been pronounced "Yohwuh" or "Yehwah," we do not know.

xlv

Some of these names such as the forty-two letter name were secret and only spoken by the High Priest at certain occasions; these were passed down from father to son or teacher to student (By the way, the letter "A" or "Aleph" is a modifier and not a vowel).

יתצאבג שטנקרע יכשנגד צתגבטר טנעחקב ופזקיגל ציתשק

Romanized this name was spelled like this; the pronunciation is not known today as the vowels between the consonants are not given.

ABG YTS QRA STV NGO YCS BTR STG CQB TNA YGL PZ SQVSYT

The seventy-two letter names of God comes from Exodus 14:19-21 and is known as the Shem Ha Mephorash or "The Divided Name." Each of these three verses contain 72 letters; combined, this is the 216 **letter name** of God. Recombined, seventy-two three **letter names** of God are also created; in the Zohar these are the 72 angels of Jacob's Ladder. It is only through coincidence, one might say, that these three verses in a row each contain the exact number of seventy-two letters.

Bible Code - ELS

Jewish mystics did not see these mysteries in Scripture as coincidence but see all of this as a mysterious code written by God throughout their Scripture of that day; this was the revelation of God in the Torah.

This code was seen in many different ways such as significant meaningful words or names of God that could be reversed, vertical or diagonally across the page. One technique used to find these "coincidences" is the process called Equidistant Letter Sequence or ELS; a way to find the hidden coded words in the Torah, very much like a crossword puzzle. One such example is that in the book of Genesis; if you start with the first letter and count fifty letters, then fifty more and so on, the Hebrew word for Torah gets spelled out. In Isaiah 53:10 beginning with the second Hebrew letter yod, if you count every 20th letter, the phrase Yeshua Shmi is found which means "Yeshua is My Name".

This in part is why the written Torah in Hebrew can never be changed; one little change in spelling or adding a word would destroy this code. This code is put in Scripture because it is the Story of God, not only holding historical truths but also written prophecy of the future in code; of things not yet taken place.

Word Alignment

This all may seem to happen by chance just like "letter name" and "name" align themselves by "chance" on the previous pages and "names of God" align by "chance" on the page before; not being intentional at all, all three have the word "name." If you look close throughout any text, you will see a sort of "code" like structure throughout it. Sometimes even the spaces between words on a page line up evenly for some mysterious reason making a straight or diagonal line.

Some words that align throughout this text have been put in bold print for awareness of this. Unlike the text of this book, the Torah is structured with strict rules of word position. The Torah is normally written with two columns of forty-two rows in each column per page; this way the alignments stay the same. The text of this book is not a new revelation, nor is it inspired by God; this text has no such structure and in the writers opinion, these aligned words simply happened by chance. Could it be possible that the words that align here are there to get our attention because of something important that is being said in the connected text?

Gematria

Another type of Jewish Biblical code is in numerology. As previously reviewed, ancient Hebrew like many other Semitic languages had no vowels. Not only did Hebrew not have vowels utilized in its writings, there also were no numbers. In Hebrew, the **letters** of their alphabet are used for the dual purpose of **letters** and numbers. This led to a practice known as Gematria where a numerical value can be given to words or phrases. Gematria values of words are often compared with other words. Since numbers and letters were the same symbols, words, or phrases could have numerical equivalence to other words or phrases and every word or phrase would have its own numerical value. Hesed or loving kindness in English for example is spelled with the three letters; Cheth **with the value** 8, Samech with the value 60, and Daleth **with the value** 4, with the sum totaling 72.

As we have already seen, the number **72** has a lot of meaning in Jewish tradition such as the **72** letter name of God and the 72 angels. The number of disciples Jesus sent out in Luke10:1 was also seventy-two.

Temurah

Another type of Biblical code is called Atbash code or Temurah which means "exchange". This was the practice of switching or exchanging out one letter for another in order to hide its true meaning. The word Atbash is derived from the first, last, second, and next-to-last letters of the Hebrew alphabet: Aleph, Taw, Beth and Shin.

The letter A may be substituted with the letter B for example and B with C or the letter A may be substituted with Z and B with Y and so on; with a "key" this code can be broken.

What we Believe

In reading this book, the fundamentals of Jewish, Islam and Christian theologies are made more clear. In understanding what the ancient Jews really believed and what certain terms meant in their day and age, we today can come to understand more of what we believe and why we believe it. We will also see that over time, influences of other nations during the time of occupation or captivity of Israel caused changes in belief and misinterpretation of old beliefs due to cultural and religious differences.

After reading this book, be aware, it may be for certain that your perspective on other people's beliefs as well as your own beliefs will change – your mind will be opened. You will begin to see people around you in a different light; that glow that you may notice in others will be understood to be that divine spark that has the potential to become a light to the world. You will notice that beauty, Tifereth, that shines on ones face, that comes from the heart, will someday bring change to the world; this is at the heart of the Kingdom of God.

Luke 17:21 ... "You see, the kingdom of God is within you."

1

Jewish Mysticism

Roots

It is believed by many that Jewish mysticism began with Moses when he was given the Law of God at Mount Sinai. Many others believe it began with Abraham and his ascension on Merkabah, the throne-chariot of God. Others yet believe that these mystic beliefs began far earlier, back to the times of Enoch and his ascension into the Seven Heavens (II Enoch 20:1).

Ancient Jewish mysticism is the source of Medieval Kabbalah, meaning "received tradition," knowledge that was only passed down only by the "elect" for centuries and branched out into Christian mysticism in the Medieval ages. Judaic mysticism attempted to reach beyond the intellectual understanding of Judaism and its teachings and tried to satisfy the human needs of many to experience a personal relationship with the Divine. A desire that strived to encounter God directly without the intercession of priests and clergy, religious liturgy and rituals. A desire to know God and attain unity with Him (Leet, pg. 158).

Jewish Mystic Thought

The three main points of Jewish mystic thought are:

The Almighty God referred to as Ein-Sof, the limitless, unknowable God, is a God without beginning or end. He is the Endless One, the Alpha and Omega who cannot be comprehended and is far above the ability of man to understand.

1

The Creator God of the Bible is viewed as a "Limited" God, one who is described in such a way that can be somewhat understood. A "knowable" God; a God that could walk and talk with Adam in the Garden before the fall of man (Ponce' pg. 15).

The Ten Sefiroth – these are the ten attributes of the "incomprehensible God" (Ein-Sof) divided up into four worlds (Ponce' pg. 67-68): Ancient Jewish teachings had Seven Heavens and even Ten Heavens (II Enoch 22).

Atziluth (First World – Spiritual)

1) Kether – "Crown"
2) Hokhmah – "Wisdom"
3) Binah – "Understanding"

Beri'ah (Second World – Moral)

1) Hesed – "Kindness"
2) Gevurah – "Severity"
3) Tifereth – "Beauty"

Yetzirah (Third World –Sensual)

1) Netsah – "Eternity"
2) Hod – "Splendor"
3) Yesod – "Foundation"

Assiah (Fourth World – Bridegroom)

1) Malkuth – "Earthly Kingdom"

Schools of Thought

The main branches of Jewish mysticism are the Practical or magical school of thought and the Speculative or philosophical school of thought.

Practical Mysticism

The practical school of thought involved heavily guarded teachings and focused on the ability to invoke the powers of God for spiritual knowledge. Abuse of such power for selfish gain was considered black magic; white magic utilized these powers for furthering ones spiritual needs. These powers were invoked by using the names of God and His angels within the secret constructs of the Jewish faith and rituals.

The simple act of prayer and saying a blessing utilizing the name of God is a form of white magic as well as the ritual of breaking a glass in a Jewish wedding. These were powers derived from God and not one's self; these were for Predictive, Preventative, Curative, and Creative reasons that were beneficial to individuals and society. Because the world was believed to be filled with evil, these rituals helped protect from malevolent forces (Sherwin, pg. 197-198).

During the Medieval period, the Christian Church condemned such practices as Satanic, leading to the execution of millions of people in what is called the Inquisition today. This was an attempt by the Roman Catholic Church to wage a war against heresy of which lasted for about two hundred years. This involved witch hunts and searches for heretical teachings in which in many people were being "burned at the stake" Mass burnings of books were also held resulting in the loss of many ancient manuscripts forever.

Speculative Mysticism

The speculative or contemplative school of thought in Jewish mysticism had its beginnings in Babylonia and focuses on the theological or philosophical aspects of the Jewish religion. Seeking only to understand, they mostly have not been supportive of the magical and practical aspects of the practice. Instead of magic, they study the working organization of the **ten Sefiroth**, the doctrine of Gnosis or spiritual knowledge; the feeding Ein-Sof's, the Almighty God's life force (Ponce', p 15) and creativeness down into the fourth world of man. Here the incomprehensible Divine spirit is revealed to His creation and God can be "known." Here the relationship of finite man and his soul with an infinite God is sought to be understood.

Although this "division" of God into the ten Sefiroth seems to be pantheistic, Judaism strongly believes in God's Oneness, that there is only one God; these Sefiroth are ten of God's attributes, emanations or "names" of God. This doctrine merely strives to read between the lines and explain what is not ordinarily explained, how that God before creation was "unexplainable," so much so that He did not even have a name. Simply stated as *Ehyeh Asher Ehyeh*, "I am that I am" (Ponce' pg. 174).

It was during creation that God created man in His own image and in His likeness; in such a way that they could commune, walk and talk together in the Garden. These ten Sefiroth are ten ways that God makes Himself, the "incomprehensible" God, "knowable" to mankind.

The Prophetic Prayer

Ehyeh Asher Ehyeh Crown me (Kether).

Yah, grant me Wisdom (Hokhmah).

Elohim Chaim, grant me Understanding (Binah).

El, with the right hand of His Love, make me great (Hesed).

Elohim, from the Terror of His Judgment, protect me (Gevurah).

YHWH, with His mercy, grant me Beauty (Tifereth).

Adonai Tzevaot, watch me Forever (Netsah)

Elohim Tzevaot, grant me beatitude from His Splendor (Hod).

El Chai, make His covenant my Foundation (Yesod).

*Adonai, open my lips and my mouth will speak of Your praise and Kingdom (*Malkuth*)*

(Kaplan, pg. 165)

Visions of the Merkabah Riders

Ten Sefiroth

There are ten of God's attributes or Sefiroth that are shared with man in creation; *Kether* – Crown or Knowledge (Da'at), *Hokhmah* - Wisdom, *Binah* - Understanding, *Hesed* - Kindness, *Gevurah* - Power, *Tifereth* - Beauty, *Netsah* - Eternity, *Hod* - Splendor, *Yesod* - Foundation and *Malkuth* - Kingdom.

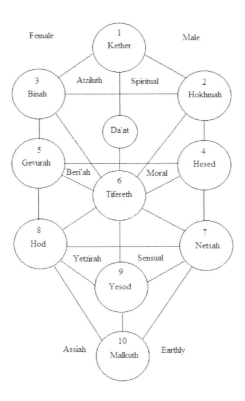

Tree of Life

These ten Sefiroth are split up into Four Worlds by three's known as triads in the Judaic Tree of Life. These four worlds are *Atziluth*, the Spiritual World and the highest of these worlds; *Beri'ah*, the Moral World; *Yetzirah* the Material and Sensual World and *Assiah*, the Earthly Kingdom.

The ten attributes can be seen as both the attributes of God and the good attributes of mankind; this is the Light of the World spoken of by Jesus. Darkness came upon man through evil and negative attributes by disobedience to God; through these came pain, suffering and death; thus the need for salvation. Only through the life giving light of God shining down through His "knowable" attributes and the life giving light of God shining out from those among mankind who let the light of God shine through them, can the world have Life. This is the Tree of Life from which Living Water flows.

Three Pillars

The Tree of Life is vertically in the form of three pillars (Ponce' pg. 143); the right side is considered masculine, the Pillar of Mercy. On the left side of the Tree of Life is the feminine attributes of God, the Pillar of Strength. In the center is a pillar that is neutral in gender attributes, the Middle Pillar, the pillar of Equilibrium, Mildness and Compassion. This neutral, central pillar as well as the other two pillars rests on Yesod, the Foundation or Cornerstone that all other attributes of God rest. Each triad of this tree therefore horizontally has its male and female attributes, balanced counterparts which are all attributes of God; mankind, being created in God's image is likewise male and female.

Hebrew is read right to left, therefore these Sefiroth are shown numbered right to left. The light of God descends vertically down to man in *Malkuth* through these three pillars of the Tree of Life; spiritually man in his commune with God in meditation and prayer, attempts to ascend vertically to God through these three pillars. These pillars can be viewed as the support to the Temple or House of God, the palaces that the Merkabah Riders ascend to in their visions of God's throne-chariot.

Psalm 23:6 ...Surely, **Compassion** *and* **Loving-kindness** *shall follow me all the days of my life; and I will dwell in* **the house of Lord** *forever.*

Another perspective of the Tree of Life figuratively combines the Tree of Life with the Tree of Knowledge of Good and Evil. In this illustration, the tree of Life is the center pillar, the "narrow road" or the "eye of the needle" (Prophet, pg. 30). The pillar on the right signifies the "knowledge of Good" and the pillar on the left signifies the "knowledge of Evil" (Waite, pg. 201).

Positive and Negative Attributes

The positive and good attributes of Light are Spiritual Leadership, Royalty and Knowledge; Wisdom, Understanding; Kindness, Mercy, Strength, Power, Beauty, Glory, Compassion; Eternity, Splendor, Foundation and Earthly leadership and royalty.

Negative and Dark attributes of man after the Fall are Inability, Weakness, Subservience, Powerlessness, Ignorance, Thoughtlessness, Instability, Cowardice, Idleness, Hatred, Anger, Carelessness, Ugliness, Finiteness, Fear, Lost-ness and Frustration.

This is the Kingdom of Darkness vs. the Kingdom of Light. A longing to be rescued or saved from the pain and agony of this world lives in the heart of every man.

Jesus makes reference to these human attributes that are in the heart of man in the book of Matthew:

Matthew 15:19 ...For from the heart come evil thoughts, murder, adultery, all sexual immorality, theft, lying, and slander.

Paul speaks of the two kingdoms in the book of Colossians:

*Colossians 1:13 ...For he has **rescued** us from the **kingdom of darkness** and brought us into the **kingdom of the Son** he loves.*

The Four Worlds

Spiritual World of Atziluth

Atziluth, the Spiritual World, is where the three spheres or triad's of *Kether, Hokhmah* and *Binah* are found and where the Sefiroth originally dwelled at the time of creation. This was a hidden incomprehensible God; in this world, God and his Shekinah glory or light, His feminine side, became the union that would create the next three worlds. During the "Fall" of mankind, this Shekinah became separated from God just as man became separated from Him. This is the spiritual world as in the power of the Spirit seen in the book of Numbers.

Numbers 11:17 ...I will come down and speak with you there, and I will take some of the power of the Spirit that is on you and put it on them.

Sefiroth Kether

Kether, meaning "Crown," is the first and highest attribute of God in the first world of Atziluth, and is the most hidden of God's attributes; beyond the ability of the mind of man to grasp, the "Hidden Light." This is Adonai, the *Tetragrammaton* seen in the Hebrew letters YHWH, thought to be pronounced Yahweh, (Ponce' pg. 174) translated into English as "Lord" or "Jehovah", the "Cause for the Effect," the reason for creation, where the plan for the universe began.

Kether is the first impulse of God Almighty, it is the manifestation of Ein-Sof, God's primal will where all opposites exist in peaceful unexplainable unity; the "will to will," where there is no need for balance as of yet (Ponce', pg. 115). This is *Ehyeh Asher Ehyeh*, "I am that I am." It is the "Divine Emanation," the "Divine Will" that is known as *Macroprosopus* from which all other Sefiroth come.

In Scriptural references, this was visualized as the *Ancient of Days* in the book of Daniel and Revelation, and the *Head of Days* with hair like wool in the books of Enoch:

> *Daniel 7:9 ...As I looked, thrones were set in place, and the **Ancient of Days** took his seat.*

> *I Enoch 47:3 ...In those days I saw the **Head of Days** when He seated himself on the throne of His glory.*

Sefiroth Hokhmah

Hokhmah, below and to the right of Kether (since Hebrew is read right to left), is the second attribute or *utterance* of God, meaning "Wisdom."

Wisdom spoke of in Proverbs:

> *Proverbs 8:1, 2 ...Does not **wisdom** call out? Does not understanding raise her voice? At the highest point along the way, where the paths meet, she takes her stand...*

*Proverbs 8:22, 23 ...The Lord brought me (wisdom) forth as **the first of his works**, before his deeds of old; I was formed long ages ago, at the very beginning, when the world came to be.*

Hokhmah is a masculine term and related to as the "**Father**," representing the will or desire to create; the spark of life, the "beginning." Here the plan of creation was put in place. In Kether we see the "will to will" and in Hokhmah we see the "desire to express that will," the "Father" of all creation (Ponce', pg. 119). In the books of Psalm and Proverbs we see this wisdom of God expressed:

*Psalm 104:24 ...How countless are Your works, Lord! In **wisdom** You have made them all; the earth is full of Your creatures.*

Sefiroth Binah

Binah, to the left of Kether, is the third attribute of God in the highest realm, meaning "Understanding," or "Intelligence," being feminine in nature, the "Higher **Mother**" (Ponce', pg. 122). She is symbolized as a white dove and is also seen as the womb from which creation is born, giving shape to the "Spirit" of God, the giver of life. She is also associated with another name of God, *Elohim* meaning "spirit" or "spiritual powers."

John 1:32 ...I saw the Spirit come down from heaven as a dove and remain on him.

This is the third part of the first "triad," composed of male and female, mother and father. Kether can be considered as neither or male; it is however pictured as male in that it is the "Bridegroom" in the highest world and Malkuth is the "Bride" in the lowest world.

Proverbs 3:19 ...By wisdom (Hokhmah) the Lord laid the earth's foundations, by understanding (Binah) he set the heavens in place (Creation or *Malkuth).*

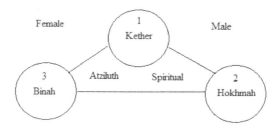

The Trinity of Atziluth

The union of *Hokhmah* (Wisdom), *Abba* or "Spirit Father" with the *Imma* or "Spirit Mother" *Binah* (Understanding) produces *Da'at,* which means "Reason" or "Revealed Knowledge." This has the same meaning as the Greek word *"Logos,"* which is "doctrine," "argument from reason" or "word;" roots for theology, the "doctrine of God" (Jacobs, pg. 108).

This triad or "spiritual trinity," represents God in the Spiritual World of Atziluth, above the "abyss" of the seven spheres (seven heavens) of the of the created world. *Hokhmah, Binah and Da'at* therefore together

14

represent *Kether* who contains all that is "known" in *Ein-Sof*. He is the "Almighty," the "Alpha and Omega," the one without beginning or end who cannot be "known" or comprehended.

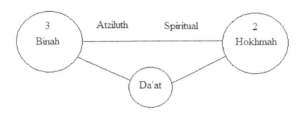

The Hebrew letter Shin represents this Spiritual Trinity as well as the number three and is the word for light, fire or spirit. The symbol of the Star of David consists of an interlocked pair of triangles, one pointed up and the other down.

The triangle pointing up represents the word for fire symbolizing the spiritual triad of Kether, Hokhmah and Binah. The triangle pointing down represents the Hebrew word for water symbolizing the material triad of Father, Mother and Son. Also symbolizing the six days of creation with the center the seventh day, the day of rest (Gauding, pg. 71).

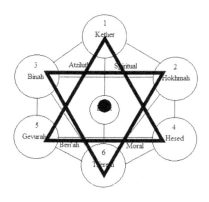

Da'at

Although the Jewish Tree of Life contains ten Sefiroth, some are shown with *Kether* and some are shown with *Da'at*; but always the warning is given, "ten Sefiroth, not nine, not eleven" (Scholem, pg. 274).

Da'at in fact, is not normally shown with the "ten utterances" or "attributes of God" as he is not truly a Sefiroth. It in turn represents all of the seven lower Sefiroth in one; it is only through this "**Son**" of the *Abba* and *Imma*, *Da'at* who is manifested through Sefiroth **Tifereth**, that humans, if they are humble, can see the light of God. This is the "Divine Light" or the "Hidden Light," that is shining down to *Malkuth*, the earthly kingdom, through Him. Da'at can be seen as the "knowledge of God" embedded in humankind. The lower seven Sefiroth can also be viewed as the seven days of creation; Malkuth or earthly kingdom can also be seen as the **bride** of Tifereth.

Moral World of Beri'ah

The next world is *Beri'ah*, the second world known as the Moral World. Beri'ah is also composed of a triad of three Sefiroth; *Hesed* (Kindness), *Gevurah* (Power) and *Tifereth* (Beauty). Beri'ah is the first world of the creation and is at the top of the "abyss" of seven Sefiroth and is created for the righteous and the highest of the angels.

The Abyss

The Abyss here is sometimes viewed as the "symbol of a moment or glimpse within God" (Scholem, pg. 428). Others taught that this Abyss is the "empty" area between the Spiritual World of Atziluth and Moral World of Beri'ah (Prophet, pg. 19). Beri'ah is the higher Garden of Eden; where the Throne of God's Justice resides (Ponce', pg. 66), the first of God's creation yet without shape or form, where self-awareness first took place.

Isaiah 43:7 ...Bring all who claim me as their God, for I have made them for my glory. It was I who created them.

Sefiroth Hesed

Hesed is the first Sefiroth of the Beri'ah moral world meaning Kindness, Love and Mercy and is a masculine term and is at the center of the Pillar of Mercy. It is a product of Wisdom and Understanding in the spiritual triad above it. Being the first of the lower seven Sefiroth, Hesed represents the first day of creation when God created light, separating the darkness from light. It is interesting that light existed in creation before the sun and moon and stars, therefore this light must have been emanating from Ein-Sof (God) Himself (Ponce, p. 126).

Sefiroth Gevurah

Gevurah is the second Sefiroth in the realm of Beri'ah and is feminine in nature, representing the Power and Strength of God, Judgment, Justice and Control and is at the center of the Pillar of Strength. It is an opposite to Mercy and limits the amount of mercy bestowed (Prophet, pg. 54); likewise this power is tempered by mercy by limiting the punishment of God's power. It is through the balance of power and mercy that the next Sefiroth exists; *Tifereth* (Beauty). Gevurah represents the second day of creation when God separated the waters of the heavens from the waters of the earth with the sky.

Sefiroth Tifereth

Tifereth is the third Sefiroth in the realm of Beri'ah and is neutral in nature, meaning Beauty, Graciousness and Compassion (Prophet, pg. 54); this is the beauty of the heart. It is in the center of the Middle Pillar, the pillar of Equilibrium and Compassion. Its function is to mediate between Judgment and Mercy and represents the third day of creation when dry land appeared.

Tifereth also can be viewed as the mediator between **God and man**, the bridge across the Abyss that divides **God and mankind** (Prophet, pg. 65).

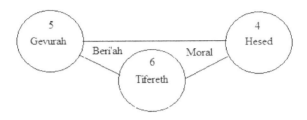

The book of I Enoch explains both the *Macroprosopus* with **Microprosopus, or Ze`ir Anpin,** the **Son**: the Lesser Countenance; the name, the Lesser YHWH (Yahweh). This is *Tifereth*, the Son, the revealed image of God as human; the mediator and **bridegroom**, the **Messiah** with Shekinah (Malkuth) as the **bride**.

> *I Enoch 46:1-3 ...And there I saw One who had a **head of days** and His head was white like wool, and with Him was **another being** whose countenance had the **appearance of a man**, and his **face was full of graciousness**, like one of the holy angels.*
>
> *And I asked the angel who went with me and showed me all the hidden things concerning that **Son of Man**, who he was, and from where he was, and why he went with the **Head of Days**.*

Throne of God

It is in I Enoch chapter 1 and Isaiah chapter 6 that we see the Throne of God described in thorough detail. In Jewish mysticism the throne is called Merkabah or the Chariot-Throne.

This throne resides in the Beri'ah world in order to be perceived in vessels of lower Worlds. A similar Throne is portrayed in the books of Daniel and Revelation

*I Enoch 6:25 ...And I looked and saw in it was an **elevated throne**. Its appearance was as crystal and the wheels of it as the shining sun, and there was the vision of cherubim.*

*Isaiah 6:1 ...In the year that King Uzziah died I saw the **Lord sitting upon a throne, high and lifted up;** and the train of his robe filled the temple.*

It was here that the Throne of God was challenged by Satan:

*I Enoch 29:3-4 ...And one from out the order of angels, having turned away with the order that was under him, conceived an impossible thought, to **place his throne higher than the clouds** above the earth, that he might become equal in rank to my power.*

Babel

In much the same way, mankind tried to reach up to the heavens when they built the tower of Babel; God likewise was unhappy with this attempt and scattered mankind.

*Genesis 11:4-9 ...Then they said, "Come, let us build ourselves a city, with a **tower that reaches to the heavens,** so that we may **make a name for ourselves;** otherwise we will be scattered over the face of the whole earth."*

But the Lord came down to see the city and the tower the people were building.

The Lord said, "If as one people speaking the same language they have begun to do this, then nothing they plan to do will be impossible for them.

Come, let us go down and confuse their language so they will not understand each other."

So the Lord scattered them from there over all the earth, and they stopped building the city.

That is why it was called Babel (Babylon).

Metatron

Metatron, the angel whom Enoch was transformed into, also inhabits this world of Beri'ah after Enoch's body ascended into heaven; we see this when God took him in Genesis chapter 5 and the books of Enoch.

Genesis 5:24 ...And Enoch walked with God: and he was not; for God took him.

To the Jewish mystics, Enoch is a celestial scribe and is the highest of the Archangels. Many believe that the angel referred to in Exodus chapter 23 was Metatron (Halperin, pg. 258).

*Exodus 23:21, 22 ...See, I am sending **an angel** ahead of you to guard you along the way and to bring you to the place I have prepared.*

*Pay attention to him and listen to what he says. Do not rebel against him; he will not forgive your rebellion, since my **Name is in him**.*

Seven Heavens

Jewish mysticism teaches that the seven heavens spoke of in the book of I Enoch are all part of the second world of Beri'ah. These multiple layered heavens contain the seven palaces or throne rooms of God; these represent the created world, the seven days of creation. Through the proper utilization of the names of God, fasting and praying, mystics are able attain visions of ascent into these heavenly palaces.

It is in the books of Enoch that Enoch himself is guided through these heavens:

II Enoch 20:1 ...And those two men lifted me up from there on to the seventh heaven, and I saw there a very great light, and fiery troops of great archangels.

Here in Beri'ah there is a true separation between Divinity and its creation, a place where self-awareness can exist; where awareness of dark and light, good and evil exists within the constructs of space and time.

Isaiah 45:7 ...I form the light, and create darkness. **I make peace and create evil***: I the Lord do all these things.*

Two Kingdoms

Beri'ah is the Kingdom of Heaven also known as *Shamayim* of the seven heavens, whereas Malkuth is the earthly kingdom, the kingdom of mankind. Beri'ah is the "third heaven" spoken of by St. Paul in 2 Corinthians perceived from the earthly level; Beri'ah, the Moral World; Yetzirah, the world of the Senses and Assiah, the earthly kingdom where Malkuth resides.

2 Corinthians 12:2 ...I know a man in Christ who was caught up into the **third heaven** *14 years ago. Whether he was in the body or out of the body, I don't know, God knows.*

Material and Sensual World of Yetzirah

Yetzirah the Formed, Material and Sensual World is composed of *Netsah* which is Eternity, *Hod* being Splendor and *Yesod* which is Foundation.

Sefiroth Netsah

Sefiroth Netsah is the first sphere of the World of Yetzirah. It is masculine in nature and means Eternity, Endurance or Victory; it represents the fourth day of creation when the sun and moon are created for their light. It is the base of the Mercy Pillar, under Wisdom and Loving-kindness on the right side of the Tree of life.

Sefiroth Hod

Hod is the second Sefiroth in the World of the Senses. It is feminine in nature and means Majesty or Glory; it represents the fifth day of creation when God created life in the sea and air. It is also the foundation of the Pillar of Strength under Understanding and Strength on the left side of the Tree of life.

Sefiroth Yesod

Sefiroth Yesod is the third Sefiroth in the World of the Senses. It is both male and female in nature and means Foundation; it represents the sixth day of creation when God created Adam and Eve; the union of Endurance and Glory. It is the Foundation of the center pillar, the Pillar of Compassion which supports Beauty and Crown. Yesod also supports the feminine Pillar of Severity on the left and the masculine Mercy Pillar on the right, making it the true foundation. It could be considered the Corner Stone that is the Foundation to God's creation, connecting the earthly kingdom of Malkuth with all of the other attributes of God; the ninth of the ten Sefiroth.

Yesod is said to the "straight gate," the "narrow way, " the "eye of the needle;" the pathway of Shekinah (Prophet, pg. 82).

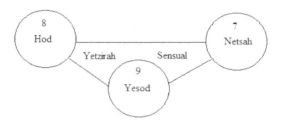

Earthly Kingdom of Assiah and Malkuth

Assiah, the Earthly Kingdom contains in it the tenth and last Sefiroth. It is in the form of Malkuth, meaning Kingship or Kingdom in the human realm. The Sefiroth is feminine in nature but without a male pair as it alone exists in this earthly world. It is however vertically paired and considered to be the **Bride** or God's feminine counterpart, the Shekinah; her union with God Almighty was creation itself. She is the gateway to the upper spiritual world and also represents the seventh day of creation when God saw that it was good and rested.

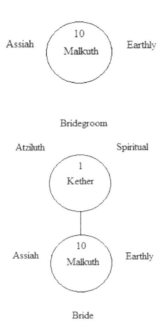

The Greater and Lesser Countenance
=

The Greater and Lesser Countenance

Assiah's male counterparts can be viewed in two ways; as Macroprosopus, also known as Arich Anpin, and Microprosopus, also known as Ze`ir Anpin. These two differing aspects of God are drawn from the Tree of Life diagram with two different combinations of the Sefiroth; the image of a "Extended Countenance" and a "Lesser Countenance." Another view is the Greater and Lesser YHWH, God the Almighty and the "limited" image or reflection of God in human form; the perfect man, seen in Adam Kadmon before creation and for the Christians in Jesus Christ.

Macroprosopus

Macroprosopus or Arich Anpin, is the hidden God, the Extended or Greater Countenance, the Greater YHWH. the "I am" and the **Father** of Creation. His hair and beard is white like wool as we see depicted in the book of Daniel and the books of Enoch and the book of Revelation. His eyes wide open as He never slumbers or sleeps and from His nostrils he breaths out life into the lower worlds (Ponce', p. 114).

> *Daniel 7:9 ...As I looked, "thrones were set in place, and the **Ancient of Days** took his seat. His clothing was as white as snow; the **hair** of his head was **white like wool**. His throne was flaming with fire, and its wheels were all ablaze.*

His first manifestation is through Kether, the head and crown, from which all other Sefiroth are manifested. His arms are the Pillars of Mercy and Strength and his torso is the Middle Pillar; his feet planted in Malkuth, the earthly kingdom.

Microprosopus

Microprosopus, or Ze`ir Anpin, is the un-manifested and manifested God, the Lesser Countenance; He has a name, the Lesser YHWH (Yahweh). He is pictured as having black hair with both masculine and feminine characteristics and is contained in six of the lower Sefiroth or "Partzufim;" this contains the six expressive Sefiroth characteristics of Hesed, Gevurah, Tifereth,

Netsah, Hod and Yesod. Ze`ir Anpin, the **Bridegroom** is the **Son** of Kether or Abba, the **Father** of creation and Binah or Imma the **Mother** of creation. Partzufim Nukvah or Shekinah is the spiritual **Daughter** or **Bride** in the form of mankind (Leet, pg. 62).

The masculine image is described with his right arm as Mercy, His left arm as Power, His trunk as Beauty, His right leg as Victory, left leg as Glory and Foundation (Yesod) His reproductive organs. The feminine image is of one with Beauty (Tifereth) as the head with long black hair and the breasts of Hod and Netsah (Ponce', p. 128, 129).

Microprosopus is also very similar to what is expressed in Enoch's vision in the book of I Enoch. This explains Macroprosopus or Arich Anpin, the "Higher Countenance," the "Hidden Light" as the "*Head of Days*" whose "*head was white like wool.*" Microprosopus or Ze`ir Anpin is seen here in the form of the Son of Man; the Lesser Countenance, God manifested to mankind, the one who manifest the Hidden Light of God to man and gives him life. He mediates between the Hidden God and mankind.

John 14:6 ...I am the Way, the Truth and the Life, no man can come to the Father but by me.

*I Enoch 46:1-3 ...And there I saw One who had a head of days and **His head was white** like **wool**, and with Him was **another being** whose countenance had the **appearance of a man.**

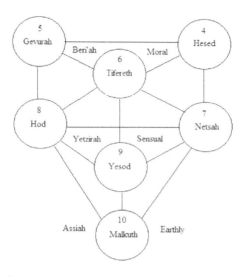

The Light

God Almighty, Ein-Sof, is the originator of all creation. This Almighty God exists in everything and everything exists within Him. This creation however spiritually, is something that stands alone, separate from God, existing outside of Him because of the fall and cannot comprehend Him.

God also however, emanates a light that flows from Him and is sustained by Him and does not exist separate or outside of Him. His light or life giving energy is what flows down through these Sefiroth; these are ten knowable attributes of God, shining down to mankind, giving creation and mankind Life.

Shekinah

God's Shekinah glory or *Kavod*, is expressed throughout Jewish writings, mostly hidden in poetry or narratives. Shekinah means to "live within" or to "indwell" in Hebrew (Ponce', p. 721). She is not God but a manifestation of Him as His first creation. The "Higher Kavod" is the glory of God that man cannot comprehend or endure. The "Lower Kavod" is the glory of God that man can both absorb and understand. She is seen in the Torah as the pillar of cloud that led Israel through the wilderness, in the burning bush with Moses, in the glory of God on Mount Sinai that radiated from Moses face and in the glory that filled the Hebrew tabernacle and temple (Ponce', p. 61).

This glory is expressed as the feminine side of God, as the Light of the World, as a the Bride of God. Literature such as in the narrative of Esther, queen of Babylon, is a figurative representation in Jewish tradition of the Shekinah of God as a Bride; the book of Song of Solomon also an allegorical representation of God's Bride and Shekinah glory. The Christian New Testament takes this further and sees the Church as the Bride of Christ.

The Sacred Union Prayer is prayed by the Jewish mystics and prays for the union of God's feminine Shekinah, pictured as a forlorn lover in exile, eager to return to Ein-Sof, the Eternal One (Cardin pg. 48). This in effect is a prayer for redemption. Mankind is in dire need for healing and to be reunited with God.

30

The prayer pleads for a reunion of God and mankind pictured in the unification of His name: Yod Hei, (Y-H) with the last two letters of God's ineffable name, Vav Hei, (W-H) which creates His name – YHWH.

Sacred Union Prayer

> *In the name of the Holy One, blessed be He, and His Shekinah, in prayer and for mercy, for the sake of the union of the first two letters of God's ineffable name, Yod Hei, (Y-H) with the last two letters of God's ineffable name, Vav Hei, (V-H) a complete and total union for the sake of all Israel.*

She can be seen in a couple of ways; as the Heavenly Shekinah and as the Earthly Shekinah. She is seen as the "Spiritual Mother" or *Imma*, through the Spiritual Sefiroth of the Crown, Wisdom, and Understanding; she is the "Shekinah above" and the mother or womb of creation. In Malkuth, the kingdom of mankind, she is seen as the "Shekinah below" called the Bride. She is seen as transiting between the Spiritual and the Physical worlds along the center Pillar of Mildness of the Tree of Life (Ponce', p. 216). In this physical world, this is the indwelling of God's glory, God's divine presence within mankind that can only be seen as through a "cloudy lens;" in the next world it will be face to face.

Paul refers to this in I Corinthians 13:

1 Corinthians 13:12 ...For now we see through a glass, darkly; but then face to face: now I know in part; but then shall I know even as also I am known.

Shekinah is also expressed in all of the Sefiroth on the left side of the tree of life, in the Pillar of Severity, as each of these represent an attribute of God with feminine qualities. These are *Binah* - Understanding, *Gevurah* - Power and *Hod* - Majesty. It's ultimate expression however is in Malkuth, the earthly kingdom of mankind and expressed as the **Bride** of God.

There are also three "Mother Letters" of Jewish mysticism are Aleph, Mem and Shin representing the primordial elements. The **letter** Aleph represents the element air, the **letter** Shin represents the element of fire and the **letter** Mem, the element water. The twenty two **letters** of the Hebrew alphabet are broken up into three categories represented by these three Mother Letters; these three are based on the three types of sounds the letters make - mutes, sibilants and aspirates.

Second Temple Mysticism

Second Temple style of mysticism goes back to the time of the Babylonian captivity of Israel. These were the times of Ezekiel, Daniel, Isaiah, Joel and Zechariah. It was these prophets that had the first visions of God's throne recorded in Jewish literature. Over the centuries, devoted mystics attempted to achieve the same vision;

attempting to ascend into the Seven Heavens of these worlds, and to enter the divine throne room through fasting, prayer and meditation. In Jewish mysticism, it is the *Merkabah Riders* who ascend in visions into the palaces, to the throne of God, The Shekinah is seen as the "Divine Presence," a light that descends down from heaven to accompany them in their visions of ascent; the life giving energy that links man with God.

Visions of the Merkabah Riders

Chariot Mysticism

Jewish Literature

Chariot of Fire

The most ancient of Jewish mysticism goes back as far as the 6th century BC and is known as Throne - Chariot (Ponce' pg. 55) mysticism or *Merkabah* which means "to ride in." Its literature describes many mystical ascents into the seven heavenly palaces known as *Hekhalot* and is full of angelic glory expressed in the transcendent languages of hymns, poems, and the petitions of angels. It is centered on the mystical adoration of the Throne Chariot of God, with doctrine that has been heavily guarded for centuries; the foundation for the magic of Practical Kabbalah in the middle ages. Those who ascend through the seven heavens to the throne in these visions are called *Merkabah Riders* and the chariot, the Chariot of Fire.

This mystic faith is founded in the visions of the book of Ezekiel (Ponce' pg. 35), primarily Ezekiel chapter 1, and in chapter 10; a book that was originally written by Ezekiel and his sages almost 500 years before Christ. Many believe it may have had its roots much earlier in the books of Enoch, stories passed down through memorization long before they were put down into words. Many books were most likely re-written by scribes either from orally memorized passages or ancient manuscripts during the time of Ezra; this was not too long after the return of Israel from their captivity in Babylon. The books of Isaiah and Daniel which have similar visions to Ezekiel were probably written in Babylon around the same time as Ezekiel. Ezekiel clearly was written after Daniel as Daniel's wisdom is mentioned in Ezekiel chapter 28.

Great Assembly

Some scholars believe that it was during Ezra's time that scribes who were highly educated in Babylon, were tasked to put together the Jewish canon (Collins, pg. 3). Ezra, was the priest and scribe who gathered together the *Great Assembly* of one hundred and twenty scribes, sages, and prophets after his return to Jerusalem from the Great Captivity. It was this assembly that divided up the recovered Hebrew Scriptures into three major parts (the *Torah* - Teachings, the *Nevi'im* - the Prophets and the *Kethuvim* – the Writings); twenty two individual ancient books were chosen as the canon of Jewish Scripture.

This Scripture that was assembled from scattered ancient writings and memorized passages and is what we know as the Tanakh or Old Testament today. Many writings may have come from old decaying papyrus or leather scrolls hidden away during the siege and destruction of Jerusalem in 586 BC. Of these writings, **Enoch** was not canonized but Ezekiel was. Although **Enoch** was not included in these Scriptures, it still was highly influential in Jewish culture, even till today. The books of Ezra and Nehemiah, document this time period of the rebuilding of the Second Jewish Temple and the walls of Jerusalem.

Prior to the captivity, almost all Scripture such as the Torah, was passed down orally from generation to generation. It wasn't until the time of the captivity in Babylon that well educated Jews started putting their revelations into writing; these were the days of Ezekiel and Daniel.

Babylonian Influences

Many of these writings had been written in Babylon by men of great stature, such as Daniel, Ezekiel and Ezra who were educated in Nebuchadnezzar's court as well as the Persians. Because these scribes were educated in Babylon, they were heavily influenced by its culture and religions. Other books containing this Second Temple style of mysticism are the books of Isaiah, Joel, Zechariah and later the Apocalypse of Abraham and the New Testament book of Revelation. These became the center of focus for the Merkabah mystics from 100 BC till around 1000 AD as well as the Kabbalah mystics of the Middle Ages and their "white" magic.

Magi

In Babylon, mysticism was part of normal society. The magicians, sorcerers, astrologers and Chaldeans (Magi) were commonly called to advise the king. It was in the interpretation of dreams that Daniel himself became known as Belteshazzar under King Nebuchadnezzar. Daniel became *"chief over all the magicians, enchanters, astrologers, and fortune-tellers of Babylon"* as we see in Daniel 5:11.

After the fall of Babylon to the Persian Empire, followers of Zoroaster, also believers in a monotheistic religion of one God, supported the Jews in returning to Jerusalem to rebuild the city and the temple. The Median priests of Zoroastrianism were the Magi, the Athravan, keepers of the fire, of which later in the New Testament came searching for the young Jesus.

Melchizedek

One of the first influences of this Jewish mysticism is the story of Melchizedek, king of Salem and priest of the Most High God. Long before Moses, Salem was the city that is called Jerusalem today. The story of Melchizedek meeting with Abraham is at the heart of this faith; in Genesis he is called the High Priest of El Elyon, the Most High One (YHWH).

Genesis 14:19 ...Then Melchizedek king of Salem brought out bread and wine. He was priest of God Most High, and he blessed Abram, saying, "Blessed be Abram by God Most High, Creator of heaven and earth

His story is also in the book of II Enoch and his priesthood is also mentioned in the New Testament book of Hebrews several times.

*Hebrews 5:9-10 ...In this way, God qualified him (Jesus) as a perfect High Priest, and he became the source of **eternal salvation** for all those who obey him and was designated by God to be high priest in the order of Melchizedek.*

Other books such as the book of Revelation and the Apocalypse of Abraham were written around the time of Christ and have the same theme. Melchizedek is a major theme in the New Testament book of Hebrews where his name is mentioned fifteen times. The Old Testament mentions his name in only three verses of Genesis 14 and once in Psalm 110.

The "Exaltation of Melchizedek" in the book of I Enoch is a whole chapter dedicated to Melchizedek, describing his miraculous birth and destined as a High Priest to the Most High. These writings were most likely common readings for the Jews while in Synagogue and were highly influential in the teachings of the New Testament. While reading the details of Melchizedek's birth, one cannot help but reflect on the stories of John the Baptist's and Jesus' birth in the Gospel of Luke (See Mark Dennis - The Apocalypse of Enoch).

The Dead Sea Scrolls Translated

It is in the book of *Songs of the Sabbath Sacrifice,* written some 100 years before Christ (found in the Dead Sea Scrolls of Qumran) that we see a different picture of Melchizedek. Here he is visualized as a "Angelic" High Priest in the "Celestial Temple" and is the most plausible source for the message in the books of Hebrews (Barnard, pg. 128).

*Hebrews 8:1 ...We do have such a **high priest**, who sat down at the right hand of the throne of the majestic God in heaven*

Songs of the Sabbath Sacrifice
Melchizedek 11Q13 *(Martínez pg. 140)*

Then the "Day of Atonement" shall follow after the tenth jubilee period, when he shall atone for all the holy ones (Sons of God), and the men of the order of Melchizedek.

And on the heights (highest of heavens) he will declare it is the time for the "Year of grace for Melchizedek", and by his power he will judge God`s holy ones and so establish a holy kingdom, as it is written about him in the Songs of David;

"A godlike being (Elohim) will stand up in the assembly of God; in the midst of holy ones he holds judgment" (Psalm 82:1).

Scripture also says about him; "Return to your seat in the highest of heavens; God will judge the nations" (Psalm 7:7-8).

The Chariot Throne is quite explicitly shown in these Dead Sea writings, which is sometimes called "Angelic Liturgy." Much of this text describes the celestial temple, the throne room and throne-chariot of God.

The cherubim lie prostrate before him and they bless when they raise themselves, the voice of divine silence is heard and roar of excitement;

At the rising of their wings, the voice of divine silence. They bless the image of a throne-chariot above the vault of the cherubim.

And they sing the splendor of the shining vault from beneath the Throne of his glory.

(Martínez pg. 429)

Moses

Another major influence in Jewish mysticism is Moses. The first instance in the Bible of the Lord descending in the clouds was in Exodus 34:5 where Moses sees the Lord descending in the clouds at Mount Sinai.

Exodus 34:5 ...Then the Lord came down in the cloud and stood there with him and proclaimed his name, the Lord.

Deuteronomy 33:2 ...And He came from the midst of ten thousand holy ones. At His right hand there was flashing lightning for them.

Also see 1 Enoch 1:9 and Jude 1:14.

Enoch, the seventh from Adam, prophesied about them: "See, the Lord is coming with thousands upon thousands of his holy ones."

Mount Sinai was a burning mountain with smoke and fire. It was there that the Torah, the oral Law was given to Moses and the Ten Commandments were chiseled into the stone tablets. Jewish mystics believe that the Torah, although given to Moses orally, had always existed as the Word of God, but the letters where incoherent and "jumbled up" until the creation. As events began to take place, the words took form; these words took form from a fixed amount of letters which cannot be added to or subtracted from.

The Torah was therefore treated as a living organism, the secret life of God Himself (Ponce' pg. 28). As scribes over the centuries copied the Torah into new scrolls, this belief was so strong that not one "jot or tittle" could be changed, leading to virtually no change at all to the words of the Torah for centuries.

Many orthodox Jews believe that God orally gave secret knowledge to Moses who passed this knowledge from teacher to teacher or priest to priest. It was the brother of Moses of whom the twenty-four priestly families of Israel descended from; many believe this was a continuation of the order of Melchizedek.

Psalm 110:4 ...You are a priest forever, in the order of Melchizedek.

Hebrews 6:20 ...He (Jesus) has become a high priest forever, in the order of Melchizedek.

Names of God

The 22 letter name of God

Hear O Israel, the Lord is our God, the Lord is One

שְׁמַע יִשְׂרָאֵל יהוה אֱלֹהֵינוּ יהוה אֶחָד

The 42 letter name of God

The Talmud refers to the "forty-two-letter name of God" but does not say what it is. "This name of forty-two letters is exceedingly holy; it can only be entrusted to him who is modest, in the midway of life, not easily provoked to anger, temperate, gentle, and who speaks kindly to his fellow men" (Alter, pg. 108). It is derived from the first forty-two letters of the Torah. The daily recitation of the prayer *ana becho'ach* is said to contain the secret forty-two letter name of God.

יתץ	אבג
שטן	קרע
יכש	נגד
צתג	בטר
טנע	חקב
פזק	יגל
צית	שקו

Ana b'khoach g'dulat yeminkha tatir ts'rura
Kabel rinat am'kha sagvenu taha'renu nora
Na gibor dor'shei yichu'd'kha k'vavat shomrem
Bar'khem taharem rachamei tzid'kat'kha tamid gom'lem
Chasin kadosh b'rov tuvkha nahel ada'tekha
Yachid ge'eh l'am'kha p'heh zokhrei k'dusha'tekha
Shv'ateinu kabel ushma tza'akateinu yode'a ta'alumot

The 72 letter name of God

The 72 letter name of God, the Shem Ha Mephorash, "the precise name," comes from the 72 Hebrew letters written by Moses in Exodus 14 which is used in for meditation in Jewish mysticism.

Exodus 14:19-21 ...Then the angel of God, who had been traveling in front of Israel's army, withdrew and went behind them. The pillar of cloud also moved from in front and stood behind them, coming between the armies of Egypt and Israel.

Throughout the night the cloud brought darkness to the one side and light to the other side; so neither went near the other all night long.

Then Moses stretched out his hand over the sea, and all that night the Lord drove the sea back with a strong east wind and turned it into dry land. The waters were divided, and the Israelites went through the sea on dry ground, with a wall of water on their right and on their left.

וְהַחֹשֶׁךְ הֶעָנָן וַיְהִי יִשְׂרָאֵל מַחֲנֵה וּבֵין מִצְרַיִם מַחֲנֵה ׀ בֵּין יָבֹא
מֹשֶׁה וַיֵּט כָּל־הַלַּיְלָה: אֶל־זֶה זֶה וְלֹא־קָרַב אֶת־הַלַּיְלָה וַיָּאֶר
עַזָּה קָדִים בְּרוּחַ אֶת־הַיָּם ׀ יְהֹוָה וַיּוֹלֶךְ עַל־הַיָּם אֶת־יָדֹו
הַמָּיִם: וַיִּבָּקְעוּ לֶחָרָבָה אֶת־הַיָּם וַיָּשֶׂם כָּל־הַלַּיְלָה

When these three verses are combined in a specific way, 72 unique three letter names are produced. Some refer to these as the 72 names of God and others attribute these names to 72 angels of Jacob's ladder. In Genesis Jacob has a dream of a ladder with angels going up and down from heaven.

*Genesis 28:10-11 ...And he dreamed there was a **ladder** a set up on the earth, and the top of it reached to heaven. And behold, **the angels of God were ascending and descending on it!***

72 Names of God/ Angels

Aehaiah	Hahaziah	Lauiah	Nelchael
Aladiah	Hahuiah	Lecabel	Nemamaih
Aniel	Haiaiel	Lehahiah	Nithael
Annauel	Hakamiah	Lelahel	Nithaiah
Ariel	Harahel	Leuuiah	Omael
Asaliah	Hariel	Leviah	Pahaliah
Cahethel	Haziel	Mahasiah	Poiel
Caliel	Iahhel	Mebahel	Rehael
Chavakiak	Iehuiah	Mebahiah	Reiiel
Damabiah	Ieiaiel	Mehekiel	Rochel
Daniel	Ieiazel	Melahel	Sealiah
Eiael	Ieilael	Meniel	Seehiah
Elemiah	Ielahiah	Michael	Sitael
Haaiah	Ieliel	Mihael	Umabel
Haamiah	Ierathel	Mizrael	Vasiariah
Habuiah	Ihiazel	Monadel	Vehuel
Hahahel	Iibamiah	Mumiah	Vehuiah
Hahaziah	Imamiah	Nanael	Vevaliah

The First Merkabah Riders

Enoch Taken

Chronologically, Enoch is first of these Merkabah Riders and is seen in the book of Genesis as the seventh in line from Adam. He is the first to have mysteriously disappeared… Genesis simply says that God took him. This story is explained much further in the ancient books of I, II and III Enoch.

> *Genesis 5:24 …Enoch walked faithfully with God; then he was no more, because God took him away.*

Enoch in 1 Enoch 39:3 is taken up into the heavens by a whirlwind; up to the *Hekhalot*, the dwelling places of the righteous.

> *1 Enoch 39:3-4 …And in those days a whirlwind carried me off from the earth, and set me down at the end of the heavens.*
>
> *And there I saw another vision, the dwelling-places of the holy, and the resting-places of the righteous.*
>
> *Isaiah 66:15 …See, the Lord is coming with fire, and his chariots are like a whirlwind; he will bring down his anger with fury, and his rebuke with flames of fire.*

Enoch's Throne Vision

The book of I Enoch, looks back at the Enoch of Genesis, the seventh descendant of Adam. This book is believed to have been written during or shortly after the time of Ezekiel and Daniel in Babylon. The book most likely was written by several authors and over a relatively long time period.

In this book, Enoch is taken by the Spirit into heaven and enters into something like a large palace or temple where we also see the throne of God, a throne that seems to have shining wheels of crystal, shining like the sun much like the writings of Ezekiel and Daniel.

I Enoch chapter 14 says:

"And in every respect it so excelled in splendor and magnificence and extent that I cannot describe to you its splendor and its extent.

And its floor was of fire, and above it was lightning and the path of the stars, and its ceiling also was flaming fire.

And I looked and saw in it was an elevated throne. Its appearance was as crystal and the wheels of it as the shining sun, and there was the vision of cherubim...

*And the Great Glory sat on the throne, and His
robe shone brighter than the sun and was whiter
than any snow.*

*None of the angels could enter or could see His
face because of the magnificence and glory and
no flesh could see Him.*

*And ten thousand times ten thousand stood
before Him, yet He needed no counselor. And
the most holy ones who were near Him did not
leave Him by night nor go from Him.*

Melchizedek

The book of Hebrews talks about Melchizedek at
great lengths. He is introduced as the king of Salem
and priest of God Most High and met with Abraham.
His name means "king of righteousness" or "king of
peace,' and is described as "without father or mother,
without genealogy, without beginning of days or end of
life, **resembling the Son of God**, who remains a priest
forever" (Hebrews 7:3).

Melchizedek too is envisioned as one who does not
die and as in the books of Ezekiel and Daniel, is one
that resembles the "Son of God." He is also described
in gnostic gospels as the "Light-Bringer" or "Light-
Maker." This is another picture of Da'at, the entity in
which the light of God shines down through; the light
that separates us from the animal world, the divine
knowledge within us that helps discern good from evil.

The book of Hebrews 7:15 attributes Jesus to this same priesthood:

*Hebrews 7:15 ...A different priest, who is like Melchizedek, has appeared. Jesus became a priest, not by meeting the physical requirement of belonging to the **tribe of Levi**, but by the power of a life that cannot be destroyed.*

And the psalmist pointed this out when he prophesied,

"You are a priest forever in the order of Melchizedek." (Psalm 110:4)

There is also an eerie similarity between the story in II Enoch, *The Exaltation of Melchizedek,* and the description of the birth John the Baptist and the birth of Jesus in the beginning of Luke. Both fathers were High Priest; both mothers were barren and all very old and with a strong similarity to the story of Abram and Sarai in Genesis chapter 16.

Also in all of these stories, both the women and the men are visited by the archangel Gabriel. Melchizedek in this text is the son of Nir (not mentioned in the Bible), the brother of Noah. Both were Lamech's sons; Lamech being the son of Methuselah, the son of Enoch. **Melchizedek** would show up in Genesis chapter 14 as **Melchizedek** king of Salem, priest of God the Most High and met with Abram. Ancient Salem is believed to be what Jerusalem is today.

The book of Hebrews in the New Testament has a heavy emphasis on Melchizedek (See Mark Dennis - The Apocalypse of Enoch).

II Enoch 72 ...And Melchizedek will be the head of the priests in that generation

Hebrews 7 ...This Melchizedek was king of Salem and priest of God Most High.

Abraham's Throne Vision

The Apocalypse of Abraham, is a Jewish texts attributed Abraham but most likely written in the first century AD. It provides an exclusive insight into Jewish teachings and apocalyptic writings at and around the time of Christ.

The Apocalypse of Abraham is the story of the young Abram who travels to a heavenly temple and the celestial sanctuary of the divine Throne Chariot.

Apocalypse of Abraham, chapter 18

And as I was still reciting the song, the mouth of the fire which was on the firmament was rising up on high.

And I heard a voice like the roaring of the sea, and it did not cease from the plentitude of the fire.

And as the fire rose up, soaring to the highest point, I saw under the fire, a throne of fire and the many-eyed ones round about, reciting the song, under the throne **four fiery living creatures***, singing.*

And the appearance of each of them was the same, each having four faces, And this (was) the aspect of their faces: of a **lion***, of a* **man***, of an* **ox***, and of an* **eagle** *...*

And while I was still standing and watching, I saw behind the living creatures a chariot with fiery wheels.

Each wheel was full of eyes round about. And above the wheels was the throne which I had seen.

And it was covered with fire and the fire encircled it round about, and an indescribable light surrounded the fiery crowd.

And I heard the voice of their sanctification like the voice of a single man.

Moses Vision

Although Moses was not taken up in a whirlwind and brought before a throne of God, he did see the Lord descending from heaven on Mt Sinai. The throne that Moses met and talked with God at was the "Mercy

Seat" on top of the Ark of the Covenant within the Holy of Holies inside of the Tabernacle. The first instance in the Bible of the Lord descending in the clouds was in Exodus 34:5 where Moses sees the Lord descending in the clouds at Mount Sinai. Also see 1 Enoch 1:9 and Jude 1:14.

> *Deuteronomy 33:2 ...And He came from the midst of ten thousand holy ones. At His right hand there was flashing lightning for them"*

Moses later appears with Elijah at the Mount of Transfiguration where they met and talked with Jesus.

> *Luke 9:30 ...Two men, Moses and Elijah, appeared in glorious splendor, talking with Jesus.*

Although Deuteronomy 34:6 says that "He (God) buried him (Moses) in Moab," it also says "to this day no one knows where his grave is." Babylonian Talmud: Tractate Sotah 13b indicates that many believe that Moses like Enoch and Elijah never died. This portion could not have been written by Moses as it refers to his death and had to be added to this book of Moses.

Elijah Taken

Elijah is the next rider where in 2 Kings, Elisha and Elijah are walking together and almost exactly as Ezekiel chapter 1, Elijah is also taken in a whirlwind on a *"chariot of fire."*

2 Kings 2:11 ...As they were walking along and talking together, suddenly a chariot of fire and horses of fire appeared and separated the two of them, and Elijah went up to heaven in a whirlwind.

As mentioned previously, Elijah is taken in a whirlwind on a *"chariot of fire."*

2 Kings 2:11 ...suddenly a chariot of fire and horses of fire appeared and separated the two of them, and Elijah went up to heaven in a whirlwind.

The book of Malachi concludes with these words:

Malachi 4:5 ...See, I will send the prophet Elijah to you before that great and dreadful day of the Lord comes.

Jesus, in Matthew 11:14 says:

"And if you are willing to accept it, John himself is Elijah who was to come."

Isaiah's Throne Vision

Although Isaiah the prophet lived in the 8th century BC, the writing of the book of Isaiah most likely also was written by several people during the Babylonian captivity as Daniel and Ezekiel were. In Isaiah chapter 6, Isaiah too sees a vision of God on his throne.

Isaiah 6:1-3 ...In the year that King Uzziah died, (742 BC), Isaiah saw the Lord in a vision, high and lifted up, seated on a throne; and the train of his robe filled the temple.

Above him were Seraphim, each with six wings. With two wings they covered their faces, with two they covered their feet, and with two they were flying.

And they were calling to one another, "Holy, holy, holy is the Lord Almighty; the whole earth is full of his glory."

In I Enoch we see the angels sing:

I Enoch 39:12 ...Holy, holy, holy, Lord of the spirits"

In II Enoch chapter 21 we also see a reference to the creatures in front of the throne and the "many eyed ones" singing:

II Enoch 21:1 ... "Holy, holy, holy, Lord Ruler of Sabbath."

The only other place in Scripture where we see the phrase, "Holy, holy, holy" other than in Isaiah chapter 6 verse 3 is in the New Testament book of Revelation.

Revelation 4:8 ... "In the center and all around the throne were four living beings, each covered with eyes, front and back, who day after day and night after night they keep on saying:

Holy, holy, holy is the Lord God, the Almighty; the one who always was, who is, and who is still to come."

And they did not rest day and night, saying, "Holy, holy, holy, Lord God Almighty, which was, and is, and is to come"

Daniel's Throne Vision

In Daniel chapter 7 and 10 Daniel has visions of God, the Ancient of Days, on his throne where there were other thrones set up as well, similar to Ezekiel and the book of Revelation.

Here, Daniel sees a man clothed in white linen and a belt of fine gold with hair like wool and his throne on fire with burning wheels. His body also was like topaz and his face looked like lightning and his eyes like torches. His arms and his feet were like in color to polished brass and the voice of his words like the voice of a multitude of people. Fire is seen streaming from his throne and ten thousand times ten thousand minister to him and the books were opened.

Daniel 7:9 ...His throne was aflame with fire, and its wheels were all ablaze. A river of fire was flowing, coming out from before him.

Thousands upon thousands attended him; ten thousand times ten thousand stood before him.

Then, much like in the book of Enoch, the one referred to as the "Son of Man" and "coming in the clouds" comes to the Ancient of Days and power is given to him over all things. This vision causes him to become faint and everyone with him runs and hides.

> *Daniel 7:13 ...I saw in the night visions, and, I saw, one like the Son of Man came with the clouds of heaven, and came to the Ancient of Days, and they brought him near before him.*

> *I Enoch 70 ...for that Son of Man has appeared, and has seated himself on the throne of his glory, and all evil will pass away before his face, and the Word of that Son of Man will go out and be strong before the Lord of Spirits.*

To the Jewish mystics, this was a reference to the *Greater* and *Lesser Countenance* with the Ancient of Days as *Macroprosopus*, also known as Arich Anpin (the Almighty God), and the Son of Man as Microprosopus, also known as Ze`ir Anpin (representation of God, His attributes in human form).

Ezekiel's Throne Vision

Ezekiel chapter 1 reveals a vision of Ezekiel similar to other visions of God's throne such as in Daniel's and Enoch. Here Ezekiel is taken in a whirlwind and ascended into heavenly palaces or *Hekhalot* in Hebrew and before God's Throne.

This throne in Ezekiel looked like sapphire and on the throne was someone that looked like a man. And from underneath the throne came *"streams of flaming fire so that I could not look on it."*

*Ezekiel 1:26-27 ...Above the vault over their heads was what looked like **a throne** of lapis lazuli and high above on the throne was a **figure like that of a man**.*

I saw that from what appeared to be his waist up he looked like glowing metal, as if full of fire and that from there down he looked like fire; and brilliant light surrounded him.

John's Throne Vision

In the book of Revelation, the Apostle John is shown the things that will come in the future much like Enoch is show the *"secrets of the ends of the heavens."* He is *taken in the spirit* and set before the throne of God where he explains what he sees just as Enoch, Ezekiel and Daniel do. John's vision is of Christ sitting on a great throne made of all kinds of precious stones, a rainbow around it and a sea of glass or crystal around the throne.

Revelation 4:5 ...From the throne came flashes of lightning, rumblings and peals of thunder. In front of the throne, seven lamps were blazing. These are the seven spirits of God.

Also in front of the throne there was what looked like a sea of glass, clear as crystal. In the center, around the throne, were four living creatures, and they were covered with eyes

The glory of Christ is explained here as his feet were like brass; eyes were like lamps and his hair like wool and referred to as the *"Son of Man"* and *"coming in the clouds"*; all pictures identical to visions of Moses, Daniel and Enoch.

Revelation 22:1 ...Then the angel showed me the river of the water of life, as clear as crystal, flowing from the throne of God and of the Lamb.

I Enoch 14 ...And from underneath the throne came streams of flaming fire so that I could not look on it.

Revelation then describes that in front of God's throne are seen *"many eyed creatures"* just as in Ezekiel 1 and several times in 2 Enoch. John sees different types of winged part man creatures like **lions, eagles** and **oxen** similar to carvings and sculptors around the throne of Solomon and Zeus/ Jupiter as we will see next. Cherubim and Seraphim are there as well, just as in these other books. We can go on and on with almost word for word similarities already shown in the Review of Literature (See Mark Dennis - The Revelation of John).

Solomon's Temple

Jewish Temple

The only reference in biblical Scripture that we see the *fiery wheels* of the throne of God is in Daniel 7 where:

> Daniel 7:9 ... *"His throne was aflame with fire and its wheels were all ablaze."*

The only other biblical reference that has any similarity with Ezekiel's writings of wheels and a temple and those of Daniel and the book of Revelation is found in I Kings chapter 7. Here we see the construction of the ten bronze water carts in front of Solomon's temple built for Solomon by Hiram, king of Tyre. Each of these carts had *"four wheels"* made of *"burnished bronze."* Each of these carts was decorated with carvings of *oxen, lions* and *cherubim's* with wreaths. Some believe that these ten carts represent the ten Sefiroth and the four wheels, the four realms or worlds.

> *1 Kings 7:27-30 ...Hiram also made ten bronze water carts, each 6 feet long, 6 feet wide, and 4-1/2 feet tall... Each of these carts had four bronze wheels and bronze axles.*

The components of Solomon's Temple would be the bronze *Sea* that was in front of the Temple, the *Altar of Incense* with *four horns.* We have the description of the *bowl* of pure olive oil and the menorah with *seven candles* or lamps. In between the altar and the lampstand is the table of the showbread and then the *two angels* that stand over the Ark inside the inner sanctuary.

The Sea which was in front of the temple was a great bronze basin placed on a base of twelve bronze oxen that all faced outward. Three faced north, three faced east, three faced south, and three faced west just as we see Jerusalem's walls and gates were built in Ezekiel 48. The walls of the Sea were about three inches thick and its rim flared out like a cup resembling a water lily.

The use of this imagery in Ezekiel and Revelation of the Sea in front of the throne of God, the fiery wheels, the oxen, lions and cherubim facing in four directions cannot be ignored. Hiram, the Phoenician king of Tyre, built much more of what we see in the temple for Solomon. Two great bronze pillars were erected in Solomon's Temple, the gold altar, the five lampstands of solid gold, the bowls and incense burners, all of solid gold.

In both cases of Ezekiel and Revelation, the temple of God had recently been destroyed; first by the Babylonians and next by the Romans and the people of Israel and their prophets longed for its return. This cannot be a coincidence; there must be a direct correlation between what is written in 1 King's chapter 7 and the imagery of Ezekiel which is clearly the origin of John's writings in the book of Revelation.

Sea of Glass

The sea of glass in Solomon's temple was a giant laver, a great bronze basin called the Sea that held 17,000 gallons of water used to purify one's self. It was broken up and taken into Babylon during the destruction of Jerusalem in 597 BC.

I Kings 7:23-26 ... And he made the Sea of cast bronze, ten cubits from one brim to the other; it was completely round.

Its height was five cubits, and a line of thirty cubits measured its circumference. Below its brim were ornamental buds encircling it all around, ten to a cubit, all the way around the Sea.

The ornamental buds were cast in two rows when it was cast.

It stood on twelve oxen: three looking toward the north, three looking toward the west, three looking toward the south, and three looking toward the east.

The Sea was set upon them, and all their back parts pointed inward. It was a handbreadth thick; and its brim was shaped like the brim of a cup, like a lily blossom. It contained two thousand baths (17,000 gallons).

Wheels of King Solomon's Throne

Ancient writings known as Jewish Midrash and the Babylonian Targum Sheni, an expansion of the book of Esther, describe the throne of Solomon to be made of ivory and covered with jewels. It had six golden steps and on each step were twelve golden lions facing twelve golden eagles. Many types of animals including **lions, eagles** and **oxen** were carved on these steps.

Above this throne was a seven branched lampstand of the menorah which represented the seven patriarchs of Israel. Above this was a golden bowl filled with olive oil which acted as a reservoir for the seven branched lamp. Above the throne yet was constructed something that resembled twenty-four golden vines to shade the king from the hot mid-day sun.

1 Kings 10 ...Then the king made a huge throne, decorated with ivory and overlaid with fine gold. The throne had six steps and a rounded back.

There were armrests on both sides of the seat, and the figure of a lion stood on each side of the throne.

There were also twelve other lions, one standing on each end of the six steps. No other throne in the entire world could be compared with it!

(See Mark Dennis - The Revelation of John)

Solomon's Temple

Solomon's throne was possibly stolen by Pharaoh Sheshak I in a campaign against Israel around 920 BC when he ransacked the temple and took its treasure sometime after Solomon's death. It is believed that this throne eventually ended up in Babylon and was used by Nebuchadnezzar, Cyrus, Darius, Alexander the Great and eventually to Antiochus Epiphanes (Flood, pg.85).

John, in the book of Revelation chapter 4, puts the throne, the colors around the throne, the seven horned lamp, the lion, calf and eagle as well as the twenty four elders all in one place. It is not clear if the Babylonian writings illustrating Solomon's throne influenced John or not but the resemblance cannot be ignored.

Revelation 4:5 ...*From the throne flashes of lightning came, rumblings and peals of thunder. In front of the throne, seven lamps were blazing. These are the seven spirits of God.*

The king's throne was also set up with four wheels on it so that it could be quickly moved to whatever function that King Solomon would have to preside over. It is said that the wheels of his throne and the creatures on the designed on his throne would move and make sounds by some mechanical means in order to paralyze and intimidate those being judged. This was a huge throne and being made of ivory was evidently white. Being that Solomon was well known for his wisdom; could it be that John is alluding to the throne of Solomon in Revelation chapter 20? No other place is there a reference to a white throne in Scripture.

Enoch's Temple Visions

In I Enoch Chapter 14 we see this beautiful vision of the temple:

See, in the vision clouds invited me and a mist called me and the course of the stars and the lightning sped and hurried me, and the winds in the vision caused me to fly and lifted me upward, and bore me into heaven.

And I went in until I drew near to a wall which is built of crystals and surrounded by tongues of fire and it began to frighten me. And I went into the tongues of fire and drew near to a large house which was built of crystals; and the walls of the house were like a tessellated floor made of crystals, and its foundation was of crystal.

Its ceiling was like the path of the stars with lightning, and between them were fiery cherubim, and their heaven was clear as water. A flaming fire surrounded the walls, and its entries blazed with fire.

And I entered into that house, and it was hot as fire and cold as ice; there were no pleasures of life in it.

Fear then covered me, and trembling got hold on me and as I quaked and trembled, I fell on my face.

And I saw a vision, and look! There was a second house, greater than the former, and the entire doorway stood open before me, and it was built of flames of fire.

And in every respect it so excelled in splendor and magnificence and extent that I cannot describe to you its splendor and its extent.

And its floor was of fire, and above it was lightning and the path of the stars, and its ceiling also was flaming fire.

And I looked and saw in it was an elevated throne. Its appearance was as crystal and the wheels of it as the shining sun, and there was the vision of cherubim.

And from underneath the throne came streams of flaming fire so that I could not look on it.

And the Great Glory sat on the throne, and His robe shone brighter than the sun and was whiter than any snow.

None of the angels could enter or could see His face because of the magnificence and glory and no flesh could see Him.

The flaming fire was all around Him, and a great fire stood before Him and none around could draw near Him.

*And **ten thousand times ten thousand** stood before Him, yet He needed no counselor. And the most holy ones who were near Him did not leave Him by night nor go from Him.*

Ezekiel's Temple Visions

On a couple occasions in the book of Ezekiel, someone who looks like a man takes Ezekiel in a vision from Babylon to Jerusalem. In Ezekiel 8 we see this:

I looked, and I saw a figure like that of a man. From what appeared to be his waist down he was like fire, and from there up his appearance was as bright as glowing metal.

He stretched out what looked like a hand and took me by the hair of my head.

The Spirit lifted me up between earth and heaven and in visions of God he took me to Jerusalem

In Ezekiel 10 we see this:

I looked, and I saw the likeness of a throne of lapis lazuli above the vault that was over the heads of the cherubim.

The Lord said to the man clothed in linen, "Go in among the wheels beneath the cherubim.

Fill your hands with burning coals from among the cherubim and scatter them over the city." And as I watched, he went in.

Now the cherubim were standing on the south side of the temple when the man went in, and a cloud filled the inner court.

Then the glory of the Lord rose from above the cherubim and moved to the threshold of the temple. The cloud filled the temple, and the court was full of the radiance of the glory of the Lord.

The sound of the wings of the cherubim could be heard as far away as the outer court, like the voice of God Almighty when he speaks...

Later on in Ezekiel chapter 10 the glory of God leaves the temple:

...Then the glory of the Lord departed from over the threshold of the temple and stopped above the cherubim.

While I watched, the cherubim spread their wings and rose from the ground, and as they went, the wheels went with them.

In the twenty fifth year of the Jewish captivity in Babylon and fourteen years after Jerusalem was destroyed, Ezekiel was again taken in a vision to the land of Israel. He was set on a high mountain with the city to the south. There he saw a man, whose appearance was like the appearance of brass, with a measuring line in his hand standing by the gate of the city. The man takes him to the Holy Temple and this is what Ezekiel sees:

Ezekiel 43:1-4 ...Then the man brought me to the gate facing east, and I saw the glory of the God of Israel coming from the east.

His voice was like the roar of rushing waters, and the land was radiant with his glory.

The vision I saw was like the vision I had seen when he came to destroy the city and like the visions I had seen by the Kebar River, and I fell facedown.

The glory of the Lord entered the temple through the gate facing east. Then the Spirit lifted me up and brought me into the inner court, and the glory of the Lord filled the temple.

Zechariah's Seven Candlesticks

In the book of Zechariah, in a vision, an angel announces that the seven candlesticks, which are the image of the seven-branched menorah of the temple, are the *"seven lamps representing the seven eyes of the Lord that search all around the world."*

Solomon's Temple

These *"seven eyes will be glad when they see the plumb line in the hand of Zerubbabel"* when the Temple in Jerusalem is being rebuilt after being destroyed in the Babylonian captivity. The seven candles of the menorah may also have originally represented the seven days of God's creation, just like we see in the lower seven Sefiroth in Jewish mysticism.

Just like what was above King Solomon's throne, Zechariah's illustration here is of a single bowl of olive oil sitting above a seven-branched menorah with seven pipes feeding the lamp with the oil (Zechariah 4). Although the oil could have easily been simply fed by gravity as the bowl is pictured above the lamp, some believe that his might have been a more complex device.

Recent scientific research has shown that many temples of the ancient world had "fire pumps" (Kline, pg. 38) such as those described by Hero of Alexandria, that were generated by the heat of a fire lit on the altars. Air in a seal box heated by this fire would expand and force fluids to flow through copper pipes from reservoirs. Some temples had blood pumped to the eyes of statues for a dramatic magical effect on believers; others forced milk from the breasts of the statue of Artemis (Diana) in the temple of Ephesus in ancient Asia Minor.

This vision of Zechariah seems to some researchers as such a device that automatically pumped oil from the bowl to the lamps, reducing the work load of the priest. Solomon's throne as we saw was also mechanized.

Throne of Zeus

Some scholars believe that these ancient description of God's throne in the books of Enoch, Ezekiel, Daniel, and Revelation, were an ancient description of the temple of Zeus in Olympia Greece and Antioch Syria or of the Roman equivalent, Jupiter in Rome. This great temple in Olympia was built around 450 BC, about the same era as the Jewish priest Ezra who had scribes pen, copy and re-write many ancient books.

The ivory statue of Zeus had an *eagle* perched over him, his robe and sandals are made of gleaming fine gold and his garments where white and carved with lilies; it was one of the seven wonders of the ancient world. The magnificent forty foot ivory throne was carved with figures of Greek gods and mystical animals such as the sphinx which was half *lion* and half *man*.

Above the great support columns were sculpture depicting the twelve labors of Heracles, six on each side of the temple. His throne was adorned with precious stones, ivory, ebony and gold. In his right hand, Zeus held the winged figure of Nike, the goddess of victory and a scepter in the left.

In order to keep the ivory statue from deteriorating in the damp weather of Olympus, the statue of Zeus was continuously bathed with olive oil (MacKendrick, pg. 244). The Olive oil used to preserve it came from a large reflecting pool of oil, like a sea of glass in front of the throne of Zeus that reflected light from the doorway illuminating it.

Intoxicants, Religion and Visions

From a non-religious, natural perspective, the visions of these prophets simply may have been hallucinations generated naturally through an illness and high fever, or though the ingestion of natural toxins in the food supply. While reading the descriptions of these visions, many have noted that they seem very psychedelic, as if they had eaten some psilocybin mushrooms which are abundant in that region.

One ancient Greek practice that these Merkabah Riders might have been exposed to was that of Greek philosophers such as Plato and Sophocles some 300-400 years before Christ. It was common practice for these philosophers and debaters and priests in the temples, to burn Frankincense to enhance mental stimulation and debate in close quarters for hours. Frankincense contains mind altering chemicals that have a similar affect to cannabinoids that can stimulate the brain and cause the hallucinations; this is linked with many religious visions and spiritual experiences in ceremonies throughout the ages (Ruck, pg. 94).

Others suggest that these "visionaries" may have consumed the Greek drink Eleusinian Kykeon (Ruck, pg. 19). This was a drink made from barley infused with the parasitic ergot fungi; the psychoactive properties of the chemical ergonovine in this drink triggers intense experiences, a practice of hierophantic priests of that time. Lysergic acid derived from ergot sclerotia naturally contains some amounts of lysergic acid diethylamide or LSD.

Visions of the Merkabah Riders

Although such ideas may be postulated by many well educated scholars throughout the centuries, all such possibilities are blasphemy, an anathema and an abomination to most faithful Jewish and Christian believers who believe that the Torah and the entire Scripture as the inspired Word of God.

(See Mark Dennis - The Revelation of John)

Mystical Visions

Mansions of the Elect

In I Enoch chapter 14 we see Enoch's vision of entering into two large houses or palaces:

*And I entered into that **mansion** (palace), and it was hot as fire and cold as ice; there were no pleasures of life in it.*

Fear then covered me, and trembling got hold on me and as I quaked and trembled, I fell on my face.

*And I saw a vision, and look! There was a second **mansion** (palace), greater than the former, and the entire doorway stood open before me, and it was built of flames of fire.*

In I Enoch chapter 41 we see that in the celestial heavens Enoch sees mansion built for the righteous; the *Hekhalot* or heavenly palaces.

I Enoch 41:2 ... *And after that I saw all the secrets of the heavens, and how the kingdom is divided, and how the actions of men are weighed in the balance. And there I saw the **mansions of the Elect.***

In the Gospel of John, Jesus speaks of these heavenly mansions that his Father has built for the righteous.

John 14:2-3 ...*In my Father's house are many* **mansions***: if it were not so, I would have told you. I go to prepare a place for you.*

And if I go and prepare a place for you, I will come again, and receive you unto myself; that where I am, there you may be also.

Ezekiel's Wheel in a Wheel

In this vision in Ezekiel chapter 1, Ezekiel sees four creatures that each have a wheel standing next to them and each of these wheels rims are full of eyes and sparkle like the crystals. All four wheels looked alike and were made the same; each wheel had a second wheel turning crosswise within it. The rims of the four wheels were tall and frightening, and they were covered with eyes all around, moving alongside of the four creatures which ever direction they moved; up or down, left or right.

Again in Ezekiel chapter 10 we see the same imagery. Each of the four cherubim had a wheel beside them sparkling like crystal. All four wheels looked alike and were made the same; each wheel had a second wheel turning crosswise within it. The cherubim could move in any of the four directions they faced, without turning as they moved. They went straight in the direction they faced, never turning aside. Here, Ezekiel says that both the cherubim and the wheels were covered with eyes and the cherubim had eyes all over their bodies, including their hands, their backs, and their wings. Ezekiel hears someone refer to the wheels as "the whirling wheels."

The most likely source of Ezekiel's writings here possibly can be found in the ancient book of I Enoch chapter 14 and chapter 40 and in II Enoch chapter 21; all written possibly much earlier and passed down orally until the time of Ezra. This vision of God's throne is almost identical to Ezekiel chapter 1 and chapter 10, Daniel chapter 7 and Revelation chapter 4.

Four Living Creatures

These four wheels and four creatures also could be imagery associated with the mystical four worlds. In Revelation 5 we see the vision describing the four living creatures again but this time with *the twenty four elders*. These are seemingly identical to the four living creatures of Ezekiel 1, the only other almost identical reference in the Bible.

> *Ezekiel 1:4 ...I looked, and I saw a windstorm coming out of the north--an immense cloud with flashing lightning and surrounded by brilliant light. The center of the fire looked like glowing metal, and in the fire was what looked like **four living creatures**...*

*Their faces looked like this: Each of the four had the face of a **human** being, and on the right side each had the face of a **lion**, and on the left the face of an **ox**; each also had the face of an **eagle**.*

In the first book of Enoch, chapter 40, however, we see that the four creatures in front of Gods throne are four archangels:

I Enoch 40:1-10 ...And on the four sides of the Lord of Spirits I saw four presences, different from those who do not sleep.

And I learned their names; for the angel that went with me told to me their names, and showed me all the hidden things.

*And he said to me, "This first is **Michael**, the merciful and patient.*

*The second, who is set over all the diseases and all the wounds of the children of men, is **Raphael**.*

*The third, who is set over all the powers, is **Gabriel**.*

*And the fourth, which is set over the repentance to hope of those who inherit eternal life, is named **Phanuel**.*

*And these are the **four angels** of the Lord of Spirits and the four voices I heard in those days.*

The Four Presences

Later on in 1 Enoch chapter 40 we see a reference to the "four presence" that stand in front of God's throne.

*"And on the four sides of the Lord of Spirits I saw **four presences**, different from those who do not sleep.*

*And I learned their names; for the angel that went with me told to me their names, and **showed me all the hidden things**."*

Shamash

In many cultures throughout history, there are also similar beings of four known as the Four Guardians of the directions or the Four Heavenly Kings representing the four cardinal directions. As for the wheel within a wheel, the *Shamash*, also known as the **Babylonian Sun Wheel**, closely resembles Ezekiel's wheel within a wheel (Wright, pg. 36).

One wheel is vertical and one wheel intersects the other wheel horizontally, also an image of a circle indicating the four directions of north, east, south and west. *Shamash* is the sun god of the ancient Assyrians and Babylonians of which we see references to in the ancient writings of "*The Epic of Gilgamesh*" and in the writings of Hammurabi, king of the Sumerians in Mesopotamia.

This symbol is clearly depicted on the Tablet of Shamash, a stone tablet discovered in southern Iraq from the 7th century BC. Ezekiel was a contemporary of Daniel and both books were written in the 6th century BC in the land of Babylon and possibly influenced with the imagery and symbolism of the Babylonian culture of that day.

Twenty-four Elders of Revelation

In Christianity throughout the centuries, many teachers and believers have believed that these four living beings are symbols for the four writers of the Gospels; Matthew, Mark, Luke and John. Many scholars believe the twenty-four elders are simply representative of the 24 books of the Masoretic Text or the *Tanakh* of the Old Testament.

These are the *Torah* or the five "books of Moses", the eight books of the *Nevi'im* or "Prophets" (counting the twelve Minor Prophets as one book) and the eleven Kethuvim or "Writings." The first and second books such as Samuel are all combined into single books.

There are other twenty-fours such the **twenty-four** thousand priests that served in the temple, **twenty-four** oxen offered as a sacrifice. There are the **twenty-four** hours in a day or the twenty four ornaments worn by a Jewish bride (listed in Isaiah 3). Of course twenty four is twice twelve; the number of months and the number of tribes of Israel, each having a priest representing them twice a day for the morning and evening sacrifices (Twenty-four elders?). Also in a similar context, Ezekiel in a vision immediately after his vision of God's glory meets with twenty–five elders of the city. These however were plotting mischief and were giving wicked council in the city.

This is the closest reference in Scripture to the number twenty four outside of the book of Revelation and a giant with twenty-four fingers and toes in the second book of Samuel.

2 Samuel 21:20 ...In a battle at Gath, there was a huge man with six fingers on each hand and six toes on each foot, twenty-four in all.

Most symbolic of all of these *"twenty-fours"* is that there were *twenty-four priestly divisions* known as *Mishmarot* who took weekly shifts in temple service. We see this practice continued for some time as recorded in Luke 1:5 over five-hundred years later; here John the Baptist's father, Zechariah, was of the priestly division of Abijah. One of Zechariah's divisional duties was to serve as a priest at the altar of God in the Temple where the angel Gabriel appeared to him. Each division was on duty twice a year for a one-week period in the Temple at Jerusalem and all participated in the major feasts Passover, Pentecost, and Tabernacles.

These priests were assigned the *twenty-four priestly gifts* or sacrifices of which ten were given in the temple, four in Jerusalem and the remaining ten, outside of the city of Jerusalem. The twenty-four priestly families who these gifts were assigned to were the descendants of the High Priest Aaron, the brother of Moses and are listed in 1 Chronicles 24. This was a priestly line set up during King David's reign just before he died.

Priestly Lineage

This priestly lineage was almost destroyed during the Jewish diaspora, the second captivity of the nation of Israel under Nebuchadnezzar. During the seventy years of captivity, the Israelites were dispersed all over the Babylonian Empire, Persia and the known world of that time. During the return to Jerusalem under Governor Zerubbabel, only some of the Jews returned. Many stayed in the "new world" as we see with the Jewish queen of Persia, Queen Esther, wife of King Ahasuerus, also known as Xerxes.

Interestingly enough, under Zerubbabel, only four priestly tribes returned to Jerusalem (Ezra chapter 2). These were the children of Jedaiah, which were of the house of Jeshua the High Priest; the children of Immer, the children of Pash'hur and the children of Harim. These four, which were the Chiefs of the priests of the four Davidic orders, were then divided up into the *twenty-four* original divisions and given the same names, continuing their duties according to the same tradition.

1 Chron. 24:4–5 ...Since more chief men were found from the descendants of Eleazar than the descendants of Ithamar, they divided them thus:

*There were **sixteen** heads of fathers' households of the descendants of Eleazar and **eight** of the descendants of Ithamar, according to their fathers' households.*

Could there be an association here? Is this possibly the source of this vision or analogy in Revelation chapter 5 and the twenty-four elders?

*Revelation 5:6 ...Then I saw a Lamb, looking as if it had been slain, standing at the center of the throne, encircled by the **four living creatures** and the **twenty-four elders**.*

Jewish mysticism also utilized the name of God, Adonai in twenty-four variations both in magic and in meditation.

They can be written in twenty-four different ways:

ADNY, ADYN, ANDY, ANYD, AYND, AYDN, DNYA, DNAY, DYNA, DYAN, DAYN, DANY, NYAD, NYDA, NAYD, NADY, NDAY, NDYA, YADN, YAND, YDAN, YDNA, YNDA and YNAD

$$4^2 = 24$$

Each of these twenty-four arrangements are individually associated with three parts of the seventy-two names of God (Name of Seventy-two Names) which are made into a "magic seal" known as a chotam.

Daniel's Image

In Daniel chapters 2, the king of Babylon, King Nebuchadnezzar, had a dream of a great image with a head of gold, arms of silver, torso of brass and legs of iron representing four kingdoms. These four Kingdoms possibly represent the Four Worlds of Jewish mysticism previously reviewed. At the base of this image were feet with ten toes; is this the image of Microprosopus, or Ze`ir Anpin and the ten Sefiroth so imbedded in Jewish mysticism?

Daniel also contains a story of the Fiery Furnace in which a "**son of God**" is seen Daniel 3:25, possibly the representation of Da'at or Tifereth. Later on Daniel himself sees a vision of the **Son of Man** before the throne of God.

Daniel 7:9 ...I watched until the thrones were set down and the Ancient of days did sit; whose clothing was white as snow and the hair of his head was like the pure wool...

*Daniel 7:13 ...I saw in the night visions, and, I saw, one like the **Son of Man** came with the clouds of heaven, and came to the Ancient of Days, and they brought him near before him.*

John's Vision

In Revelation 4, John is first called as Enoch was called to *"come up here."* John sees a door open in heaven just as Enoch does. He is brought before the *"twenty four elders"* and Enoch before the elders and *"rulers of the stellar orders."* John is shown the things that will come in the future much like Enoch is show the *"secrets of the ends of the heavens."*

He is *taken in the spirit* and set before the throne of God where he explains what he sees just as Enoch, Ezekiel and Daniel do; visions of *Merkabah Riders.* In Revelation, Christ is sitting on a great throne made of all kinds of precious stones, a rainbow around it and a sea of glass or crystal around the throne and so on.

The vision continues with a visual account of the four living creatures. The first is like a *lion*, the second like a *calf*, the third like a *man* and the fourth like a flying *eagle*. This is identical almost word for word out of Ezekiel chapter 1 where Ezekiel is taken in a whirlwind (see 1 Enoch 39:3).

Daniel's Vision

Daniel's vision of God in white clothing and with hair like wool is not new as in this illustration of God. The Son of Man and other spiritual beings are shown in a similar fashion in other Scriptures and ancient text. Even Noah in the book of Enoch has similar features. Enoch makes reference to God as the Head of Days and Daniel the Ancient of Days, possibly only different in translation. In ancient Aramaic these two phrases Head of Days and the Ancient of Days or "atik yomin" simply mean "the aged one."

The Image of Adam

The image of Adam Kadmon, the First Adam in Jewish mysticism is seen in the same fashion in contrast with Adam Ha-Rishon of the "Fall." Jesus is given the title of "The Last Adam," "Second Adam" or "New Adam" in the New Testament as seen in 1 Corinthians 15:45.

So it is written: "The first man Adam became a living being"; the last Adam, a life-giving spirit.

The Zohar:
Adam; who is the holy and supreme, who rules over all, and gives spirit and life to all.

Jewish mysticism also speaks of Adam Elyon as the "supreme man." Interestingly enough, the letters of Adam have the numerical value of 45, as does the letters of the Tetragrammaton (YHWH), when spelled out in full.

Daniel's Last Vision

Then Daniel sees two others that looked like men, one on this side of the bank of the river and the other on the opposite side of the river. Interestingly enough, the book of Enoch is full of references to two men that escort Enoch through the heavens and explain his visions to him. Then one of two men calls out to a man clothed in linen who was standing on the waters of the river, how long will it be to the end of these wonders? Jesus walking on the water in the Gospels can clearly be associated with this text. Then the man clothed in linen that was standing on the waters of the river, held up his right and left hand to heaven and swore by him that lives forever that it will be for a "time, times and an half." And when he will have accomplished to scatter the power of the holy people, all these things will be finished. But Daniel did not understand what this meant.

Then Daniel said, "Oh my Lord, what will be the end of these things?" And he said, "Go your way, Daniel. For the words are closed up and sealed until the "time of the end." Many will be refined and cleansed and made pure; but the wicked will do wickedly. And none of the wicked will understand; but the wise will understand." Then the man standing on the water said, "From the time that the daily sacrifice will be taken away to the abomination that makes desecration, there will be 1,290 days. Blessed is he that waits and comes to 1,335 days."

It is believed by some that the sacrifices were band for seven years in Jerusalem under the rule of Antiochus Epiphanes and oppression of the Jewish people during that time. It would be midway into the seven year period, about 1,300 days that Antiochus Epiphanes sacrifices a pig on the altar of the Jewish temple. Many would die in the blood bath that took place afterward. (See Mark Dennis - The Revelation of Daniel and The Revelation of John)

Visions of the Merkabah Riders

The Book of Zechariah

The book of Zechariah is the second to the last book in the Christian Old Testament and the eleventh book of Nevi'im or the "Prophets" in the Jewish Tanakh. According to Zechariah 1:1, the prophet Zechariah begins his dialog in the second year of Darius, King of the Persian Empire sometime around 520 BC.

Zechariah is an apocryphal writing that is full of visions and warnings of judgment with a call to repentance. The text seems to be split up into what might be called "First" and "Second" Zechariah with a contextual change in chapter 9, possibly due to a different scribe writing the text or simply a change in the date that the text was written. The second part is believed by some to be written by a student of Zechariah with a focus on historical writings of other prophets such as Isaiah and Jeremiah during the fall and destruction of Jerusalem.

John's book of Revelation clearly has much of its visionary source in the book of Zechariah. The first references are with the seven candlesticks of Revelation chapter 1 which originate in Zechariah chapter 4.

"I answered, "I see a solid gold lampstand with a bowl at the top and seven lights on it, with seven channels to the lights."

Seven Candlesticks

In Revelation chapter one, John writes of seven angels that represent the "seven candlesticks" or "lamps" of Zechariah chapter 4; these are John's "seven churches" of Asia. In the book of Zechariah, the angel announces that the seven candlesticks, which are the image of the seven-branched menorah of the temple, and are the *"seven lamps* representing the seven eyes of the Lord that search all around the world." Also, *"these seven eyes* will be glad when they see the plumb line in the hand of Zerubbabel" when the Temple in Jerusalem is being rebuilt after being destroyed during the Babylonian captivity. Like the seven stars of Revelation, the seven candles of the menorah may also have originally represented the seven days of God's creation.

The Two Anointed Ones

Zechariah's seven golden candlesticks are just one of Zechariah's symbols used in the Revelation of John. Seven bowls and two olive trees are also blended into the visions that John sees.

Zechariah chapter 4 says:

"Also there are two olive trees by it, one on the right of the bowl and the other on its left…

So he said, "These are the two who are anointed to serve the Lord of all the earth."

On each side of this bowl or reservoir of olive oil are two olive trees that keep the bowl filled with oil. It seems that Zechariah had been given a vision that appeared to keep the lamp burning continually through the power of God. The bowl possibly represents the power of God that sustained Israel in the time of restoration. The seven candles or lamps of the menorah represent the seven eyes of God, or the seven Archangels in front of the throne of God, which are well known in ancient Judaic mysticism.

The only two "anointed" persons of Zechariah's day were the High Priest Jeshua, and the Governor Zerubbabel who was the grandson of Judean king Jehoiachin. Their job was to keep the building of the walls and Temple going during the restoration of Jerusalem after the return of Israel from captivity. Zerubbabel was appointed as governor by the King of Persia; Darius the Great in 522 BC not long after the Persians dethroned the Babylonian King Belshazzar during a revolt. Darius who was a Zoroastrian in religion was also a monotheist as the Jews were and was receptive to the Jewish faith.

In Revelation chapter 11, John describes these two olive trees in a totally different way; these two olive trees are the two witnesses of God in the latter days. This is the most common belief today among Evangelical fundamental believing Christians in conjunction with the "rapture" of the Church.

Revelation 11:3 ...And I will grant authority to my two witnesses ...

These are the two olive trees and the two lampstands that stand before the Lord of the earth.

And if anyone wants to harm them, fire flows out of their mouth and devours their enemies.

Seven Horns and Seven Eyes

The *seven horns that have seven eyes* of Revelation 5:6 come right out of Zechariah 4:10, *"these are the eyes of the Lord which range to and fro throughout the earth.* Unlike the ten horns on the beasts of Daniel and Revelation, these *seven horns* are clearly the seven branches of the menorah with the seven lamps lit by pure olive oil, the seven eyes of the Lord who are the seven Archangels of God.

Four Horses

In Revelation chapter 6 we also see three colors of horses, white, red, black and pale horse. Zechariah also has a similar vision of the same color horses with chariots and an additional fourth speckled horse as well. These were to conquer, take peace from the earth and produce famine with the symbol of the balance, a similar image used in Enoch. Zechariah 6:2 says,

"In the first chariot were red horses; and in the second chariot black horses; and in the third chariot white horses; and in the fourth chariot speckled bay horses."

Again, in Zechariah these four horses represent the four spirits that are in front of Gods throne.

*Zechariah 6:4, says, "The angel answered me, "These are the **four spirits** of heaven, going out from standing in the presence of the Lord of the whole world."*

(See Mark Dennis - The Revelation of John)

Visions of the Merkabah Riders

The Book of Isaiah

Holy, Holy, Holy

Isaiah is also a source of some of much of Jewish mystic imagery. It is only in Isaiah chapter 6 that we see any other reference to the words, "*Holy, Holy, Holy*" other than in the books of Enoch which is most likely the original source of this text in Revelation

Revelation 4:8 ... "Day and night they never stop saying, "'Holy, holy, holy is the Lord God Almighty,' who was, and is, and is to come".

Isaiah 6:3 ... "And they were calling to one another, "Holy, holy, holy is the Lord Almighty; the whole earth is full of his glory."

In Isaiah chapter 14 we see the origin of text of the Dragon being cast out of heaven, another Jewish mystic story also seen in Revelation chapter 12.

*Isaiah 14:12-15 ... "How you have fallen from heaven, **O Morning Star**, son of the dawn! You have been cast down to the earth, you who once laid low the nations!*

You said in your heart, "I will ascend to heaven; I will raise my throne above the stars of God;

I will sit enthroned on the mount of assembly, on the utmost heights of the sacred mountain.

I will ascend above the tops of the clouds; I will make myself like the Most High."

But you are brought down to the grave, to the depths of the pit."

Babylon has Fallen, has Fallen

The true origin is II Enoch 29. Most readers do not know that the context of this text is to the Babylonians and their defeat by the hands of the Medes and the Persians. It is Babylon that is viewed as one that has *"fallen from heaven."* It is again Babylon who is *"Babylon is fallen—that great city is fallen"* in Revelation chapter 14, a direct quote from Isaiah 21:9, *"Babylon has fallen, has fallen!"*

The term, "a new name" is only used in Scripture in Revelation chapters 2 and 3 and in Isaiah chapter 62. *"I will also write on them my new name"* and, *"I will also give that person a white stone with a new name written on it."* White stones were used as an amulet or breast piece worn by the Levite priests with the tribes names.

Isaiah 62:2 ..."And the Gentiles shall see thy righteousness, and all kings thy glory: and thou shalt be called by a new name, which the mouth of the Lord shall name."

Exodus 28:21 ...There shall be twelve stones with their names according to the names of the sons of Israel. They shall be like signets, each engraved with its name, for the twelve tribes.

96

*Isaiah 11:1 …"And there shall come forth a root out of the **stem of Jesse**, and a Branch shall grow out of his roots."*

Revelation has similar text with its source in Isaiah.

*Revelation 22:16 …"I, Jesus, have sent my angel to give you this... I am the root and the **offspring of David**, and the **bright Morning Star**."*

*Revelation 5:5, "See, the Lion of the tribe of Judah, the **Root of David**, has triumphed."*

Ancient Jewish mystic belief was in a Savior, a Messiah that would come from the House of Jesse, the father of King David and free Israel from oppression. This became the Kingly lineage that the Jewish kings of Judah would come from and from which they believed the Messiah would also come from. It was from this belief that early Christians would point out the genealogy of Jesus, how that he would come from the lineage of David, therefore proof that he was the Messiah.

Islam however points out the Priestly Line of Amram of whom Mary in the Qur'an is a descendant of, indicating that both Jesus and his cousin John the Baptist (son of the Levite priest Zechariah) were both Levites and of the Priestly lineage of Aaron, son of Amram; possibly the priesthood of the order of Melchizedek

One strange thing to point out in the preceding passages is that both Jesus and Lucifer (Satan) are referred to as the **Morning Star.**

(See Mark Dennis - The Revelation of John)

The Books of Enoch

Enoch I, II and III

History

The books of Enoch are several works that are attributed to the Enoch of Genesis, son of Jared, father of Methuselah and great-grandfather of Noah. Parts of the first book, I Enoch, are dated between the 3rd and 1st century BC (up to three hundred years before Christ) and primarily written in Ge'ez or the Ethiopic language; therefore also known as the Ethiopian Enoch. Recently small fragments have been found in both Aramaic and Greek in the Dead Sea Scrolls. Parts of the book were rumored to have been found in the early 1700's but it wasn't until 1821 that the first book of Enoch was finally translated into English by Richard Laurence.

The second book of Enoch or II Enoch was preserved solely in the Slavonic language and also known as the Slavic Enoch, most likely translated from Greek. Upon discovery of the second book, it was thought to be another version of the Ethiopian Enoch. However, after translation was completed in the late 1800's, it was evident that the text was from a totally different source and written closer to or during the Christian era. Because of the references to the temple and temple traditions, it clearly was written before the destruction of Jerusalem and the temple in 70 AD.

Enoch III was written well after the time of Jesus but is influential in Judaism with its references to Melchizedek. Although the books of Enoch (I, II and II) were not in either of the Jewish or Christian canons and were not considered to be inspired by either religion, they were very influential in ancient Jewish society. There are many similarities that can be shown between verses in the books of Enoch and both the Biblical Old Testament and New Testament. Many of the texts are clearly influenced or even direct references to Biblical verses. Many phrases such as "sons of God," "Son of Man," "Watchers," "King of Kings," "Lord of lords," "Most High" and so on, are common religious terms in ancient Jewish literature and even modern Christianity today.

Many entire chapters in the books of Enoch cover the stories of Creation or of the Flood. One chapter covers the whole history of Israel metaphorically as sheep with the Lord of the Sheep referencing God or possibly the Messiah. The book also covers in detail the fall of Satan as seen in Isaiah 14:12 and Luke 10:18. It is believed that many of these books were considered heretical books and denounced, banned and destroyed by the early Christian church along with the Gnostic Gospels and many other ancient books.

Son of Man

There is a clear distinction in the books of Enoch between the Most High who is called the Lord of the Spirits and the "Son of Man" as seen in Enoch I, chapter

105. This is possibly the first clear manifestation of the "Messiah" or "Anointed One of God" in ancient writings; the one who will rule in God's kingdom which was a common belief and hope in the time of Jesus. Unlike anywhere else in the Scriptures, the words "Son of Man" occur in the books of Enoch sixteen times and are clearly identified with the context of Enoch I, chapter 105, "My Son". Here it is used in a spiritual context yet not truly "divine" and is not a reference to "human being" as can we see in Ezekiel 2, Psalm 144 and other places in the Old Testament; possibly a reference to Adam Kadmon.

Jesus describes himself as the "Son of Man" over seventy times, seemingly emphasizing his "humanity." However, with so few Old Testament references with this phrase and the book of Enoch's link of this term to "the spiritual realm" it is highly likely that Jesus used the term "Son of Man" in the same context; knowing this book well and fulfilling the prophecy of this book. During the baptism of Jesus and the Transfiguration, God calls Jesus "My Son." According to Enoch, it is he, the Son of Man (the term Jesus uses for himself) who will return and judge sinners in the last days at the Day of Judgment. The term son of man is used, almost without exception, in the Old Testament in reference to "human being" (not divinity) such as in Ezekiel.

As far as the New Testament goes, many of the passages in the Gospels have clear commonality with the book of Enoch. Many of the parables of Jesus have identical themes and phrases such as "Let your yea be yea, and your nay be nay;" especially in reference to a common theme in the book of Enoch, Judgment Day.

Holy, Holy, Holy

The books of Enoch are clearly the foundation for the mystical beliefs of many Jewish people in the time of Jesus and the early Christian Church. This is evident in the many direct and indirect references of terms, phrases and topics to these books also in the Gospels, the books of Paul and other New Testament writings.

There are words and phrases such as "Holy, Holy, Holy," "King of kings and Lord of lords" and the visions of "many eyed creatures" before the throne and the "Great Judgment" where the evil ones are thrown into the fiery pit that are very similar in Old and New Testament Scripture. The most evident of these references is in the book of Jude which word for word quotes the first book of Enoch:

> *Enoch chapter 2 ...Behold, he comes with **ten thousands** of his saints, to execute judgment upon them, and destroy the wicked, and reprove all the carnal for everything which the sinful and ungodly have done, and committed against him.*

> *Jude14, 15 ...Enoch, the seventh from Adam, prophesied, saying, "Behold, the Lord comes with **ten thousands** of his holy ones.*

Other references are not as clear as direct quotes but are evident in the teachings of the Apostles and Jesus himself. The major theme of Enoch is Judgment and the end times when God reigns and rules on the earth. The verse above speaks of this return, a return shown throughout the New Testament as the Second Coming of Jesus; spoke of by Jesus himself, Paul, John and other writers in the early Christian church. This of course has its origin in the Torah at Mount Sinai.

*Deuteronomy 33:2 ...And He came from the midst of **ten thousand** holy ones. At His right hand there was flashing lightning for them...*

Influences of Enoch

Enoch and Revelation

The book of Revelation is the most similar to Enoch with a parallel description of heaven and Gods throne, the angels and other creatures around his throne. The term Elect is used in both as well as Holy, holy, holy, Lord of the Spirits and Son of Man. Seven mountains and seven stars are also used in both as well as a blood drenched robe, blood up to the horse's bridles, and the destruction of tens of thousands of evil ones fighting against God. John was taken into heaven in the spirit similar to Enoch, and was told "come here" as John also was in Revelation. Enoch and John, as well as Daniel fall as dead men before the Almighty God and told not to fear.

Revelation 1:17 ...When I saw him, I fell at his feet as though dead. Then he placed his right hand on me and said: "Do not be afraid."

103

The great "abyss" as the "Lake of Fire" is also a common topic in both, where the devil and his angels are thrown. The "Tree of Life" is discussed at great length as well and the descending of the New Jerusalem on the earth where the righteous will live and where God will rule and live with them. Also, a time of Great Tribulation is described in Enoch where the mountains turn to wax, great pestilence and plagues on the earth; where the moon turns red and the sun is darkened and great earthquakes. The elders before the throne, the four creatures, the two prophets, the creatures with many eyes, the trumpets, the Book of Life and the angels singing holy, holy, holy, are all common themes in both Revelation and Enoch.

It is not clear whether or not John was primarily influenced by the book of Enoch or the strong similarities that are also in the books of Job, Ezekiel, Daniel, Jeremiah, Joel and Zechariah. The books of Enoch were highly likely to have been written by many scribes, possibly some parts even before the above books were written, influencing them. Some fragments were clearly written after these books were written due to references that put their writing at about the time of Christ but before the destruction of Jerusalem and the Temple.

Book of Hebrews

Melchizedek is a major theme in the New Testament book of Hebrews where his name is mentioned fifteen times. The Old Testament mentions his name in only three verses of Genesis 14 and once in Psalm 110. The story of the Exaltation of Melchizedek in the book of I Enoch describes Melchizedek's extra ordinary extraordinarybirth and how he became a High Priest of the Most High. The stories in the books of Enoch were common stories that all the Jews knew so well even in the time of Jesus. The birth of Melchizedek as stated earlier is very similar to the stories of Jesus and his cousin John the Baptist's birth.

Paul's Writings

In similar context of influence, Paul's writings of predestination in Romans and Ephesians have a strong correlation with teachings of predestination in Enoch and were possibly influences on Paul during his upbringing and religious training as a Pharisee. Tongues of fire described in Enoch likewise may have had an influence on the writings of Acts and the Day of Pentecost. The Hebrew word for fire is Shin שׁ, and is used to depict the power of God and the Spirit of God.

Teachings of Jesus

Many of the teachings of Jesus are represented as doctrine taught in the books of Enoch. The story of Lazarus and the rich man that speaks of a great Gulf between them was a picture of what happens after death already in the Jewish mind, influenced by these books.

The parables that Jesus taught may have also been influenced by these writings, such as building you house on solid rock. Jesus made reference to the spirit of Abel calling out from the earth; a reference clearly brought out from these books of Enoch. Jesus taught that he himself saw Satan fall from heaven, a story spoke of at great length in Enoch but with only a glimpse in the Old Testament, also possibly influenced by the book of Enoch themselves.

The Beatitudes from Jesus' sermons and many parables also are very similar to teachings in Enoch, phrases such as *"the meek will inherit the earth"* or *"do not swear by heaven or earth"* for example. The book of Enoch clearly teaches the same message the Jesus taught about those who are rich and how their riches will lead to their destruction. The parable about the rich man and his need to build larger barns clearly comes from Enoch. Enoch is full of *"Blessed is the man"* and full of *"Woe's."*

Jesus also speaks of mansions that he will prepare for his followers; a story clearly spoken of in Enoch. The transfiguration of Jesus is also identical to Enoch's transfiguration when he ascended into heaven before God himself. The words *"it had been better that he had never been born"* was spoken by Jesus and in Enoch as well as *"how can a man return into his mother womb"* when Jesus speaks or being born again. Jesus speaks of *"Living Water"* and *"eternal life,"* both common themes in Enoch. The term *"Lord of the Sheep"* in Enoch is very similar to Jesus' reference to the *"Good Shepherd."*

Enoch and the Old Testament

Since the books of Enoch are religious Jewish writings, many stories have come directly from the Old Testament. The story of the fallen angels who *"mingled with the daughters of men"* mentioned briefly in Genesis is explained at great length in the books of Enoch; to the point of actually naming the angels who left heaven and married these women by name. Jude also makes reference to the book of Enoch recognizing this story.

Jude 1:6 ...And the angels who did not keep their positions of authority but abandoned their own home...

In the second book of Enoch chapter 29 we see a similar story of the fall of Satan explained at some length, describing how Satan (Azazel) thought he could become more powerful then God, but is only mentioned briefly in both Old and New Testaments of the Bible.

Luke10:18 ....Jesus said, "I beheld Satan as lightning fall from heaven."

II Enoch 29 ...conceived an impossible thought, to place his throne higher than the clouds above the earth, that he might become equal in rank to my power.

And I threw him out from the height with his angels, and he was flying in the air continuously above the bottomless Abyss.

Isaiah 14:12... *How you have fallen from heaven, morning star, son of the dawn! You have been cast down to the earth, you who once laid low the nations!*

Other Old Testament terms and phrases are commonly used in the books of Enoch, borrowed from Psalms, Song of Solomon, Job and possibly Ezekiel and Daniel; these books however were written after the return of Israel to Jerusalem and it is not clear which book influenced which. It also must be stated that many of these stories were passed down over the centuries by word of mouth and were common beliefs and possibly influenced all the writers equally.

Whole stories from the Old Testament are also replicated in the books of Enoch such as creation and the flood, likewise passed down from generation to generation and finally written down by a scribe in the time of Ezra, after the captivity.

Enoch Lifespan

It is interesting that Enoch in the book of Genesis, in the book of II Enoch and in the book of Jude is the 7th in line from Adam. Also curiously, he lived for 365 years; 365 is clearly a reference to the solar year and known thousands of years ago as seen in II Enoch chapter 14.

Genesis 5:23 *...Altogether, Enoch lived a total of **365 years***

In the first chapter if II Enoch this is reiterated:

II Enoch 1:3 *...After this too I lived two hundred years and completed of all the years of my life **three hundred and sixty five years**.*

This is clearly stated II Enoch:

II Enoch 14:1 *...Again those men led me away to the western parts, and showed me six great gates open corresponding to the eastern gates, opposite to **where the sun sets**, according to the number of the days, **three hundred and sixty five and a <u>quarter</u>**.*

Who was Enoch

According to III Enoch, after Enoch's ascension, he became Metatron. According to the Zohar, Metatron is Shaddai, which is the Shekinah light of God (Yoḥai, pg. 273). When Adam sinned, he lost touch with this divine light; this divine light was given to Enoch when he ascended into the heavens and became the heavenly "High Priest" who is associated with Melchizedek, also a heavenly "High Priest."

In Jewish numerology both Metatron and Shaddai have Hebrew letters in their names that add up to 314 (Marġolies, pg. 81). Shaddai is a name of God found written in piece of parchment which Jews call the Mezuzot, it is rolled up and placed inside a case place on their right doorposts. In it are verses from the book of Deuteronomy "Hear, O Israel, the Lord our God, the Lord is One." The name Shaddai and the Hebrew letter Shin ש are written on it.

Metatron is seen as the guardian of the gates in some earlier writings and was perceived as the "Lesser YHWH" or Ze'ir Anpin; this spiritual '**Son**'. This mystical thought comes from Exodus 23 where God speaks to Moses from a cloud on Mount Sinai:

> Exodus 23:20-21 ...*See,* ***I am sending an angel** ahead of you to guard you along the way and to bring you to the place I have **prepared**.*
>
> ***Listen to him** and listen to what he says. Do not rebel against him; he will not forgive your rebellion, since my **Name is in him**.*
>
> III Enoch 12:5 ...*And He called me the "**Lesser YHWH**" in the presence of all His heavenly household; as it is written, "**For my name is in him.**"*

The book of Luke directly links these same verses in Exodus to Jesus and John the Baptist; angels being sons of God and the messengers of God.

> Luke 9:35 ...*A voice came from the cloud, saying, **"This is my 'Son'**, whom I have chosen; **listen to him."***
>
> Luke 7:27 ...*John is the one about whom Scripture says, '**I am sending my messenger** ahead of you to **prepare the way in front of you**'.*

Isaiah 40:3 ...The voice of one crying in the desert: **Prepare ye the way of the Lord, make straight in the wilderness** *the way of our God.*

John 1:23 ...And John said, "I am the voice of one crying out **in the wilderness, 'Make straight the way of the Lord,'**

Metatron, Melchizedek and Michael

Among the Dead Sea Scrolls found in Qumran is a book called *Songs of the Sabbath Sacrifice*, written some 100 years before Christ. In these writings we see a picture of Melchizedek, like Enoch, visualized as an angelic or heavenly "High Priest" in the **Celestial Temple** as well; it is highly likely the source for the book of Hebrews (Barnard, pg. 128).

In the book of Daniel 10:21, Daniel calls the archangel Michael, the **"Prince of Israel"** and in the book of III Enoch 1:4, Metatron is called the **"Prince of the Presence"** or Sar Hapanim; many believe that *Michael*, *Metatron* and *Melchizedek* are one in the same. The name Michael means, "one who is like God" and is mentioned in the books of Daniel, Jude and Revelation; Metatron means "one who shares the throne," and Melchizedek is interpreted as the "King of Righteousness."

Jesus, also likened to Melchizedek, is called a "High Priest" the "Son of God," (Lesser YHWH). Jesus is also called the "Second Adam" and shared the throne with his Father (Abba). Jesus is Yeshua ישוע in Hebrew meaning "to deliver" or "savior."

Revelation 3:21 ... *To the one who is victorious, I will give the right to* **sit with me on my throne,** *just as I was victorious and* **sat down with my Father on his throne.**

Metatron who Enoch became after his ascension into heaven is explained in the oral Torah, the Talmud and in several other ancient Jewish books such as III Enoch. In Rabbi Ishmael's Merkabah vision of III Enoch, he sees Metatron in the palace halls of heaven. A subtle link to the celestial High Priest Melchizedek, King of Salem, (peace) is shown, referencing the priesthood of Aaron.

III Enoch 1:1-4 ... *Rabbi Ishmael said: When I ascended on high to behold the* **vision of the Merkabah,** *I had entered the six Halls, one within the other.*

As soon as I reached the door of the seventh Hall I stood still in prayer before the Holy One, blessed be He, and, lifting up my eyes on high, I said:

"Lord of the Universe, I pray thee, that the merit of **Aaron, the son of Amram,** *the* **lover of peace** *and pursuer of peace,*

Who received the **crown of priesthood** *from thy Glory on the mount of Sinai, be valid for me in this hour.*

So that Kaziel, the prince, and the angels with him may not gain power over me and throw me down from the heavens.

Then the Holy One, blessed be He, sent to me **Metatron***, his servant the angel, the* **Prince of the Presence.**

And he, spreading his wings, and with great joy came to meet me so as to save me from their hand.

Is the story of the "First Adam" related to the story of Enoch who became Metatron (same as Michael?), and the story of Melchizedek and the story of Jesus? It seems that across these different writings, the roles of Metatron, Melchizedek, Michael and Jesus seem to be overlapping in in many ways. All ascend or descent from heaven and provide the light of God to the world and their names are very similar in reference to God.

Hermes and Enoch

In Greek theology, it was *Hermes, son of Zeus* that was the *messenger of the god's*, a messenger sending communication between the worlds. He was an *intercessor for mankind* to the god's and *transcended the divine and physical worlds.* As Roman gods mostly corresponded with Greek gods, Mercury best depicted his same attributes. Hermes was also known as the *teacher of all secret wisdoms* and was the god that carries the souls of those who have departed to Hades.

1 Peter 3:18-19 ... Because Christ also died once for the sake of our sins, The Righteous One in the place of sinners, to bring you to God, and he died in body and lived in his Spirit. And he preached to those souls who were in Hades.

In Greek literature, Hermes description is similar to the archangel **Michael** as well. The Paul the Apostle was mistaken for Hermes while visiting Lystra.

Act 14:12 ...Barnabas (a Levite) they called Zeus, and Paul they called Hermes because he was the chief speaker.

An **Egyptian priest king** known as *Hermes Trismegistus,* author of the Emerald Tablet, is associated with **Toth**, the Egyptian god of wisdom and magic. Toth like *Hermes* was the god of magic, the development of wisdom and the judging the dead. Toth is commonly associated with **Moses**, **Enoch** and **Metatron;** Metatron was also an alternate name for **Hermes** in Gnostic writings.

Atenism

Atenism or **Amenism** can also be indirectly linked to **Toth** by the Israelites who came out of Egypt. Egyptian monotheism began with Atenism and Pharaoh Akhenaten. It was after the Pharaoh's death that Atenism immediately fell apart and Egypt went back to pagan polytheism and Atenism was stifled. Some believe that under this religious oppression, it is highly probable that true believers were driven underground where it survived in the desert in Qumran. From there it would prosper and flourish under the priesthood of Melchizedek in Salem and the priesthood of Jethro in the land of Midian; it was brought to Israel under Moses and Aaron from Midian (Feather, pg. xiii).

A copper scroll found in Qumran has been directly linked the city Amarna and the Pharaoh Akhenaten. Robert Feather, author of *The Mystery of the Copper Scroll of Qumran,* states that the basic doctrines of Judaism, Christianity and Islam, came out of Egyptian Atenism (related to Amenism).

It would be Moses who would grow up in Pharaoh's household, in many ways like Joseph before him, in great luxury and being royalty, he was well educated; he also most likely knew the Egyptian monotheistic religion and rituals of Amenism well. Some researchers indicate that the ancient Hebrews may have been influenced by Amenism in Egypt during Moses' up bringing in Pharaohs court and in the land of Midian.

The word Amen was first mentioned in 1 Kings at the end of King David's rule, and was used in prayer; it had not been long since the Exodus of the Jews from Egypt. It has also been adopted by many religions around the world who end prayers with "Amen" just like as the day ended in Egypt with the chanting "Amun" at the setting of the sun. A hymn written in Amarna Egypt says:

How manifold it is, what thou hast made! They are hidden from man's face. You are the only god, like whom there is no other!

*Psalm 104:24 ...O Lord, **how manifold are thy works**! In wisdom hast thou made them all: the earth is full of thy riches.*

Some scholars believe that it was this very belief that continued in the desert by the Dead Sea and was sustained in the Priesthood of Melchizedek through the Priesthood of Aaron and on through Christ, the "Amen." The Nazarenes and followers of Jesus knew these "hidden" things as seen in the book of Hebrews and other New Testament writings.

*Revelation 3:14 ...These are the words of **the Amen**, the faithful and true witness, the ruler of God's creation.*

*2 Corinthians 1:20 ...Therefore, the "**Amen**" is also spoken through Him by us for God's glory.*

Ten heavens of Enoch

Similar in nature to the ten Sefiroth of Jewish mysticism, the books of Enoch very vividly describe ten heavens that Enoch is taken to. These are quite different in many ways then the Sefiroth as these are places and are not to be confused with God's attributes. This vision of Enoch is typical of the other Merkabah riders, Ezekiel, Daniel and John.

From the earth, Enoch is taken to the **first heaven** described as a spiritual realm above the clouds where the winged angels inhabit. This a place where the rulers and elders of the stellar orders with 200 other angels who lend their services to the heavens reside. A place with store houses that shower the earth with snow, flowers and olive oil; store house that are opened and close from time to time as services by these angels.

The **second heaven** represents judgment; it is a dismal place of darkness greater than any earthly darkness. Here are God's apostate angels, who did not obey God's commands, but took counsel with their own will, and turned away with their prince, who is held on the fifth heaven. They are seen here hanging and weeping. As Enoch envisions this sad place, he felt great pity for them as they greeted him saying, "Man of God, pray for us to the Lord."

The **third heaven** Enoch was taken to was Paradise, a place of Mercy and Justice; a garden full of sweet flowering trees with fruits that were sweet smelling and bubbling with fragrance. The Tree of Life is in the center of the garden where the Lord rest when he goes up into paradise. Two springs come out of its roots which send out milk and honey and there are also more springs sending out oil and wine which separate into four parts and go down into the Paradise of Eden, separating corruptibility and incorruptibility. This is a sweet place, where three hundred very bright angels keep the Garden, who's incessant sweet singing voices serve the Lord throughout all days and hours. This is the "third heaven" that Paul mentions in 2 Cor.12:2.

In the **fourth heaven**, Enoch observes and even measures the sun and the moon, timing their orbits and comparing their light. Their orbits and the wheels on which they turn never stop, like the wind going past with very marvelous speed, day and night they have no rest. There are four great stars to the right of the sun's wheel, and four to the left, each having under it a thousand stars, altogether eight thousand, dancing with the sun continually. And by day fifteen myriads of angels attend them, and by night a thousand. And six winged ones go with the angels before the sun's wheel into the fiery flames, and a hundred angels kindle the sun and set it alight. He sees the twelve great gates of the Moon, six in the eastern gates and six in the western gates of the Sun. He sees the marvelous and wonderful Phoenixes and Chalkydri, with feet and tails in the form of a lion, and a crocodile's head, and their appearance is colored like the rainbow. At the Lord's command, they break into song, causing every bird to flutter with its wings, rejoicing at the giver of light.

As Enoch was carried on toward the fifth heaven, in the midst of the heavens he was delighted by armed soldiers, serving the Lord with percussion and organs and with sweet incessant voices and various singing, impossible to describe. Music that astonishes every mind, so wonderful and marvelous is the singing of those angels.

The **fifth heaven** Enoch encounters was also a place of judgment, a sad place as the second heaven was. There Enoch saw countless Grigori, huge human like soldiers residing in solemn silence and gloom, their faces withered. Like the apostate angels who turned away with their prince, rejecting the Lord of light, these are the angels of Genesis chapter 6, who broke through their vows and saw the daughters of men how good they are, and took them as wives, and contaminated the earth with their deeds. They who in all times of their age made lawlessness, mixing with mankind and giants were born from them, marvelously huge men with great hostility.

The **sixth heaven** is a spiritual home to the angels like the first heaven is. There are seven groups of angels here that set the timings of the earth, learning from the stars, and the moon and sun, and govern of the world likewise. These are the archangels who are above angels, measuring all life in heaven and on earth, the angels who are appointed over seasons and years.

These are also the angels who write down all the souls of men, and all their deeds, and their lives before the Lord's face. In their midst are six Phoenixes and six Cherubim and six winged ones continually singing with one voice, and it is not possible to describe their singing, for they rejoice before the Lord at his footstool.

In the **seventh heaven**, Enoch becomes fearful when he sees a very great light and fiery troops of great archangels, Cherubim and Seraphim, thrones and many eyed ones with nine regiments bowing before God. Enoch is told by the archangel Gabriel not to be afraid and is shown the Lord from a distance, sitting on His very high throne on the tenth heaven. Then he sees the Cherubim and Seraphim standing about the throne, the six winged and many eyed ones do not depart, standing before the Lord's face doing his will, and cover his whole throne. They were singing with gentle voice before the Lord's face, "Holy, holy, holy, Lord Ruler of Sabbath, the heavens and earth are full of Your glory."

The **eighth heaven** is called in the Hebrew tongue Mazzaroth, the changer of the seasons, of drought, and of rain, and of the twelve constellations of the circle of the expanse, which are above the seventh heaven.

The **ninth heaven** is called in Hebrew Kuchavim, where are the heavenly homes of the twelve constellations of the circle of the expanse.

The **tenth heaven** is the highest heaven which is called Aravoth or Araboth; this is where the throne-chariot of the Lord God Almighty is. Here Enoch in the vision, in a moment of eternity sees Lord's face. It was indescribable, marvelous and very awful, and very, very terrible; like iron made to glow in fire, and brought out, emitting sparks as it burns. Then he falls prone and bowed down to the Lord, and the Lord with his lips said to him, "Have courage, Enoch, do not fear, arise and stand before my face into eternity. And the Supreme Commander, archangel Michael, lifted him up, and led him to before the Lord's face.

(See Mark Dennis - The Revelation of John)
(See Mark Dennis - The Apocalypse of Enoch)
(See Mark Dennis – World of the Forsaken)

Jewish Priesthood

History of the Priesthood

Many scholars believe that the priesthood of Israel began with Moses in the land of Midian. Moses had lived there for many years and his wife Zipporah, was the daughter of the priest of Midian. These scholars believe that it was through Jethro the priest, that Moses was introduced to the term Yahweh or YHWH.

Exodus 6:2–3 ...I revealed myself to Abraham, to Isaac, and to Jacob as Ēl Shaddāi, but was not known to them by my name, YHWH.

This became the new name for the God of Israel, introduced to them by Moses as this name for God was not used in Scripture before that time; we remember that the Torah was written by Moses or scribes after Moses. It was the brother of Moses, Aaron of the tribe of Levi, whom the twenty-four priestly families of Israel descended from, also known as Amramites as they were sons of Amram. All priests were Levites but not all Levites were priests as they are descendants of Levi, son of Jacob. Traditionally priests could only marry Levites, keeping the priestly line uncontaminated.

During the forty years of wandering in the wilderness up until the time of Solomon, the Levite priests performed their daily duties in the Tabernacle, a portable temple which housed the sacred artifacts of the

Jewish faith such as the Ark of the Covenant. King David in 1 Chronicles 24:3-5 divided Aaron's descendants into groups according to their various duties. Each group carried out its appointed duties in the Temple according to the procedures established by their ancestor Aaron. In this chapter we see that Eleazar's descendants were divided into sixteen groups and Ithamar's into eight for a total of twenty-four priestly groups.

These were known as *Mishmarot*; all tasks were assigned to them by means of casting lots so that no preference would be shown. It is interesting to see that in the Islamic *Qur'an*, in the chapter of *The Family of Amram*, we see the story of the priests casting lots to see who would be in charge of caring for the young Mary (mother of Jesus) in the Temple. The lot fell on Zechariah, the father of John who was Mary's uncle.

These twenty-four groups of priests were chosen to serve in the temple because twenty-four is twice twelve; the number of tribes of Israel, each having a priest representing them twice a day for the morning and evening sacrifices. Each division was on duty twice a year for a one-week period in the Temple at Jerusalem and all participated in the major feasts of Passover, Pentecost, and Tabernacles.

Was Jesus a Levite?

It is traditionally believed that Levites and Cohen's who were in the priestly line of Aaron, could not marry outside of their tribe. We see this priestly practice continued for some time as recorded in the book of Luke chapter 1 over five-hundred years later. Here John the Baptist's father, Zechariah, was of the priestly division of Abijah, the eighth to be chosen. One of Zechariah's divisional duties was to serve as a priest at the altar of God in the Temple where the angel Gabriel appeared to him. Leviticus chapter 21 speaks of Levite marriage rules and says the High Priest wife:

> *...must be a virgin from his own clan, so that he will not dishonor descendants of his clan.*

If Zechariah married a Levite and Elizabeth and Mary were cousins, then Mary was a Levite as well, an Amramite, the descendants of Aaron and his father Amram. In the story of Mary, the mother of Jesus in the Qur'an, it begins with Mary's mother, an Amramite woman, a descendant of Amram, the father of Aaron and Moses. In this story she says a vow to God concerning the baby girl in her womb; when the baby was born she named her Mary, who was cared for by Zechariah in the Temple.

But Hebrews 7:14 says this of Jesus:

> *For it is evident that our Lord sprang out of Judah; of which tribe Moses spoke nothing concerning priesthood.*

Both Matthew chapter 1 and Luke chapter 2 show the genealogy of Jesus going through King David, assuring him of his kingly line. However, both are

123

making reference to his "father" Joseph and are slightly different. An explanation is normally given that Joseph's name is given because he was his "legal" father even though Jesus was of virgin birth. Most scholars today do believe that both genealogies are through Joseph; one legal, the kingly line of David and the other is the true genealogy of Joseph. If this is the case, Mary and therefore Jesus, truly may have been of the family of Amram, of priestly order after all. Even though this may be genetically true, we have to remember, that from a Jewish religious perspective, the status of a Levite priest is dependent upon being biologically a male descendant of Aaron.

Another perspective is that in Matthew's genealogy there were three Kings that were descended from David who had Levite mothers in the lineage of Jesus. King Abijah's mother was Michaiah the daughter of Uriel the Levite (2 Chronicles 13:1-2). King Jotham's mother was Jerushah the daughter of Zadok the Levite (2 Chronicles 27:1), and King Hezekiah whose mother was Abia the daughter of Zechariah the Levite (2 Chronicles 29:1).

The Priests were to be very knowledgeable in the laws and traditions of the Torah. Jesus as a child at the age of twelve, sat in the temple courts, sitting among the teachers, listening to them and asking them questions. As he began his ministry, he would teach in the synagogue and in the temple almost every day according to the book of Luke, commonly quoting Scriptures.

Jesus and John in Qumran

Many believe that Jesus and his cousin John the Baptist may have lived a secretive life in their early years with the devout Jewish sect known as the Essenes at Qumran in the desert by the Dead Sea. Although Jesus may have not been a Levite in the religious eyes of the Jewish Temple of his day, John, the son of the priest Zechariah, was. Jesus, growing up close to John and related to him, had Levite in his blood and certainly aspired to learn what he could in this respect.

The Essenes community goes way back to even before 580 BC with the returned of the Jews from Babylonian exile. Here in the wilderness by the Dead Sea, only a day's journey from Jerusalem, they had managed to sustain their way of life in abstinence from worldly pleasures. They lived a communal life style as we see in John 17:14–16 where Jesus encouraged the rejection of the world. Their intention was a pursuit of religious and spiritual goals, seeking divine knowledge, to know God, with a desire to become one with the Almighty. Years of study, prayer and meditation as well as servitude to their fellow man slowly developed into quite a large community of priests, mainly Levites. These men spent their days studying and writing as scribes and were the source of the Dead Sea Scrolls recently found.

These Essenes were highly agitated with the occupation of Rome in Judea and Jerusalem. They turned away from their everyday life in the city and focused their minds on the Messiah whom they expected to come any day. From the Dead Sea Scrolls, we see that the Essenes of Qumran appeared to be a priestly line going back to the time of Solomon and First Temple in Jerusalem. This priestly order is referred to by some as the order of Melchizedek referred to in Psalms, long before Jesus. Theirs was a Messianic message with the Messiah symbolized in the figure of Melchizedek. Psalm 110:1-4, attributed to King David, refers to the future "King of kings" and "Messiah" as a descendant of Melchizedek's priestly line.

> Psalm 110:1-4 ...*The **Lord** says to my **lord**, "Sit at my right hand until I make your enemies a footstool for your feet."*
>
> *The Lord will extend your mighty scepter from Zion, saying, "Rule in the midst of your enemies!"*
>
> *Your troops will be willing on your day of battle. Arrayed in holy splendor, your young men will come to you like dew from the morning's womb.*
>
> *The Lord has sworn and will not change his mind: "You are a priest forever, in the order of Melchizedek."*

Many believe that this is a reference to the Greater and Lesser YHWH as being, *"The **Lord** says to my **lord**, "Sit at my right hand*... God Almighty speaking to the Son of Man seen in Enoch:

*1 Enoch 70 ...for that **Son of Man** has appeared and has seated himself on the throne of His glory...*

This was written long before Christ and is an illustration for the ancient Jews of the Almighty God, the Greater YHWH with Adam Kadmon, the Son of Man, the human made in the image of God, in His likeness, the Lesser YHWH; the Messiah to come, the Celestial High Priest. This Adam was not deity or divinity, simply a reflection of the divine in human form; perfect in every way but restricted to space and time. In the New Testament, Jesus is painted in exactly the same light, as the Son of God, human, yet perfect in every way.

In John Jesus paints a similar picture:

John 14:28 ... I am going to the Father, for the Father is greater than I.

Some believe that the book*, Songs of the Sabbath Sacrifice* found here in Qumran, written some 100 years before Christ is possibly the source for the theme of Melchizedek in the book of Hebrews (Barnard, pg. 128). The book of Hebrews says that this Melchizedek was king of Salem and was the priest of Most High God. Salem was the city of Peace, the ancient city of Jerusalem, some 30 miles from Qumran.

Hebrews 6:20 ...*Jesus, has entered on our behalf. He has become a high priest forever, in the order of Melchizedek.*

Cult of Aten

Some scholars believe that there is also a link even further back, back to the time of Amenhotep IV around 1340 BC; possibly the time of Moses. Amenhotep IV introduced one of the oldest monotheistic religions known as the Cult of Aten, the worship of a universal spiritual being, the sole creator. Atenism appears in Egyptian texts dating as far back as the 1300's B.C. during Egypt's 12th dynasty (Appleton, pg. 69). This new religion branched out of Amenism and the worship of Amun, the sun-disk god known as Horus or Ra, the God of light. Many of the prayers to Amun and Aten are similar in nature with monotheism the focus of Atenism.

Egypt was a powerful entity under Amenhotep IV, the era of the Egyptian 18th dynasty. Under this revived monotheistic religion, God's mirror image was seen in the Pharaoh who was the supreme ruler of this empire. Amenhotep IV suppressed the other Egyptian polytheistic religions, and referred to **Aten** as:

"The one and only God, other than whom there is no other."

Assman (1997), pg. 153

128

This new religion however never took hold in Egypt as the Egyptians eventually over time reverted back to the worship of Amun after Amenhotep's death. Aten is also referred to as Aton, Amun-Ra and was considered to be a **trinity**:

> *All gods are three: Amun, Ra and Ptah, whom none equals. He who hides his name as Amun, he appears to the face as Ra, his body is Ptah*

Assmann (2008), pg. 64

The Word Amen

Strangely enough and possibly not just coincidence, the ancient Jewish word Amen is believed to have originated in Egypt. With Moses being brought up in Pharaoh's court, the possibility of Amenism being introduced through Moses to the children of Israel is substantial. This belief in the one and only God, then would have moved into Canaan with the Israelites from Egypt and evolved into the religious belief structure of Judaism today.

Amen was first mentioned in 1 Kings at the end of King David's rule, being was used in prayer; it had not been long since the Exodus of the Jews from Egypt.

> 1 Kings 1:36 *...And Benaiah the son of Jehoiada answered the king, and said, **Amen**: the Lord God of my lord the king say so too.*

Amen has also been adopted not only in Judaism but also in both Christianity and Islam. These religions all end their prayers with the word "Amen" just like as the day ended in Egypt with the chanting the word "Amun" during the setting of the sun.

A hymn written in the stone of the tombs in Amarna Egypt says:

O, sole god, there's no other god beside you!

Almost identical to the hymns found in the ancient religions of Zoroastrianism, Judaism, Islam and Christianity (Assmann, 2008, pg. 81). It is eerily similar to this Psalm from King David written many years later; remember it had not been long since the Exodus out of Egypt:

Psalm 104:24 ...*O Lord,* ***how manifold are thy works!*** *In wisdom hast thou made them all: the earth is full of thy riches.*

So is this great and wide sea, wherein are things creeping innumerable, both small and great beasts.

Amara Hymn to Aten

How manifold *it is,* ***what thou hast made!*** *They are hidden from man's face.*

O sole god, like whom there is no other!

Thou didst create the world according to thy desire whilst thou wert alone: All men, cattle, and wild beasts,

Whatever is on earth, going upon its feet, and what is on high, flying with its wings.

The countries of Syria and Nubia, the land of Egypt, Thou settest every man in his place, Thou suppliest their necessities:

Everyone has his food, and his time of life is reckoned. Their tongues are separate in speech and their natures as well;

Their skins are distinguished, as thou distinguishest the foreign peoples. Thou makest a Nile in the underworld, Thou bringest forth as thou desirest.

To maintain the people according as thou madest them for thyself, the lord of all of them, wearying (himself) with them,

The lord of every land, rising for them, the Aton of the day, great of majesty.

Pritchard, pg. 227-230

Texts in ancient tombs of this time also have some of these writings that indicate monotheism such as:

"I am the god Tem in rising. I am the Only One. I came into existence in Nu."

I am Ra who rose in the beginning, the ruler of this creation... I am yesterday, I know today... I am the Great God who created himself

Budge (2009), pg. 55

Hymns and prayers sung to Aten and Amun do not sound much different from any other Biblical prayer or reading said today:

Amun (God) who comes at the voice of the poor in distress, who gives breath to him who is wretched.

You are Amun, the Lord of the silent, who comes at the voice of the poor;

I called to you in my sorrow and You came and saved me.

Assmann, 2001, pg. 225

Semitic Hyksos

Scientific studies and historical records show that it was during this period that Egypt had expelled the Asiatic, Semitic Hyksos people back into Canaan; the Hyksos had occupied Egypt for over one hundred years (Assmann, 2008, pg. 81). Just like the Biblical text of Jacob and Joseph, these people too are said to have migrated to Egypt during a famine in Canaan and had lived peacefully in Egypt. The Hyksos people however were known historically to be polytheistic, worshiping gods such as Ba'al, the god of thunder and rain as well as Seth, the god of the desert.

This ironically also possibly was at the same time of the Judges in the new monotheistic nation of Israel just north of Egypt in the land of Canaan. The Israelites had also just come out of Egypt decades before according to the Biblical text of the Exodus and now Joshua was leading this new nation.

In his 1939 book, *Moses and Monotheism*, Sigmund Freud theorized that Moses who lived during this era, 1300-1200 BCE, borrowed his monotheism from Pharaoh Akhenaten (Amenhotep IV). Freud claims that Moses was possibly not Jewish at all but could have been an Egyptian priest. The Mosaic Jewish religion had probably originated with the cult of Aten, which was introduced by Pharaoh Akhenaten. Following the Pharaoh's death and the return of polytheism, Moses is believed to have fled Egypt along with his followers (Freud, pg.61). To Freud, Atenism was most likely the foundation for the monotheistic beliefs of Judeo-Christian and even Islamic theology.

Freemasonry

Some believe that Freemasonry of today also has its roots in Atenism as well as Jewish mysticism. The Masonic Eye of Providence is symbolic of the Eye of God but possibly has its origins in ancient Egypt and the Eye of Horus or Ra. The symbol of the "Unfinished Pyramid" also clearly is rooted in Egyptian symbolism. The Masons belief in a Supreme Being is monotheist in nature but stops at naming this God.

(See Mark Dennis – World of the Forsaken)

Mormonism

The modern day Christian denomination of Mormonism has many commonalities with Jewish mysticism and clearly has its roots in ancient Judaism. Mormonism, unlike many other Christian denominations puts an emphasis on the Shekinah or Holy Presence of God or Holy Spirit, one of God's "feminine" attributes. In fact both male and female images of God are emphasized, sometimes viewing God as a warrior and at other times as a birthing mother; this of course is metaphorical in both religions, drawing on the social roles of humanity as God truly is beyond gender (Paulsen, pg. 270).

Names of God

Jewish Writings

One of the first religious writings that appear in history is the Torah, the books of Moses, believed to be written about 1,300 B.C. Today, many believe that rather than being written about 1300 BC, at the time of the Hebrew exodus from Egypt, that the books of Moses were written some 700 years later, around 900 to 600 B.C. during the time of kings David, Solomon, and possibly the kings of the second temple after the captivity and the time of Ezra. Many more books about the Israelites were written over the following centuries, books that would become the core text of the Jewish culture and religion. These books today are called the Tanakh and are comprised of the Torah (the Pentateuch, also known as books of Moses or the Law), the Nevi'im (the Prophets), and Kethuvim (the Writings).

Ancient Hebrew Names of God

In the Indiana Jones film, "The last Crusade", the question was asked, "What is the name of God?" Indiana steps on the J for Jehovah and almost falls through the floor as Gods name in Latin is IHVH beginning with I. In these ancient Jewish writings, there is not just one name but many names for God. Although these are interpreted to simply be names of God due to His various attributes, some scholars suggest that they have other origins and date back to times even before Abraham and from other areas near and around the Land of Canaan.

El

The root word El appears not only in Hebrew but also in Assyrian and Phoenician as well as, a common name for the God of Israel and most other gods in the Transjordan area of Canaan. To the Canaanites, El was the "father of all gods" and whose wife was the goddess Asherah, mother of the "bull god" Ba'al.

El Shaddai

The ancient Hebrews originated from the lineage of Abraham who left Ur in the land of Mesopotamia some 4,000 years ago for the land of Canaan. Abraham had lived for some time with his father Terah in Haran, which is in northern Syria today, before migrating south to Canaan. The people here in the north were the Amorites who were polytheistic and worshiped many gods.

The city of Haran is just north the town of Tuttul or Tell eth-Thadyen, also known as Shaddai. Many believe that the true meaning of El Shaddai in Genesis means simply what it says, the "god of Shaddai," an Amorite deity. According to Exodus 6:2, 3, Shaddai was the name by which God was known to Abraham. In the book Numbers, chapter 24, Balaam, an Amorite priest who is believed to be from the city of Shaddai has a vision where El Shaddai, the "god of Shaddai," (also known as Sadidus, son of El) spoke to him in Genesis 17:1 concerning blessing the Israelites (Mendenhall, pg. 117).

Today in Biblical terms, El-Shaddai is interpreted as *"The God who is sufficient for the needs of His people"*. The Canaanite term however was *"to treat with violence," "to lay waste," "devastator,"* or *"destroyer."*

> *Genesis 17:1... "And when Abram was ninety years old and nine, the Lord appeared to Abram, and said unto him, I am El Shaddai; walk before me, and be thou perfect."*

This is the God used in most Biblical references with Abraham, Isaac, and Jacob. Jacobs's wife Rachel, who also came from Haran, stole her father Laban's idols in Genesis 31:19. These gods evidently according to the text were very important to these people, enough to risk even one's life in desperation; one of these idols may have been the representation of El Shaddai.

El-Elyon

El-Elyon (the high god of the Canaanite pantheon) is used in Genesis by the King of Salem (Jerusalem today) Melchizedek who comes and blesses Abraham after returning from a battle with the King of Elam. The Phoenicians at this time also used what appears to be the same word for God. The name "Most High God" would indicate the belief in other lesser "gods".

> *Genesis 14:18 ...And Melchizedek king of Salem brought forth bread and wine: and he was the priest of the El-Elyon (the most high God).*

137

Elohim

Elohim or Eloah is the most common biblical name of God and is plural in form. It is many times used for "the gods". For example when Abraham speaks to the Philistine king Abimelech:

> *Genesis 20:13 ...And it came to pass, when "elohim" (the gods) caused me to wander from my father's house...*

Interestingly enough, this same plural word elohim is used in Genesis:

> *Genesis 1:26 ...And "elohim" said; Let **us** make man in **our** image after **our** likeness...*

Also when Moses is spoken to by God from the burning bush and in the Ten Commandments:

> *Exodus 20:3 ... "Thou shalt have no other "elohim"(gods) before me".*

"Elohim" possibly can be a reference to the supreme beings (or whoever these "sons of the gods" where).

> *Genesis 6:2 ...And the sons of "elohim" (the gods) saw the daughters of men that they were fair; and they took them for wives...*

Similar use of plurals for the Canaanite god Ba'al and Adon or "lord of the gods" (very similar to the Egyptian god "Aton", or "Aten" as in the Cult of Aten) are found in the Canaanite and Ugaritic languages. The same word for God is found in the Arabic language "ilah" (Allah) and in Aramaic "elah", in the Assyrian "ilu". The Jewish interpretation of Elohim means "He who is feared or reverenced," or "He who one is afraid of and takes refuge from."

El-Olam -- The Everlasting God
Elohim - He who is feared
El Shaddai - God Almighty
El Ḥai - Living God
El Ro'i - God of seeing
El Elohe Israel - God of Israel
El Gibbor - Hero God
El-Elyon – Most High God
Elihu - He is my God

YHWH (Jehovah)

YHWH is the name of God that which occurs 6,823 times in the Bible, known as the Tetragrammaton, a word made up of only four letters; a way of treating His name special. Ancient Hebrew text in fact did not have vowels and the way the word was pronounced was many times assumed. Modern translations assume what vowels were used and pronounce His name as "Jehovah" or Yahweh which means "He who is self-existing", "self-sufficient."

Some scholars believe the word comes from the Kenites from the land of Midian with whom Moses once lived. It was Jethro the Priest of Midian, Moses' father in law, who may have introduced Moses and Aaron to the worship of YHWH. It was here that Moses met God at the burning bush, where God calls himself Ehyeh-Asher-Ehyeh, "I will be because I will be," or "I AM THAT I AM".

As we saw previously, the book of Exodus seems to indicate that Moses introduced the name YHWH as this name was not known to them before Moses.

Exodus 6:2–3 ...I ...was not known to them by my name, YHWH.

(See Mark Dennis – World of the Forsaken)

Mount Sinai

Just after Moses defeated the Arabian tribe of Amalek (Al-'Amālīq were early inhabitants Mecca), Jethro, the priest of Midian who evidently was in close proximity to Moses, traveled from Midian in Arabia to Sinai, the Mountain of God, to see Moses bringing wife Zipporah and his sons. Many believe that the Mount Sinai in the Sinai Peninsula was much too far away, and this Mountain of God was probably in Arabia, not too far from Midian.

Exodus 18:5 ...Jethro, Moses' father-in-law, together with Moses' sons and wife, came to him in the wilderness where he was camped near the mountain of God.

The Bible speaks of Mount Sinai as a mountain of fire and smoke; a mountain that rumbled and quaked with thunder and lightning. This was where God gave Moses the Torah – the revelation of God or the Word of God and the Ten Commandments; this was where God made His Covenant or promise with Israel. During their journey to the Mountain of God, the Israelites would follow or walk toward a pillar of cloud by day and a pillar of fire by night.

All of these visuals put together what clearly seems to show that the Mountain of God was a volcano off in the distance that they were traveling toward. The Mount Sinai of the Sinai Peninsula does not appear to have been an active volcano during this time period. However, Moses had spent many years in the Land of Midian in Arabia where there are many volcanoes. Is it possible he brought the Israelites back to the land of Midian, his former home?

Exodus 19:18 ...The whole of Mount Sinai smoked, because Jehovah descended on it in fire; and its smoke ascended as the smoke of a furnace; and the whole mountain shook greatly.

In the area of Midian, there are several volcanoes, Mount Harrat Rahat is a volcano just outside of the city of Medina and Mount Badr or Hala-'l Badr, where the Mohammed's Battle of Badr was fought as told in the Qur'an was also a volcano which last erupted in 640 AD; it was possibly active during the time of Moses (Frankfurter, pg. 209).

The book of Habakkuk chapter 3 in the Hebrew Bible also alludes to Mount Sinai as being in Arabia. The text refers to the land of Teman in north western Arabia (meaning "towards Yemen") and the description gives a destructive picture of the mountain crumbling and shaking, destroying Midian dwellings. Teman was a name of a place half way between Damascus in Syria and Mecca in Arabia (Douglas, pg. 1428).

> *Habakkuk 3:4-7 ...God came from Teman, the Holy One from Mount Paran. His glory covered the heavens and his praise filled the earth...*
>
> *He stood, and shook the earth; he looked, and made the nations tremble.*
>
> *The ancient mountains crumbled and the age-old hills collapsed but he marches on forever.*
>
> *I saw the tents of Cush in distress and the dwellings of Midian in anguish.*

Many researchers and scholars indicate in their studies that the ancient Hebrews may have not been monotheistic after all, reflecting what they call early Judaic polytheism. It may have been the influence of Amenism in Egypt during Moses' upbringing in Pharaohs court as well as the influence of the Midian Kenites through his father-in-law Jethro that Moses guided the Israelites into monotheism.

(See Mark Dennis – Visions in the Desert)

Names of God

El Replaced by YHWH:

YHWH - Elohe Zeba'ot - God of Hosts or "the God of the armies of Israel"

YHWH - Adonai - The Lord our Sovereign; Ba'al is equivalent for YHWH in Canaanite text. Adonai and Ba'al both mean "my Lord"; very similar to the Egyptian Adon or Aton, god of light.

BA'AL - The great leader and judge of Israel Gideon was also called Jerubaʿal, a name which seems to mean 'Baʿal strives'.

YHWH-Elohim - The Eternal Creator
YHWH-Jireh - The Lord our Provider
YHWH-Nissi - The Lord our Banner
YHWH-Ropheka - The Lord our Healer
YHWH-Shalom - The Lord our Peace
YHWH-Tsidkenu - The Lord our Righteousness
YHWH-Mekaddishkem - The Lord our Sanctifier
YHWH-Sabaoth - The Lord of Hosts
YHWH-Shammah - The Lord is Present
YHWH-Rohi - The Lord our Shepherd
YHWH-Hoseenu - The Lord our Maker
YHWH-Eloheenu - The Lord our God

Other Names of God:

Abir – "Strong One" of Jacob or Israel
Kedosh Yisrael - Holy One of Israel
Zur Yisrael - Rock of Israel

143

Eben Yisrael - Stone of Israel
Ha-Geburah - The Majesty
Ha-Makom - The Omnipresence
Baruk-hu - Praised be He.
Ein-Sof - Infinite or Endless one
Azilut – Animation, Life or Spirit

(See Mark Dennis – World of the Forsaken)

Divine Light

First and Second Adam

Paul speaks of the first and last Adam in 1 Corinthians chapter 15 relating Jesus to Adam.

1 Corinthians 15:44-49 …If there is a natural body, there is also a spiritual body.

*So it is written: "The **first man Adam** became a **living being**"; **the last Adam**, a **life-giving spirit**. The spiritual did not come first, but the natural, and after that the spiritual.*

*The **first man** was of the dust of the **earth**; the **second man** is of **heaven**. As was the earthly man, so are those who are of the earth; and as is the heavenly man, so also are those who are of heaven.*

*And just as we have borne the image of the earthly man, so shall we bear the **image of the heavenly man**.*

Divine Light

Philo of Alexandria, 20 BC - 50 AD, a Hellenistic Jew living in Alexandria Egypt, had a strong influence on Judaism and the early Christian Church during the time of Christ. He attempted to take Jewish mystic Wisdom doctrine and apply Greek philosophy to it. Philo's emphasis was on wisdom and equated it with the Greek word *Logos* which means "wisdom," "reason" or "logic" directly translated means "word."

145

It was this Wisdom or "Word" that was in the beginning with God, and all things were made by him as we see in the Bible in John chapter 1.

John 1:1 ...In the beginning was Logos (the Word).

In the heart of Greek philosophy is the Greek story of creation. Many philosophers such as Carl Jung, in the past associated *Logos* with the Greek god of Love, *Eros*. We see this story of Greek Creation in the Greek writer Aristophanes' story, *Birds,* written some 400 years before Christ (Meineck, pg. 314-315). Jung applied masculine traits to *Logos* and feminine traits to *Eros*; we see the Father and Mother concept again here in the Greek story of creation as well.

At the beginning (Arche) there was nothing but a formless void, Khaos (chaos), Nyx (Night), Erebus (Darkness), and Tartarus (the Abyss). The earth, air and heaven were nonexistent.

Then the black winged Nyx laid a wind borne egg in the heart of the infinite deeps of Erebus,

Nurtured by the ages, it hatched, and from it sprang the graceful Eros (Love) and with his glittering golden wings, he soared high in the winds.

*He mated in the depth of Tartarus and with the darkness of Khaos, all winged like himself, and from them our race hatched, the **first to see the light.***

146

Light of the World

According to Jewish mysticism, this *Divine Light*, the *Light of the World*, was the *Shekinah* that gives life to this world, shines down from God through His ten "knowable" attributes. It is a light that indwells all of mankind to some extent; contained in the human soul.

This *Divine Light* is also known as *Logos*, or *Divine Knowledge*; it is *Wisdom*, the ability to discern right from wrong; good from evil. The personification of Wisdom is seen in Proverbs chapters 8 and 9 and is seen as the only guide to salvation, a way to comprehend the revelations of God, a light on the path; simply stated it is, enlightenment. This Light is an attribute of God that embraces and combines all of His other attributes.

John 1:4-5 ...*In him was life, and that life was the **light of all mankind**. The **light** shines in the darkness, and the **darkness has not overcome it**.*

John 8:12 ...*I am the **light of the world**. Whoever follows me will never walk in darkness, but will have the **light of life**.*

Wisdom

Earlier we saw that Jewish mystics explained the union of *Hokhmah* (Wisdom), *Abba* or "Father" with the *Imma* or "Spirit Mother" *Binah* (Understanding) which produces *Da'at,* the "Son" which is "Reason" or "Revealed Knowledge." This is the same as the Greek word "*Logos*," which is "wisdom", "reason" or "word."

Through Wisdom and Understanding we have Knowledge.

Proverbs 8:1, 8-9, 17 ... *Does not **wisdom** call out? Does not **understanding** raise her voice?...*

All the words of my mouth are just; none of them is crooked or perverse.

***To the discerning,** all of them are right; they are upright to those who **have found knowledge** ....*

*I love those who love me, and those who **seek me find me.***

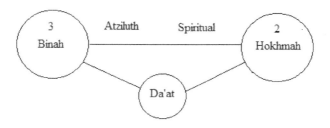

Wisdom – The Firstborn of Creation

Proverbs goes on speaking about the creation of Wisdom which is the foundation of Reason:

Proverbs 8:22-26, 35 ...*The Lord brought me (**Wisdom**) forth as the **first of his works**, before his deeds of old; **I was formed long ages ago, at the very beginning,** when the world came to be.*

*When there were no watery depths, **I was given birth,** when there were no springs overflowing with water; before the mountains were settled in place, before the hills.*

I was given birth, before he made the world...

*For those who find me (Wisdom) **find life.***

In the book of Colossians, Paul makes reference to Jesus as the **firstborn** of all creation, most likely in reference to God's "**first work**" in the creation of Wisdom seen in Proverbs 8:22. This is also a picture of the spiritual Adam known as *Adam Kadmon*, created in the image of God before the fall of man which happened through Adams disobedience.

Colossians 1:15 ...*He (Jesus) is the **image of the invisible God,** the **firstborn of all creation***

The book of Enoch makes reference to a human like person (Son of man) in the presence of the Almighty God, the Head of Days. It explains that his name was named and chosen before the Head of Days, long before creation came into being. He would take the throne and judge the world and his Word will go out and be strong before the Lord of the Spirits.

I Enoch 48 ...*And at that hour that **Son of Man** was named in the presence of the **Lord of Spirits,** and his name before the **Head of Days.***

*Yes, **before the sun and the signs were created**, before the stars of the heaven were made, **His name was named** before the Lord of Spirits...*

*And for this reason he has been chosen and **hidden** before Him, **before the creation** of the world and forevermore.*

*And the **wisdom** of the Lord of Spirits **has revealed him** to the holy and righteous; for he has **saved** all of the **righteous**.*

I Enoch 62 *...**From the beginning** the Son of Man **was hidden**, and the Most High preserved him in the presence of His might, and **revealed him to the Elect**...*

*For that **Son of Man** has appeared, and has seated himself on the **throne of his glory**, and all evil will pass away before his face,*

*And the **Word of that Son of Man** will go out and be strong **before the Lord of Spirits**.*

In Proverbs chapter 9 we see more reflection on Wisdom and Knowledge and Understanding. The Apostle Paul in 2 Timothy links wisdom to salvation.

Proverbs 9:10-11 *...The fear of the Lord is the beginning of **wisdom**, and **knowledge** of the Holy One is **understanding**.*

*For **through wisdom** your **days will be many, and years will be added to your life**.*

2 Timothy 3:15 *... You know that from childhood you have known the sacred **Scriptures**, which are able to give you **wisdom for salvation**...*

What is Salvation?

In the previous text, salvation is provided though wisdom and adds years to one's life; a salvation in this life, not in the life to come. This salvation comes through wisdom and by following the right path; wisdom helps keep us from the path of destruction.

Although there are many references in the Scriptures about eternal life and salvation from the wrath and judgment of God, many references to salvation are merely referencing an escape from danger or being rescued; deliverance and redemption. These can be applied to one's spiritual state in this life, one's soul and its emotional state and even ones physical health; this salvation being the healing power of God in our lives. This salvation can also be applied to one's family life, one's village and even the salvation of a nation.

Acts 16 :21 ...Believe in the Lord Jesus, and you will be saved; you and your whole household.

A change of one's way of life can be taken on by the whole family! If everyone in the family changes their focus to God from ones selfish life style, the whole family can be transformed and saved from that sad destructive path it once was on.

Essenes – Sons of Light

The ascetic community known as the Essenes that took refuge in the desert near Qumran, lived a celibate and hard life. They believed themselves to be the 'Sons of Light' who were at war with the 'Sons of Darkness;' a document of the same name is on scroll 1QM was found at Qumran by the Dead Sea in 1955. The scroll tells of a battle between the Sons of Light, consisting of the enemies that surrounded Israel; the Sons of Light were made up of mainly of the priestly tribe of Levi (Levites) and other tribes of Israel such as Judah and Benjamin.

It is clear that this community was occupied by priests for more than three hundred years, possibly 200 BC to 100 AD. Some scholars believe that these were remnants from a line of Levite priests that were part of the Hebrew Tabernacle during the Exodus from Egypt, a direct line from Aaron who were keepers of God's Covenant with Moses.

They were a strict sect who lived under voluntary poverty; they sought salvation by putting aside the pleasures of this world and focused on God. They daily **practiced** immersion, the same type of baptism **practiced** by John the Baptist, cousin of Jesus. John himself was a Levite, a Cohen, son of a priest. Both John and Jesus showed their feeling toward the religious elite of that day by calling them a "brood of vipers" and "of their father the devil."

The reconstructed Second Temple in Jerusalem to the Essenes was a place of corruption, perverted by the heathens, the Greeks and the Romans; these were the true 'Sons of Darkness' that they were fighting against. This anger and frustration with the corruption in the Temple clearly was evident when Jesus turned over the tables of the money changers in the Temple.

John 12:36 ...Believe in the light while you have the light, so that you may **become children of light.** *When he had finished speaking, Jesus left and hid himself from them.*

The Jewish Calendar

As seen in the books of Enoch, these mystics of the desert in Qumran also had a different calendar than the traditional priests of the Temple in Jerusalem. The Rabbinic Jewish 354 day lunar calendar was being used by the priests and leadership in Jerusalem while the Essene priests in Qumran used the 365 day solar **calendar**. It was under the Greeks that the Jewish **calendar** became "Hellenized," the Greek way of doing things. King Antiochus IV Epiphanes of the Seleucid Empire in 172 BC, selected Menelaus as the High Priest in the Temple, who slowly introduced the Hebrew people to the New Moon Calendar of the Greeks and became the Rabbinic Jewish calendar. This was a major conflict between the priests of Qumran and the Temple in Jerusalem.

Visions of the Merkabah Riders

Jewish Magic

Prohibition

Throughout the Jewish and Christian Scriptures, the practice of magic was forbidden and condemned. However, Talmudic literature suggests that it was "witchcraft" or "black magic" and not "white magic" that was forbidden. One of the most common types of magic was the social destructive "love charm," a spell cast on someone, usually by a seducing woman (witch), commonly associated with adultery in Scriptures. Another form was that of *pharmaka*, of drugs (Gideon pg. 79) and poisons used to kill or in one form or another abuse another through ensnaring or incapacitating them.

> *Deuteronomy 18:10 ...You must never sacrifice your sons or daughters by burning them alive, practice **black magic**, be a fortuneteller, witch, or sorcerer.*

> *Ezekiel 13:20 ...I am against your **magic charms** with which you ensnare people like birds and I will tear them from your arms; I will set free the people that you ensnare like birds.*

These were the secret arts as taught to the daughters of men by the sons of God (fallen angels) according to Genesis chapter 6 and I Enoch chapters 7-9:

> *Genesis 6:4 ...There were giants in the earth in those days; and also after that, when the sons of*

God came in unto the daughters of men, and they bore children to them.

I Enoch 7:1 ...And all the others (angels) together with them took themselves wives, and each chose for himself one; to defile themselves with them.

*They then **taught them various charms and enchantments,** and the **cutting of roots,** and made them **acquainted with plants**...*

*I Enoch 9:6 ...You see what Azazel has done, who has **taught all unrighteousness** on earth and **revealed the eternal secrets** which were preserved in heaven which men were striving to learn.*

Then God saw the wickedness, death and destruction that these angels had brought to the earth and decided to destroy everything on it with a flood.

I Enoch 10:1 ...Go to Noah and tell him in my name, 'Protect yourself!' Reveal to him that the end is coming, that the whole earth will be destroyed and a flood is about to come on the whole earth which will destroy all that is on it...

I Enoch 10:4 ...And again the Lord said to Raphael, "Bind Azazel hand and foot, and throw him into the darkness and make an opening in the desert which is in Dudael, and throw him in it.

Even with magic being prohibited under Jewish law, during the captivity in Babylon, under the rule of Nebuchadnezzar, Daniel had been given a new name, Belteshazzar, as the *"chief over all the magicians, enchanters, astrologers and fortune-tellers of Babylon."* It was here that Babylonian magic was learned by the Jews as well as the art of ancient Babylonian astrology. Daniel, being of the upper Jewish class, a prince of Israel as well as being a righteous man, was perfect for this position as Head of the Magicians in Babylon.

> *Daniel 5:11 ...In the time of your father he was found to have insight and intelligence and wisdom like that of the gods. Your father, King Nebuchadnezzar,* ***appointed him chief of the magicians, enchanters, astrologers and diviners.***

White Magic

Magic however, as long as it was used for good, was acceptable but only to be used by holy and pure people for the good of those being "blessed." The Hebrew term *qōḏeš* ק-ד-שׁ (Q-D-Š) is used here and refers to someone or something that is sanctified and pure; in this case, one who is consecrated or set apart for these tasks, usually a priest or rabbi. One of the main purposes of this "good" or "white" magic was to counter witchcraft and black magic.

The knowledge of "white magic" was vital to Jewish council members as well as the magistrates, priests and rabbis, much of which was learned even from the gentile world. Most of the Jewish practice of magic was for exorcism, healing or through the giving of blessings utilizing various names of God. Through these names of God, the ancient Jewish mystic was also able to call upon "good powers" which some refer to as "white" magic (Ponce' pg. 15). These were good spells meant for healing and for the blessing of a newborn, a marriage, a meal, a new house or fishing vessel and a blessing on those going to war or a long journey. Often amulets with Scripture contained in them were also worn for healing and to protect against evil and burying of incantation bowls face down in the earth to counter evil (Gideon pg. 291). Today, although we do not call it magic, we continue these very same practices of blessings and still call on the name of God, Allah or Jesus to invoke these blessings.

Classified under this category of ancient magic was also that of ancient science, sought after disciplines based on natural fact but misunderstood by the masses as magic. The word magic comes from the Zoroastrian Persian Magi; these were the "scientists" of the Persian world, monotheists who were highly respected by the Jews of that day. These Magi were the same as those who visited Jesus as a young boy (Gideon pg. 80). After all it had been the Zoroastrian Persian King who had freed the Jews from their Babylonian bondage; the one who the Jews called "The Anointed One" and Messiah.

The visionary ascent of the ancient mystic's mysterious Hekhalot literature is also classified under this "magic" because the practice also utilized the

"Divine Name" of God for their theurgic-practical ascent. The term "theurgic-practical" is defined as *"the art or technique of **compelling** or **persuading** a god or beneficent or supernatural power **to do** or **refrain from doing something**"* according to Webster's dictionary. Not only were these magical visions of God's throne acceptable magic in ancient Judaism, the revelation of "knowledge" through dreams, clairvoyant visions and the reading of faces, leaves and hands was also permitted as long as the purpose was for good.

Miracles or Magic

It is for this reason, many scholars believe that Jesus performed his miracles using Jewish mystic techniques learned from the Essenes. These were practiced only by the elect, the priests or someone that is sanctified and pure, *qodesh* שֶׁדֶק; consecrated and set apart from the sinful. These miracles were achieved only through the power of God, by calling upon the name of God. These practices of Jesus were no more "evil" than the miracles of any of the previous Jewish prophets; although the Pharisees clearly wanted to blame Beelzebub in Matthew 12, saying, *"He has Beelzebub, and by the prince of the demons casts he out demons."* Jesus' reply indicates that this was a common practice of the religious elect and the Pharisees themselves. Jesus says,

> *Matthew 12:26 ... "If Satan drives out Satan, he is divided against himself. How then can his kingdom stand?*

And if I drive out demons by Beelzebub, by whom do your people drive them out?

Most conservatives cringe at replacing the word "miracle" with the word "magic" as the word magic has occult connotations. Magic is normally interpreted as an act of a human being, miracles are an act of God. Jesus clearly gives the glory to God the Father by saying that the:

"Father is greater than I" and

"The Son can do nothing by himself; he can do only what he sees his Father doing."

Semantics

Let this be clearly stated, although the Jewish mystic may have relied on these *secret teachings* that taught what words to uses, when and how, still in order to be useful, they clearly taught as Jesus did, that this "miracle" or 'magic" was the manifestation of the **power of God and not of themselves**. The difference in these words is merely semantics; simply stated, God listens and helps those who are devoted to Him; speaking secret magical words with burning incense in chants and prayers or in simply bowing to God in humble prayer with **faith** may have the same outcome for those who have a contrite heart before God.

Many Jewish Hasidic teachings today shun the use of this magic and encourage the practice of *devekut* known as "cleaving to God"; being fully devoted to Him. This concept, much like the mystics of the past, involves the repetitive recitation of Scripture, prayer and meditation until a trance like state occurs. The use of magic is no longer condoned as the belief that one's **faith** in God and the closeness that one has with God is as strong the power as magic ever was. Jesus likewise also taught in Matthew 17 that **faith** could move mountains;

> *"If you have **faith** as small as a mustard seed, you can say to this mountain, 'Move from here to there,' and it will move. Nothing will be impossible for you.*

Origins of Magic

The origins of this magic begins in Egypt and was most likely brought to Israel by the Hebrews who left the bondage of Egypt. Qumran, where the Essenes lived for centuries was most likely inhabited from the time of the Exodus and possibly was the place of monastic study of these secret arts. After the return of the Jews from the Babylonian captivity until the time of Christ, Qumran continued to be a place of studying ancient secret teachings that clearly were also influenced by those who were educated in Babylon much like Daniel and Ezekiel were.

Jesus and John the Baptist are believed by many to have spent many years here, studying these priestly teachings. It was here in Qumran that the scroll named, *The War of the Sons of Light Against the Sons of Darkness* was found and later published in 1955.

This type of teaching was almost identical to the teachings of Jesus and his Disciples and that of the Apostle Paul;

John 12:36 ...While you have the light, believe in the light, that you may **become sons of light.**

1 Thessalonians 5:5...For you are all **sons of light** *and sons of the day. We do* **not belong to the night or the darkness.**

Was this why Jesus in the book of Hebrews was called a "perfect High Priest," and was "designated by God to be high priest in the order of Melchizedek?" Was Jesus qōḏeš ק-ד-שׁ? Someone who was sanctified and pure; a priest who came to heal?

Torah Code

Jewish Numerology

Many ancient Semitic languages such as Phoenician, Syriac and Hebrew did not have vowels utilized in its writings and are known as "consonantal alphabets." A term used for this type of language is Abjad believed to be derived from the first letters of these similar alphabets, Alef, Bet, Gimel and Dalet א ב ג ד or a, b, g, d.

Most written languages throughout history utilize both letters and numbers; many of these ancient Semitic languages, however, including ancient Greek, only have one group of characters used for both numbers and words in their alphabets. Since there are no numbers, letters in these written languages are used for the dual purpose of letters and numbers and known as Abjad numerals. For example, the number 1 is also the Hebrew letter Aleph or א (Aleph is a glottal stop not a vowel). Likewise the number 2 is the letter Bet or ב and 3 is Gimmel or ג and so on

1 Aleph א	10 Yud י	100 Qoph ק
2 Bet ב	20 Kaph כ	200 Reish ר
3 Gimmel ג	30 Lamed ל	300 Shin ש
4 Daled ד	40 Mem מ	400 Taw ת
5 He ה	50 Nun נ	500 Kaph ך
6 Vav ו	60 Samech ס	600 Mem ם
7 Zayin ז	70 Ayin ע	700 Nun ן
8 Heth ח	80 Pe פ	800 Pe ף
9 Teth ט	90 Tsade צ	900 Tsade ץ

Gematria Code

The dual use of letters and numbers led to a practice known as Gematria where a numerical value can be given to words or phrases (Ponce' pg. 170). Gematria values of words are often compared with other words. An example is Messiah or משיח (Meshiach) and the Hebrew word for snake נחש (Nachash) as in the serpent that Moses lifted up on a pole in the wilderness, both add up to 358; some attribute this to Christ, the Messiah on the cross (Ponce' pg. 170).

Messiah - Meshiach משיח

Nun (50) + Gimmel (3) + Hey (5) + Shin (300) = 358

Serpent - Nachash נחש

Nun (50) + Heth (8) + Shin (300) = 358

> *Numbers 21:8...The Lord said to Moses, "Make a **snake** and lift it up as a banner; anyone who is bitten can look at it and live.*
>
> *So Moses made a bronze snake and put it up on a pole. Then when anyone was bitten by a snake and looked at the **bronze snake**, they lived.*
>
> *John 3:14 ...As Moses lifted up the **snake** in the wilderness, so the Son of Man must be lifted up.*

Nachash נחש in Hebrew also means "shiny one" and "whisper" in an enchantment connotation. In its feminine form Nachasha means **bronze**. In the garden of Eden, this serpent could have been interpreted as the Shining Enchanter who was able to smooth talk Eve into listening to him.

Another example of Gematria is in the phrase "Shilo shall arrive," שילה יבא, with a value of 358. The Hebrew word for Messiah is משיח which also has Gematria 358.

Genesis 49:10 ...The scepter shall not depart from Judah nor a scholar from between his feet (among his descendants) until Shilo shall arrive and his will shall be an assemblage of nations.

שילה יבא כי עד רגליו מבין ומחקק מיהידה **שבט יסור** לא
עמים יקהת ולו

ELS Code

Jewish mystics do not see these mysteries as "coincidences" but see a mysterious code written throughout the Torah. Many times this code is seen in words or names of God reversed, vertical or diagonally across the page. Equidistant Letter Sequence or ELS is just one way to find the hidden code in the ancient text of the Torah, very much like a crossword puzzle.

One example is that in the book of Genesis, if you start with the first letter Taw ת and count fifty letters, then fifty more and so on, the Hebrew word for Torah (תּוֹרָה) gets spelled out (Sherman, pg. 28). In Exodus 1:1, starting with the letter Taw ת and counting by fifty as well, the Torah is also spelled out.

Taw ת – vav ו – reish ר – hei ה spells Torah (ignore spaces and punctuation).

The text below is Genesis 1 in modern Hebrew:

1 ואת השמים את אלהים ברא בראשית הארץ

2 וְרוּחַ תְהֹום עַל־פְּנֵי וְחֹשֶׁךְ וָבֹהוּ תֹהוּ הָיְתָה וְהָאָרֶץ מֵר אֱלֹהִים חֶפֵּת על־פני המים

3 ויה אור יהי אלהים ויאמר יהי־אור

4 ובין האור בין אלהים ויבדל כי־טוב את־האור אלהים וירא החשך

5 וְיְהִי־עֶרֶב לַיְלָה קָרָא וְלַחֹשֶׁךְ יֹום לָאֹור ׀ אֱלֹהִים וַיִּקְרָא ויהי־בקר יום אחד

6 מים בין מבדיל ויהי המים בתוך רקיע יהי אלהים ויאמר למים

In Leviticus when starting with the letter Yud י and counting by fifty the word Torah is reveled. In Numbers and Deuteronomy, the word Torah can be found by using the same processes by working backwards through the books.

In Leviticus, if you start with the letter Yud י, the word YHVH, spoken as **HaShem** when read is spelled out; literally translated, **HaShem** simply means, "the Name" השם. In Isaiah 53:10 beginning with the second Hebrew letter Yud י, if you count every 20th letter, the phrase Yeshua Shmi is found which means "Yeshua is My Name" (Sherman, pg. 40).

Coincidence? I think not. To the mystic, this is not chance! Divine meaning and prophecy can be learned from it and this proves to them the authorship of God. The Torah to the mystic held the key to knowledge and could foretell the future. The Torah was believed to be jumbled and without form before creation; as creation came into being, the letters and words found their place

(Ponce' pg. 27). Likewise, just as the Torah contained the story of creation before creation, the Torah today for them contains the encrypted future of the world in code.

Jesus seems to have understood this and made reference to this existing belief in Matthew 5:18.

*Matthew 5:18 ...I tell you the truth, until heaven and earth disappear, not the smallest letter, not the **least stroke** of a pen, will by any means disappear from the Law until everything is accomplished".*

Jesus even spoke of the story of Jonah as an encrypted prophecy of his own death.

*Matt. 12:39-40 ...For as Jonah was three days and three nights in the belly of the great fish, so will the **Son of Man be three days** and three nights in the **heart of the earth**."*

Temurah Code

Another type of Biblical code is *Temurah* which means "exchange". This was the practice of exchanging one letter for another in order to hide the true meaning of what is being said. The letter A may be substituted with the letter B for example and B with C or the letter A may be substituted with Z and B with Y and so on in some sort of pattern; with a "key" this code can be broken. Another word for this coding process is

Atbash which is derived from the first, last, second, and next-to-last letters of the Hebrew alphabet: Aleph א, Taw ת, Beth ב, and Shin ש (Dan, pg. 260)

There are several examples of this can be found in Scripture such as in Jeremiah 25:26 and 55:41. The words Sheshak can be derived from Babel and in knowing the code, one would know the meaning. It was Sheshak who stole many of the treasures out of the temple in Jerusalem under the reign of Rehoboam, Solomon's son and King David's grandson.

In the case of these two words being "exchanged" it is believed to have been done in order to keep from saying something slanderous that may get one killed and still send the message to those who had "understanding."

ש = ב or Sh = b
ך = ל or k = l
Sh ש sh ש k ך for
B ב b ב l ל

Key:

ב (Bet) is the second letter of the Hebrew alphabet.

ש (Shin) is the second from the last in the Hebrew alphabet.

ך (Kaf) is the eleventh letter from the beginning.

ל (Lamed) is the eleventh from the last letter of the Hebrew alphabet.

*Jeremiah 25:15 ...Take from my hand this cup filled with the wine of my wrath and make all the **nations to whom I send you drink it.***

*Jeremiah 25:26 ...and all the kings of the north, near and far, one after the other--all the kingdoms on the face of the earth. And after all of them, the king of **Sheshak** will drink it too.*

*Jeremiah 55:41 ...How **Sheshak** will be captured, the boast of the whole earth seized! How desolate **Babylon** will be among the nations!*

Jewish Numerology

As we saw previously, the seventy-two letter name of God comes from Exodus 14:19-21 and is known as the Shem Ha Mephorash or "The Divided Name." Each of these three verses contains 72 letters; combined, this is the 216 letter name of God. The numbers 72 and 216 have significant meaning in numerology.

72 is the smallest number whose fifth power is the sum of five smaller fifth powers:

$$19^5 + 43^5 + 46^5 + 47^5 + 67^5 = 72^5.$$

The number of disciples Jesus sent out in Luke10:1 was seventy-two.

The name of God YHWH (ה ו ה י) for example in Hebrew can be added sequentially and come out to equal 72 (Ponce' pg. 175):

י (10) + ה (5) + ו (6) + ה (5) = 10+15+21+26 = 72.

The Magic Cube

As we saw previously, the seventy-two letter name of God comes from Exodus 14:19-21 and is known as the Shem Ha Mephorash or "The Divided Name." Each of these three verses contains 72 letters; combined, this is the 216 letter name of God.

Remarkably, the number 216 is a multiplicative **magic square** number where specific numbers multiplied together can be put in a 9 box square.

Magic Cube:

2	9	12	**216**
36	6	1	**216**
3	4	18	**216**
216	**216**	**216**	**216**

The number 216 is the smallest cube that is also the sum of three cubes:

$$3^3 + 4^3 + 5^3 = 6^3 \text{ or } 216.$$

Its own integers can be used to create itself;

$6^{2+1}=216.$

Also in relation to 666 in the book of Revelation; this can be inserted into the same magic cube.

$6 \times 6 \times 6 = 216$

The number 216 is an untouchable number; a positive integer that cannot be expressed as the sum of all the proper divisors of any positive integer.

Value of Bible Code

The book of Daniel seems to indicate that a book would be sealed and knowledge would be held back until the "time of the end" when knowledge will be increased.

Are we in the "end times" when these coded secrets will be revealed?

*Daniel 12:4 ...But thou, O Daniel, **shut up the words**, and **seal the book** even to the **time of the end**: many shall run to and fro, and **knowledge shall be increased.***

*I Chronicles 12:32-33 ...the children of Issachar, which were **men of knowledge** and **understanding of the value the letters to tell the times** to **know what Israel ought to do.***

According to Flavius Josephus the Torah Codes were developed and interpreted by the Essenes in Qumran by the Dead Sea. These Essenes were priests that had existed in this location for hundreds of years, ever since the time of the Exodus; priests whose main focus was to study the ancient Scriptures and interpret them. It was believed by many that these priest were given the gift of Prophecy through their knowledge of their Biblical Code, both in Gematria, the encoded numerical values of letters and with Temurah, the exchanging certain letters with other letter in order to hide the true meaning. Many believe that both Jesus and John the Baptist were members of this secret sect.

History of Israel

Israel's Captivity

The land of Judah until the captivity had been ruled by the Davidic line of Kings or House of David; the northern tribes of Israel however had a different fate. After King Solomon, somewhere around 922 BC, the land of Israel was divided in a rebellion against his son, Rehoboam, into the ten tribes of the Northern Kingdom of Israel and Southern Kingdom of Judah. This Northern Kingdom survived and was ruled by their own kings until the 720's BC when it was seized by King Sargon II of the Assyrian Empire who took these ten northern tribes into slavery and scattered them all over the Assyrian empire and the known world.

Battle of Carchemish

The Assyrian Empire which had its capital cities of Nineveh and Assur continued in power until the fall of Nineveh in 612 BC after a series of bitter civil wars; this rebellion was quelled by the hands of the Babylonian Neo-Assyrian, King Nabopolassar. The new empire now ruled by Nabopolassar was constantly waging war with Egypt at that time and was continuously passing through the land of Israel and battling on the plains of the Levant; this wreaked havoc on the nations of Lebanon, Israel, Ammon, Moab and Edom. King Nabopolassar's son Nebuchadnezzar would make this journey and fight Pharaoh Necho II of Egypt at the Battle of Carchemish and later that same year become King of Babylon himself upon his father's death. In the book of Ezekiel, God tells Ezekiel to speak to Pharaoh, King of Egypt and to tell him that he will be overthrown by the Babylonians at the Battle of Carchemish which occurred in 605 BC. Egypt had just fought the Israelites at the Battle of Megiddo in 609 BC only four years earlier and had killed Israel's King Josiah. Jeremiah also has a similar account.

Megiddo

Ezekiel uses an analogy of Egypt's destruction at Megiddo where the mountains are drenched in blood and the birds would devour the bodies. Here at the Battle of Megiddo God would blot Egypt out like darkness blotting out the heavens, much like the locusts in the previous chapter and as the locust plagues of Moses. It would be in the book of Revelation that the kings of the earth would gather together again in the "Battle of that Great Day of the Lord," in the place called Armageddon meaning "Mountain of Megiddo" in Hebrew a place of many ancient battles.

Temple Destroyed

In 597, just seven years after the slaughter of the Egyptians that Nebuchadnezzar of Babylon began the deportation of the Jews from Israel. It was in the seventh year of the siege of Jerusalem, that he carried off the rest of the Jews into captivity and destroyed the first Temple and the walls of Jerusalem. It was at this time that the great bronze sea in the temple was broken up and sent to Babylon with all the lampstands, golden bowls and bronze pillars installed by King Solomon.

In the book of Daniel there is a story of the seven years that King Nebuchadnezzar loses his mind. Historically it is believed that it is King Nabonidus, the third Neo-Babylonian king and not Nebuchadnezzar who had lost his mind for seven years in the wilderness. Nabonidus is said to have gone into the Arabian Desert at Tema for "worship and looking for prophecies." Some scholars believe he was stricken with a fever and suffered mental illness and was lost for seven years of his reign. Upon return to Babylon, his rule was cut short by the conquering of Babylon by Cyrus the Great of the Medes and the Persians while his son Belshazzar was regent in his stead.

Cyrus the Great

It was in 539 BC that the armies of Cyrus the Great of Persia snuck into the city through the gates where the Euphrates River ran under the city wall; upon entering into the city and opening the gates, Persia overcame the city by surprise without a fight. Belshazzar was killed that night and Cyrus the Mede took over the Empire of the Neo-Babylonians. Cyrus died seven years later and left the kingdom to his son Cambyses II who ruled for thirty years until 522 BC. Cyrus' younger son Bardiya only ruled a very short time and was killed some seven months after taking the throne. It was Darius I, the son-in-law of Cyrus the Great who was chosen to rule in his place in 521 BC and ruled the Persian Empire until 486 BC, sixty-five years later.

Seventy years after the Babylonian Captivity began the Persians freed the Jews with a decree from **Cyrus** allowing them to return to Jerusalem; in this act, **Cyrus** had become a savior to the Jews. Persia helped finance the rebuilding of the Temple and the walls of the city of Jerusalem which began sometime around 530 BC under Governor Zerubbabel and the priest Ezra. It under the priest and scribe Ezra, with well-educated scribes, that the books of the Old Testament were written down from oral dictation and from bits of manuscripts saved and brought back to Jerusalem from Babylon. Cyrus, King of kings and Lord of lords, was considered at that time to be the anointed one, a Messiah. There were to be ten kings in total in the Persian Empire; he was the first who took over Babylon in 539 and the last, Darius III who was killed 330 BC with the conquer of Babylon by Alexander the Great.

Alexander the Great

In 330 BC Alexander the Great conquered Darius III of Persian and took his kingdom which reached all the way to India. While living in Babylon, Alexander took on this Persian title "King of kings" and started to wear the clothing of the Persian king, taking on their customs and acting as though he was a deity, sitting on King Solomon's throne. Here Alexander would die in the palace of King Nebuchadnezzar in Babylon at the young age of 32 of what many believe to be an assassination by poisoning. General Perdiccas was temporarily appointed as regent and guardian of the empire.

Not long after Alexander's death, his infant son Alexander IV would be crowned king and his wife Roxanne as his regent; however Alexander's kingdom would still be divided up between his four generals (four horns). These generals were Cassander, Lysimachus, Ptolemy and Seleucus. Cassander received Macedonia and Greece. Lysimachus would take control of Thrace and Asia Minor. Ptolemy was then offered Egypt, Palestine and Cyprus and Seleucus took control of Syria, Babylon, Persia and India. Israel would at first fall under Ptolemy of Egypt but would later come under the Seleucid rule which would maintain control of this region until the time of the Maccabees and the Jewish Hasmonean dynasty.

Seleucid Empire

The first of these Seleucid rulers was Seleucus I Nicator, Alexander the Greats Commander-in-Chief who set himself up in Babylon in 312 BC. After being assassinated by Ptolemy of Egypt in 281 BC, seven more rulers called Satraps or governors would rule this region stretching from Asia Minor to Egypt. It would be Antiochus IV Epiphanes who took control of the Seleucid Empire in 175 BC.

Antiochus IV Epiphanes

In 171 BC, the Republic of Rome declared war on Macedon (in Asia Minor); this was the beginning of Roman domination. Rome had become a controlling entity even during the rule of the last few kings of the Seleucid Empire. Rome in fact actually turned

Antiochus IV Epiphanes back from his invasion of the Ptolemaic Empire of Egypt. On the way back to Antioch, in his frustration, Antiochus IV plundered Jerusalem and imposed *Hellenistic* religious practice on the Jews and desecrated their temple. This Hellenistic way of life became pervasive in the Jewish community and continued until the fall of Jerusalem in 70 AD.

The Temple Desecrated

Antiochus IV Epiphanes suppressed the Jewish faith and defiled the temple with a pig sacrificed to the Greek god Zeus. This desecration of the temple began in 167 B.C and ended three and a half years later when Judas Maccabeus regained control of the temple and re-consecrated the altar. 1 Macc. 4:52, 54 states that this period of desecration spanned 3 years and 10 days or 1,090 days. Antiochus IV Epiphanes died of an illness while in Persia in 164 BC during the Jewish Maccabean revolt and the Seleucid Empire began disintegrating leading to the Jewish Hasmonean dynasty. After some 25 years of rebellion under the Maccabees, the Jews had finally freed themselves from Greek rule, resulting in the Jewish Hasmonean dynasty that ruled from 140 to 37 BC just before the birth of Christ when the Roman period began.

Second Temple Destroyed

According to the great Roman historian Josephus, Titus son of Roman Emperor Vespasian that took siege of Jerusalem on May 10th, 70 CE, three and a half years into the seven year Jewish and Roman War. Titus surrounded the city for five months, stripping the hills bare of all plant life as if stripped by locusts as seen in Revelation chapter 9. He let pilgrims into the city but let no one out causing the city to run short on food and water, creating a famine and chaos within the city just like Jeremiah described the siege of Jerusalem under Nebuchadnezzar in 597 BC. The Roman Jewish War had started in 66 AD, just four years earlier and lasted for about seven years.

Masada

This seven year period was a time of great tribulation for the Jews that lived in Israel in these days. With the fall of Jerusalem, the Jews "fled to the hills" to hide from the slaughter of the Romans. Seven years after the fall of Jerusalem the mountain fortress of Masada near the Dead Sea was assaulted by the Romans. The remnant of the Jewish zealots had fled here in an attempt to gain safe haven from the Romans. Here at Masada in 73 CE, very close to Qumran where the Dead Sea Scrolls were discovered, 960 Jews were found dead, most by suicide. When the Romans finally breached the wall by creating a great ramp up the side of the cliff, no one was found alive.

(See Mark Dennis – The Revelation of John)

Visions of the Merkabah Riders

The Rise of Gnosticism

Gnosticism

Gnosticism comes from the Greek word, *gnostikos*, which means "to know." Gnostic religious belief goes way back into the Jewish mystic past to the ascetic way of life. These were a people who rejected the material world and sought wisdom and desired to "know" God; striving for a union with God through prayer and meditation. Many of these people lived in the wilderness throughout Palestine and the desert regions around the Levant. To the Gnostic Christians, heavily influenced by *Hellenistic Judaism* and ancient Jewish mysticism, it was Jesus who brought *gnōsis* to mankind; it was through this *knowledge* that man has salvation.

Many of the doctrines of Jewish mysticism are found most commonly in Christian Gnosticism but can also be found in many other Western Mystical Traditions such as Kabbalah and Sufism as well as Eastern Hindu teaching.

Gnostic Symbolism

> I Enoch 47 …*In those days I saw the Head of Days when He seated himself on the throne of His glory,*
>
> *And the **books of the living** were opened before Him and all His host which is in heaven above and His counselors stood before Him*

181

*And the hearts of the holy were filled with joy; because the **number of the righteous** had been offered,*

*And the prayer of the righteous had been heard, and the **blood of the righteous** had been required before the Lord of Spirits.*

Fountains of Wisdom

*I Enoch 48 ...And in that place I saw the **Fountain of Righteousness** which was inexhaustible.*

*All around it were many **Fountains of Wisdom** and all the **thirsty drank** of them and were **filled with wisdom** and their dwellings were with the righteous and holy and Elect.*

*John 4:13-14 ...Everyone who drinks this water will be thirsty again, but whoever drinks the water I give them **will never thirst**. Indeed, the water I give them will become in them a **spring of water welling up to eternal life**."*

*Revelation 22:17 ...The Spirit and the **bride** say, "Come!" And let the one who hears say, "Come!" Let the one **who is thirsty come**; and let the one who wishes take the **free gift of the water of life**.*

*Psalm 36:10 ...For with thee is the **fountain of life**; in thy light we shall see light.*

The Elect One

I Enoch 49 ...***Wisdom is poured out like water*** *and glory fails not before him forevermore. He is mighty in all the secrets of righteousness, and unrighteousness will disappear as a shadow and have no continuance.*

*Because the **Elect One** stands before the Lord of Spirits, and his glory is forever and ever, and his might to all generations.*

*And **in him live** the **spirit of wisdom**, and the **spirit which gives insight**, and the **spirit of understanding** and **of might**, and the spirit of those who have fallen asleep in righteousness.*

*And he will judge the secret things, and none will be able to speak a lying word before him; for he is the **Elect One** before the Lord of Spirits according to His good pleasure.*

Gnostic Mysteries in the Gospel of John

The Gospel of John, first written in Greek, stands out and is much different than the Synoptic Gospels. The testimony of John the Baptist in John 1:17–18 clearly shows the message of the Gospel, that Jesus is "born" of the Father; that grace and truth came through Jesus Christ. The focus no longer was on the Law of Moses, but in the teachings of Jesus. It is interesting the in the Greek, John makes no mention of a "Son" but a "first born" or "only born" (*monogenes*) of God. Paul also makes reference to this "Firstborn" in Romans.

183

Romans 8:29-30 ... *For those God foreknew he also predestined to be conformed to **the image of his Son**, that **he** might be **the firstborn** among many brothers and sisters.*

And those he predestined, he also called; those he called, he also justified; those he justified, he also glorified.

Logos

The word Logos in Greek has been traditionally translated as "Word" as in "Word of God." If you however review the Hellenized Jewish literature of that day, you will see a direct correlation between the first chapter of John and ancient Greek myth. In Greek theology, it was Hermes, son of Zeus that was the messenger of the god's.

Hermetica are Egyptian-Greek wisdom texts, some written several hundred years before Christ. The Greek term **Logos**, meaning "intelligent speech or expression" is commonly used in Hermetic philosophy known as Hermetism, much of which was developed in the third century A.D. In the book Corpus Hermeticum, we see these verses (George Mead):

Chapter 1: Poemandres, the Shepherd of Men

*There, out of the Light, a **Holy Word (Logos)** descended on that Nature. And upwards to the height from the Moist Nature leaped forth pure Fire; light was it, swift and active too ...*

*That Light, He said, am I, thy God, Mind, prior to Moist Nature which appeared from Darkness; the Light-Word (**Logos**) that appeared from Mind is the Son of God.*

*...Know that what sees in thee and hears is the **Lord's Word (Logos)**; but Mind is **Father-God**. Not separate are they the one from other**; just in their union rather is it that Life consists.***

Chapter 13: The Secret Sermon on the Mountain

Sing thou, O Good, the Good! O Life and Light, from us to you our praises flow!

Father, I give Thee thanks, to Thee Thou Energy of all my Powers; I give Thee thanks, O God, Thou Power of all my Energies!

*Thy Reason (**Logos**) sings through me Thy praises. Take back through me the All into Thy Reason, my reasonable offering!*

The Catholic Priest Irenaeus quotes from a lengthy Gnostic commentary on the book of John referring to Divine origins being possibly explained by John. It is hard to ignore the similarities in names and persons explained here. These names are mixed and mingled, some treated as the same in many ancient gnostic texts. These are Greek names and words such as *Monogenes, Arche, Aletheia, Logos, Zoe, Phos, Anthropos* and *Charis.*

These words are throughout the Gnostic Gospels found in the Nag Hammadi Library of Egypt.

In the "Arche" was "Logos"... in which was "Zoe", which was the "Phos" of "Anthropon."

"Charis" and "Aletheia" came through Jesus Christ.

John 1:17 ..."Grace" and "truth" came through Jesus Christ.

These very words are used in the opening verses of John chapter 1.

In the "beginning" was the "Word"...In him was "life", and that "life" was the "light" of all "mankind."

Greek Cosmogony can be seen in the ancient Greek poet Hesiod's writings from around 650 BC. In the Theogony, Hesiod describes the beginning of the universe as we know it. In Greek mythology, *Arche* was also known as Monogenes, which means "the only one" but commonly interpreted as the "only begotten son." He therefore was the "first and only-begotten", begotten meaning the 'first cause' and "came into being." Begotten implies "*having been created*"...

John in verse 14 distinguishes between the Word and the only begotten by saying that the Word's glory was "like" the glory of the "only begotten" very much like Hebrews 7:3 where Melchizedek was made "like" the "Son of God" and Daniel 3:25 where someone in the fiery furnace was "like" the "Son of God."

*And **the WORD was made flesh**, and dwelt among us, and we beheld his glory, the glory **like that of the "only begotten"** of the Father.*

Hesiod writes this poem of the beginning, much like the beginning in Genesis chapter 1.

Before Arche (beginning) there was nothing but a formless void, Khaos (chaos), Nyx (Night), Erebus (Darkness), and Tartarus (the Abyss). The earth, air and heaven were nonexistent.

Then the black winged Nyx laid a wind borne egg in the heart of the infinite deeps of Erebus,

In the beginning (Arche) God created the heavens and the earth. Now the earth was formless and empty (Khaos), darkness (Nyx) was over the surface of the deep (Tartarus), and the Spirit (Eros)of God was hovering over the waters (Erebus).

In the book of John we see both the Son and the Father referenced often. In the Corpus Hermeticum, translated by George Mead, is the chapter called *The Secret Sermon on the Mountain* we see a Greek explanation of the son and father. In verse 2 Hermes and Tat, a son and disciple of his are having this discussion:

Tat says,

"I do not know from what matter and what womb Man comes to birth, or of what seed.

Hermes says,

"The material and the womb from which Man is born is "Wisdom", the kind that understands in silence. True Good is the seed."

Then Tat says,

"Who is the sower, the father? For I am altogether at a loss."

Hermes says,

"The sower is the Will of God, my son."

Tat then says,

"And of what is he that is begotten (first cause) of the father? For I have do not have that spirit in me, that which transcends the senses. The one that is begot (created) will be another one from God, God's Son?

Hermes *says,*

"All in all, it is composed out of all powers."

Then Tat says,

"Father, you are telling me a riddle, and are not speaking as a father to his son.

Son of God

"Son of God" was a common term for Kings an Emperors of that day. In fact, Caesar was *divi filius*, which in Latin means the "Son of God." Caesar Augustus was called "Son of God" and "High Priest." Nebuchadnezzar was the name the king gave to himself meaning *"firstborn son of god"*; this would be *Nehu*, the Babylonian god of "Wisdom."

Another Greek word, *pleroma*, is commonly used in reference to Jesus in John and Paul's writings. It is in reference to the "totality" of God's powers, His "completeness" or "fullness" in direct relationship to the "empty and void" in the beginning of creation. Jesus taught knowledge of the *pleroma* to his disciples.

> John 1:16 *...Out of his fullness (pleroma) we have all received grace in place of grace already given.*

> *Ephesians 1:22-23 ...And God placed all things under his feet and appointed him to be head over everything for the church, which is his body, the fullness (pleroma) of him who fills everything in every way.*

> *Colossians 1:19 ...For God was pleased to have all his fullness (pleroma) dwell in him*

A Knowable God

Gnostics, like the ancient Jewish mystics, believed that the God of creation was "unknowable" but that we could "know" him by his attributes through prayer and meditation. Unlike the mystics, Christian Gnostics believed that it was through Jesus that they could attain this "wisdom" and "knowledge." Jesus in the Gospel of John emphasizes being free from the law and that mankind is under the grace of God. Like the Essenes of Qumran, Jesus seems to challenge Pharisees and even encourages "disobeying" the law in healing and allowing the disciples to "harvest" wheat on the Sabbath. Paul follows the same line of thought that salvation does not come through the law.

> John 1:17 ...*For the law was given through Moses; grace and truth through Jesus Christ.*

> Ephesians 2:8 ...*For it is by grace you have been saved, through faith*

Unlike the Synoptic Gospels of Matthew, Mark and Luke, the word hell is never used in John's Gospels or in Paul's Epistles. John does not mention Jesus as a Messiah or his second coming nor is there any reference to prophecies of him as the other Gospels show. The use of the Greek *Logos* implies the pagan concept that Jesus is a "god" and as Hermes, he was the messenger of God. All of these point to a common thread of Gnosticism in the early Christian Church, a direct influence of Jewish mysticism; a spiritual kingdom and spiritual birth.

The Gospel of John speaks of Jesus as the "Light of the world" and as one who can reveal the Father (John 8:12–18). The book echoes the themes of an "unknown" God that "the world has not known" that can be known and a "spiritual kingdom" that the mystics of the past and Gnostics shared.

John 17:25 ...O righteous Father, although the world has not known You, yet I have known You

John 14:15- 17 ...If you love me, keep my commandments. And I will pray the Father, and he shall give you another Comforter, that he may abide with you forever;

*Even the **Spirit of truth**; whom the world cannot receive, because it sees him not, neither knows him: but you know him; for he dwells with you, and shall be in you.*

The Gnostics like the Jewish mystics, believed that the human existence resided in four levels. These were the spiritual, moral, sensual, and material worlds. The spiritual trinity of Wisdom, Understanding and Knowledge was the key to knowing God and becoming one with God. The Spirit of Truth was the revelation of true knowledge, the light of God within mankind. The two kingdoms that were preached are the spiritual **kingdom** of God within and the physical/ material **kingdom** of mankind; this is God and his Bride.

The Almighty God is in the invisible and inexpressible heights. He is a pre-existent God, incomprehensible, eternal and un-begotten (un-created), who throughout innumerable cycles of ages has always been; many times this is symbolized as a serpent in the form of a circle with its tail in its mouth.

Gnostic Mysticism in Paul's Epistles

Although most conservative Christian Theologians would disagree, many scholars have supposed that Paul was a Gnostic and was influenced by Jewish mysticism. After all they say, Paul points out that there was a heresy spreading in the Church at that time.

> Colossians 2:8 ...*See to it that no one takes you captive through hollow and deceptive philosophy, which depends on human tradition and the elemental spiritual forces of this world.*

Paul however, was thoroughly versed in Jewish mysticism as he was well educated as a Pharisee who studied at the feet of Gamaliel, a leading authority in the Sanhedrin. Paul's close friend Barnabas, who traveled with him, also was very knowledgeable of Jewish religious tradition being a Levite, of the priestly tribe. Paul possibly was speaking of Gnostic teachings which were heavily influenced by Greek philosophy, that also had influenced Jewish religious teachings from when the Greek way of life was forced on the Jews. This was during the Hellenization of the Jews during the Greek Seleucid rule after the fall of the Persian Empire.

Paul's Visions

Paul's vision of Jesus Christ on the road to Damascus, although he was not taken into heaven, still has its Jewish mystic elements. In the book of 2 Corinthians Paul also speaks of a man he knows that was caught up to the Third Heaven. Clearly this is a Merkabah type experience; some say he was speaking of himself.

> 2 Corinthians 12:1-4 ...*Although there is nothing to be gained, I will go on to visions and revelations from the Lord.*
>
> *I know a man in Christ who fourteen years ago was caught up to the third heaven. Whether it was in the body or out of the body I do not know, God knows.*
>
> *And I know that this man, whether in the body or apart from the body I do not know, but God knows, was caught up to paradise and heard inexpressible things, things that no one is permitted to tell.*

Other Mystic Attributes

Paul also recommended celibacy to the people of Colossae, seemingly influenced by such as the Essenes of his day. Paul also preaches God's Grace rather than focusing on the Law of Moses. This was a large departure from Judaism with the concept that one could unit with God without the intercession of priests and clergy, religious liturgy and rituals. Many Gnostic sects actually refused to follow the Mosaic Law.

Salvation, Paul says, is through faith, apart from the Law of Moses:

Ephesians 2:8 ...*God saved you by his grace when you believed. And you can't take credit for this; it is a gift from God.*

Although Paul teaches that salvation comes through faith and the grace of God, "not of yourselves," he does not imply that one does not initiate coming to God. James , the brother of Jesus most likely felt the same.

James 4:8 ...Draw near to God, and he will draw near to you.

The Gnostic practice of baptizing the dead is also seemingly to be taught by Paul in 1 Corinthians 15:

1 Corinthians 15:29 ...*Now if there is no resurrection, **what will those do who are baptized for the dead**? If the dead are not raised at all, **why are people baptized for them**?*

Paul's doctrine of the first and second Adam is clearly influenced by Jewish mysticism.

1 Corinthians 15:45-50

So also it is written, "the first man, Adam, became a living soul." The last Adam became a life-giving spirit.

However, the spiritual is not first, but the natural; then the spiritual.

The first man is from the earth, earthy; the second man is from heaven.

As is the earthy, so also are those who are earthy; and as is the heavenly, so also are those who are heavenly.

Just as we have borne the image of the earthy, we will also bear the image of the heavenly.

Extended and Lesser Countenance

In 1 Corinthians chapter 8, Paul speaks of God just as John does in John chapter 1 with the Godhead as **one God**, God the **Father**, the "Extended Countenance," "Ein-Sof" or the "Ancient of Days." This is *Arich Anpin*, God's Divine Will that comes down from God to mankind through the *Sefiroth Kether*, the "Crown." Jesus is seen as the "Lesser Countenance" as *Ze`ir Anpin,* seen here in the form of the "Son of God." This is God **manifested to mankind**, the one who reveals the "Hidden Light" of God to man and gives him life. This comes through Da'at; Knowledge and Reason.

195

This **one God is the Father**, we exist **for** Him. There is one **Lord**, Jesus Christ and we exist **through** him. Not all men have this "**Knowledge**" Paul says. This goes to the heart of Jewish mysticism and has a hint of Hermes in Gnosticism as God's Son.

> 1 Corinthians 8:4-8 ...*Therefore concerning the eating of things sacrificed to idols, we know that there is no such thing as an idol in the world, and that **there is no God but one**.*
>
> *For even if there are so-called gods whether in heaven or on earth, as indeed there are many gods and many lords, yet for us, there is but **one God, the Father**, from whom are all things and **we exist for Him**; and **one Lord**, Jesus Christ, by whom are all things, and **we exist through Him**.*
>
> *However not all men have this **knowledge**; but some, being accustomed to the idol until now, eat food as if it were sacrificed to an idol; and their conscience being weak is defiled.*
>
> *But food will not commend us to God; we are neither the worse if we do not eat, nor the better if we do eat.*

In this passage, Paul seems to imply that breaking the Mosaic Law seems to have no moral or physical consequence; stumbling a weaker brother is more of an issue to him. After all, Christianity was not just for the Jew but the Gentile as well; why focus on the Law?

196

Paul also shows some of his Jewish mystic understanding in 1 Corinthians 13. Here he hits at the mystic doctrine of God's divine presence within mankind that can only be seen as through a "cloudy lens;" in the next world it will be face to face.

*1 Corinthians 13:12 ...For now we **see through a glass, darkly**; but then **face to face**: now I know in part; but then shall I know even as also I am known.*

The Mediator

Paul also speaks of Jesus as a mediator for mankind. Paul's mystic approach is a unity with Jesus and Jesus as the mediator that unites us with God.

1 Timothy 2:5 ...*For there is one God and one mediator between God and mankind, the man Christ Jesus.*

To the Jewish mystic, mankind cannot know an "unknowable" God (*Arich Anpinin or Greater YHWH*) of the Spiritual World but they can gain knowledge and become unified with him through his lower six "knowable" attributes or Sefiroth. The un-knowable, "incomprehensible" God is in the upper world of Atziluth.

Atziluth (First World – Spiritual)
Kether – "Crown"
Hokhmah – "Wisdom"
Binah – "Understanding"

Again this is the figure *of Ze`ir Anpin* and *Da'at* (Lesser YHWH) as seen through the six lower Sefiroth in the manifestation of the "knowable" God through knowledge. To the mystic, this was secret knowledge reviled through the Torah, the revelation of God to Moses, the Word of God.

It is these six attributes of God that are the mediator between God and man; through which His Divine Will is given through knowledge and the light of God flows through that gives us life.

Beri'ah (Second World – Moral)
    Hesed – "Kindness"
    Gevurah – "Severity"
    Tifereth – "Beauty"

Yetzirah (Third World –Sensual)
    Netsah – "Eternity"
    Hod – "Splendor"
    Yesod – "Foundation"

Redemption

Jewish mysticism on the other hand clearly teaches that redemption comes from one personally purifying and refining themselves. Paul's mystic teachings clearly are more Jewish in nature than Hellenistic. Paul, however, broke from Judaism by insisted that a person could be a follower of Christ without circumcision or maintaining other Jewish religious laws and practices.

Paul did speak of a hidden wisdom and a mystery, maintaining the same mystic style doctrine.

*1 Corinthians 2:6-15: "But we speak the **wisdom** of God in a **mystery**, even the **hidden wisdom**, which God ordained before the world unto our glory: which none of the princes of this world knew.*

Fruit of the Spirit

*Galatians 5:9 …For the **fruit of the Spirit** is in all goodness and righteousness and truth; Proving what is acceptable unto the Lord.*

*Galatians 5:22 …But the **fruit of the Spirit** is love, joy, peace, longsuffering, gentleness, goodness, faith, meekness, temperance: against such there is no law.*

*Galatians 5:19-21 …Now the **works of the flesh** are manifest, which are these:*

Adultery, fornication, uncleanness, lustful pleasure, idolatry, witchcraft, hatred, variance, emulations, wrath, strife, seditions, heresies, envy, murders, drunkenness, orgies, and such like.

*Of the which I tell you before, as I have also told you in time past, that they which do such things shall not inherit the **kingdom of God**.*

Visions of the Merkabah Riders

Christianity

Who Really Was Jesus?

We know about Jesus and his teachings, primarily through the Gospels of the Christian Bible. The Gospels or the first four books of the Christian New Testament, Matthew, Mark, Luke and John were all written after Jesus' death which occurred around 31 AD. Matthew was apparently the first book written at about 50 AD, twenty years after Christ's death, followed by Luke ten years later around 60 AD and Mark written about 70 AD. The rest of the New Testament is primarily the books of the Apostle Paul and John, with other Epistles or letters from other disciples and followers of Jesus; this includes James and Jude, the brothers of Jesus.

Birth of Christianity

For centuries, the Gospel of Jesus Christ has been preached throughout the world. His teachings have been taught in nearly every language, dialect and nation, astonishing the wise and humbling the proud. Christ's wisdom has been praised through the centuries and exalted not only in Christendom but also in almost every religion that exists today.

Although not much is written in Jewish writings about Christ, Jesus was believed to be considered a Rabbi by many Jews and a loving and gracious teacher who helped pave the path for the Messiah.

Today, many Muslims also respect and revere Jesus as one of the greatest of God's prophets, the servant of Allah, treating his name to be holy and believing in the virgin birth.

Buddhists also have a great deal of respect for Jesus Christ and His teachings, revering the Bible as a sacred book.

Many Hindus likewise see Jesus as a Holy man (Sadhu) or Saint and revere his words as sacred text. To the Hindu, the Sermon on the Mount and turning the other cheek are very much appreciated, harmonizing with their non-violence teachings. Mahatma Gandhi believed that if Christians would really live by the teachings of Jesus, that all of India would inevitably become Christian. It is the Christ of the Christian that these religions of the world greatly admire, not the Christians of the Christ.

Christians throughout the centuries have tarnished the name of Christ, waging war against the Jews and Muslims during the Crusades in the name of Christ. In recent years, during the 1st and 2nd World wars, it was Christians against Christians in battle, and in more recent years, Catholics against Protestants in Northern Ireland killing each other in the name of Jesus Christ. Today, Christianity in a broad term, is the largest religion in the world. No matter how large the religion is, it seems that Christians no matter where they are, simply call themselves Christians but don't hear the words of Jesus, or really know what He taught.

Synoptic Gospels

Many of the stories in the first three books of the New Testament, also known as the Synoptic Gospels, are almost identical in word, having a lot of similarities, however, chronologically are somewhat quite different. The book of John seems to be written some time later, possibly around 80-90 AD, perhaps as much as 60 years after Christ's death. The book of John is written seemingly from a totally different perspective, focusing on Christ's teachings, presenting Jesus as the Son of God rather than outlining His life as the Synoptic Gospels did. Many believe that John was written as a Gnostic Gospel as it differs greatly from the Synoptic Gospels.

Gnostic Gospels

Recently, other ancient Gospels have come to light. Many of these books where known to have existed in writings but have long disappeared. Most after having been destroyed in book burnings by the Catholic Church as heresy in the middle Ages. These are known as the Gnostic Gospels and contain stories of Jesus and his disciples with a difference in theology. Gnosticism has its roots in ancient Jewish mysticism but was blended with Hellenistic myth under Greek influence. These books not only influenced some of the New Testament books but the Qur'an of Islam as well.

Arda Viraf - The first of two possible Zoroastrian influences on Christianity and Islam is the ancient Persian book of *Arda Viraf* which describes the Night

Journey of a devout Zoroastrian known as Viraf, the "upright one"; in this non-Jewish "Merkabah" vision he was guided in flight by an angel and crosses the Chinvat Bridge into the next world. Here Viraf meets the one true God, *Ahura Mazda,* who shows him heaven and those who are righteous that have entered heaven after death; very similar to the travels of Enoch to the Seventh Heaven and Muhammad's Night Flight to Jerusalem and heaven. The story of Jesus taken to the pinnacle of the Temple has similar context.

The second of two possible Zoroastrian influences are of the teachings of Paradise and Hell where a great gulf separates the two. This teaching parallels the Islamic teaching of the veil that separates Hell and Paradise and the teaching of Jesus that taught of the gulf that separates the two in the parable of the Rich Man and Lazarus (Luke 16:19-31). Both the Islamic and Christian texts explain how that those in torment ask those in Paradise for a drop of water to cool their tongues, but no one can cross over.

Books of Enoch – First, as mentioned previously, Enoch's travels to the heavens has similarities to a story covered later in the Qur'an where Muhammad flies through the night on a horse. Here two men lift him up to the seventh heaven where he saw a very great light and fiery troops of great archangels and sees God Almighty oh His throne in the tenth heaven. Several references are found in the New Testament from the book of Enoch as well as many similarities seen in Paul's teachings and in the book of Revelation.

In the books of Enoch, there are also stories of the angels that come down from heaven and corrupt the earth which also have similarities and possible origins in the books of Enoch. Here the stories of the Garden of Eden, the Serpent, and the Great Flood are told in detail; possibly the oldest book in text today that influenced cultures throughout the ages.

It is in the books of Enoch that we first see the reference to the Son of Man standing before Almighty God, the Head of Days with hair as wool, the Son of Man who is to "reveal all the treasures that are hidden" and is referred to as the Word and "chosen from the beginning." This is possibly the first reference to the Messiah who will judge the earth at the end of days as seen in I Enoch chapter 46.

The Life of Adam and Eve – an ancient writing that is the possible source of the Garden, angels bowing to Adam and serpent stories of the Qur'an. This same theme is expressed with Jesus instead of Adam in Hebrews chapter 1.

Haggadah of Pesach - The Punishment of Cain, is the story of Cain and Abel, of the raven and the burial of Abel, also told in the Qur'an.

Infancy Gospel of James – contains the story of Mary in the temple, protected by Zechariah. The casting of lots for Mary and also the story of the birth of John the Baptist, son of Zechariah also in the Qur'an.

Infancy Gospel of Jesus Christ – Jesus speaks from the cradle, also referenced in the Qur'an.

Infancy Gospel of Thomas – this is possibly the source of the text in the Qur'an where Jesus as a child created sparrows from clay and God brought them to life.

Apocalypse of Peter – where the gnostic teachings of duality and Docetism teach that Jesus really did not die on the cross, that it was someone else.

Orthodox Christian Doctrine

Christianity separates itself from both Judaism and Islam in that the most fundamental teaching of Christianity is that Jesus is the Son of God *and is God* Himself. Without faith in Christ and without his death on the cross, there is no salvation and that only in believing in Him can one attain Eternal Life. The Apostle John and the Apostle Peter both referred to Jesus as the sacrificial Lamb of God, the one who takes away the sin of the world.

Paul speaks of Jesus as the sacrifice for sin and the book of Hebrews (author unknown) spells out to the Jews that they have been made holy through the sacrifice of the body of Jesus Christ on the cross, once and for all. It was after all, they teach, the Jewish practice of the sacrifice of the spotless lamb that foretold and prophesied of the death of Jesus on the cross for the redemption of sin.

Many verses in the New Testament proclaim this very same teaching, that Jesus is the only way to salvation and that **He is God**:

*John 1:1 ...In the beginning the Word already existed. The Word was with God, **and the Word was God**.*

John 1:14 ...So the Word became human and made his home among us. He was full of unfailing love and faithfulness.

And we have seen his glory, the glory of the Father's one and only Son.

*Romans 10:9 ...That if you will confess with your mouth the Lord Jesus, and will believe in your heart that God has raised him from the dead, **you will be saved**.*

(See Mark Dennis – World of the Forsaken)

Visions of the Merkabah Riders

Mysticism in Jesus' Teachings

Jesus and the Law of Moses

Jesus clearly was passionate against the way things were, the "status quo" if you will, and had a different vision of how things should have been. Jesus challenged the Pharisees and those who wanted to enforce legalism and the Law of Moses to the limit. In Luke chapter 14 Jesus asks the Pharisees:

> *"Is it permitted in the law to heal people on the Sabbath day, or not?"...*

> *...Which of you doesn't work on the Sabbath? If your son or your cow falls into a pit, don't you rush to get him out?" Again they could not answer.*

> *Mark 10:5 ... "It was because your hearts were hard that **Moses wrote you this law**," Jesus replied.*

Jesus taught that the whole of the Law of Moses could be summed up in two of the Ten Commandments.

> *Matthew 22:36-40... Teacher, which is the most important commandment in the law of Moses?"*

> *Jesus replied, "'**You must love the Lord your God** with all your heart, all your soul, and all your mind.'*

This is the first and greatest commandment. A second is equally important: 'Love your neighbor as yourself.'

The entire law and all the demands of the prophets are based on these two commandments."

1 John 4:16 ... He who abides in love abides in God, and God in him

Knowing God

The teaching of Jesus were contrary to the traditional mainline established Jewish religion. Love or respect and honor for others was the core message of Jesus. The Law was the message of the religion.

To love God with all your of heart was the greatest commandment; but to love God, one must **know God**.

*1 John 4:7-8 ...Anyone who loves is a child of God and **knows God**. But anyone who does not love **does not know God, for God is love**.*

John 14:1-7 ...Don't let your hearts be troubled. Trust in God, and trust also in me. There is more than enough room in my Father's home.

If this were not so, would I have told you that I am going to prepare a place for you?

*When everything is ready, I will come and get you, so that you will always be with me where I am. And **you know the way to where I am going**."*

*Jesus told him, "**I am the way**, the truth, and the life. **No one can come to the Father** except **through me**.*

*If you had really **known me**, you would **know who my Father is**. From now on, **you do know him and have seen him**!"*

Gnostic Doctrine

Early Christian Gnostic faith emerged out of Jewish mysticism almost immediately after Christ's death. Many Gnostics believed that Jesus, although human, may have reached a kind of "divinity" through secret "knowledge" and that as the previous verses imply; man can "know God" or "become one with God."

This Gnostic belief did not diminished the oneness and power of God in the Jewish or Muslim faiths, it simply expressed ones level of spiritual maturity; man becoming the reflection of God. This type of teaching however was against the teachings of many Christians of that day, who believed that **Jesus was God in the flesh**, not just a reflection of God's Light.

*John 1:18 ...No one has ever seen God, but the one and only **Son**, **who is himself God** and is in **closest relationship with the Father**.*

211

The teaching that humans can become "one with God" and be able to "know God," was the foundation of the Christian Gnostics teachings and embraced by many people in the Arabian and Egyptian wilderness.

In John chapter 10, Jesus says:

John 10:30 ...I and the Father are one.

To the Jewish mystics and the early Gnostics, the "way" to God was through the "Son." This Son of God was clearly understood long before Jesus entered the stage. This was the Lesser Countenance, the Lesser YHWH; in the flesh this would be the coming Messiah who was chosen before the world was made. This concept however was also figurative and represented through the Sefiroth of Tifereth. This also represents Ze`ir Anpin, the Son of Kether or Abba (Mark 14:36), the Father of creation and Binah the Mother, Imma, from her womb creation was formed. The Son is the revealed image of God as the bridegroom, with Shekinah and Malkuth (humanity) as the bride.

It is this attribute of God that mediates between God and man across the great void of the Abyss that separates man from Almighty God. It was through prayer and meditation on God that man reaches out to God, drawing near to Him and begins to know God and become one with God. In this way Jesus was the Light of the World; in knowing God and becoming one with God, man could also be more like God, having the heart and mind of Christ Jesus and also become lights to the world. To the Gnostic, this was the "**way**" to God, Jesus **represented** this Son and was the "**way**" to the Father. This did not mean that Jesus was God or a deity, he was the reflection of God the father, the image of God as the Son, God revealed or manifested to mankind.

These teachings are also somewhat similar to the teachings of Hinduism and Buddhism in the east which flourished some five hundred years earlier. The idea of Jesus that "the kingdom of God is within you" is also a mystic and Gnostic concept; where one can "know truth beyond words." This is "finding the Dao," in Zen Buddhism, the right path, and is often referenced in the Qur'an.

The Gnostics would slowly fade away, most likely being assimilated into the Muslim community under the pressure of the Roman Church. Most of the Gnostic books such as the Infancy Gospels were destroyed under the Roman Church as the Gnostic faith was a threat to the Churches authority. These gnostic Gospels influenced Islam greatly; many recently found and are in the Gnostic Nag Hammadi library which was found in 1945, in Nag Hammadi Egypt; many other ancient mystical books have been found, some in the Dead Sea Scrolls unearthed near Qumran Israel.

The Word

To the Gnostic, Jesus was the Word, the revelation of God that was in the beginning with God. In the first chapter of John we see that the Word was in the beginning with God and that everything was made by him. To the Jewish mystic, the Word was the Torah; since the Torah is the revelation of God, the Creator and the Torah are one and were in the beginning with God. These mystic believed that the Torah always existed as it is the story of God and God always existed.

Questions

The oneness of God is the foundation of the Jewish, Christian and Islamic faiths. Christianity however seems to have a paradox as its cornerstone in that they claim to have one God but that God has three persons. The questions that many Jews and Muslims have asked the Christians who claimed the Godhood of Jesus have been:

If Jesus was God, why did he pray to God the Father as if a separate person?

If Jesus was God, why did he ask God to "take this cup" from him when he was in the garden?

When the rich young religious leader asked him, "Good Teacher, what must I do to inherit eternal life?" Why did Jesus say to him, "Why do you call me good? No one is good except God alone.

If Jesus was God, why did he say "the Father is greater than I."?

... the Son can do nothing by himself.

214

...I have not come on my own; God sent me.

If Jesus was God, why did he say, "If I glorify myself, my glory means nothing."

If Jesus was God, when Satan told him to bow down to him, why didn't Jesus say to him, "No, worship Me, I am God"?

Instead of having Satan bow to him, Jesus said:

"Thou shalt worship the Lord thy God and him only shalt thou serve"?

Jesus made this statement during the Temptation of Christ where Satan tempted Jesus with wealth and power if only he would bow to Satan, just as God told Satan to bow to Adam as we see in the ancient writing of *"The Life of Adam and Eve."* Interestingly enough, some five hundred years before Christ, Buddha, Siddhārtha Gautama, was tempted with wealth and power as well in much the same manner by *Mara the Tempter* (Buddhadasa, pg. 131).

One With God

When the Pharisees challenged Jesus when he claimed to be *"one with God,"* by saying, *"I and the Father are one,"* it seemed to them that he was claiming to be equal with God or to be God himself; this was blasphemy, worthy of death and ended up being their reason to have him crucified.

However Jesus replied to them:

Psalm 82:6 ...Is it not written in your Law, 'I have said you are "gods'?

In the context here, it seems that Jesus explains with Scripture that we are all capable of becoming "*one with God*," not just Jesus himself. This all is seemingly strong mystic doctrine.

Jesus continues to say:

"If you really know me, you know my Father" ..."Whoever has seen me has seen the Father."

And,

"I am the way the truth and the life, no one comes to the Father except through Me;"

And,

Jesus said to them, "If God were your Father, you would love me, for I have come here from God. I have not come on my own; God sent me."

Jewish Mysticism

It is believed by some that in ancient Jewish mysticism, there was a hidden, secret knowledge that was passed down over the generations that was very powerful. This Jewish "magic" was nothing more than the "invocation of benefic powers" through the use of the holy names of God and the angels (Ponce', pg. 15).

These were learned from the teaching of the Torah and never written down; only taught to those who were well versed in the Torah and in their thirties or forties; teaching the spiritually immature would be dangerous. The Jewish Talmud used by the priests and Rabbi's taught the difference between "black magic" and "white magic." Some believe that it was in Qumran with the Essenes that Jesus learned this "secret knowledge" which was the source of his miracles and through his light the hidden things would be understood – if we listen.

To the Christian evangelicals and fundamentalists, this is heresy as Jesus was the Son of God, God in the flesh, the second part of the Holy Trinity. Jesus however, was a Jew and spent much of his time, even as a child in the Synagogue and Temple, listening to the teachings of the Torah. What he spoke of as he taught the people on the hillsides and from the boat in the Sea of Galilee, was from the same Scriptures as what was taught in the places of worship. Using the same Scriptures, he taught a different theology, one of love and compassion. Much of what he taught has the same tones as Jewish mysticism in that one could know God and become one with the Father. He spoke of a spiritual kingdom, one within you.

Matthew 13 ...At this the disciples approached him and asked, Why do you talk to them in parables?

Because you have been given the chance to **understand the secrets** *of the* **kingdom of Heaven**, *replied Jesus, but they have not.*

For when a man has something, more is given to him till he has plenty. But if he has nothing even his nothing will be taken away from him.

This is why I speak to them in these parables; because they go through life with their eyes open, but **see nothing**, *and with their ears open, but* **understand nothing of what they hear**.

Light of the World

John 8:12 ...Jesus spoke to the people once more and said, "I am the **light** *of the world. If you follow me, you won't have to walk in darkness, because you will have the light that leads to life."*

Mark 4:21-25 Then Jesus asked them, "Would anyone light a lamp and then put it under a basket or under a bed? Of course not! A lamp is placed on a stand, where its **light** *will shine.*

For everything that is **hidden** *will eventually be brought into the open, and* **every secret** *will be brought to* **light**.

Anyone with ears to hear should **listen** *and* **understand**."

Then he added,

*Pay close attention to what you hear. The closer you listen, the **more understanding** you will be given—and you will receive even more.*

*To those who listen to my teaching, **more understanding will be given**. But for those who are not listening, even what little understanding they have will be taken away from them.*

*John 1:6-14 ...God sent a man, John the Baptist, to tell about the **light** so that everyone might believe because of his testimony.*

*John himself was not the light; he was simply a witness to tell about the light. The one who is the **true light**, who gives light to everyone, was coming into the world.*

***He came into the very world he created**, but the world didn't recognize him. He came to his own people, and even they rejected him.*

*But to all who believed him and accepted him, he gave the **right to become children of God**. They are **reborn**—not with a physical birth resulting from human passion or plan, but a birth that comes from God.*

*So the **Word became human** and made his home among us. He was full of unfailing love and faithfulness. And we have seen his glory, the glory of the **Father's one and only Son**.*

219

Salvation

When the rich young religious leader asked Jesus what he must do to *inherit eternal life?* Jesus told him to sell all that he had and give it to the poor and follow him. It was not through the obedience to the law that the teacher claimed to have kept, but in leaving everything behind and become devoted to God.

John 17:3 says this:

*And this is the way to have eternal life, to **know you,** the only true God, and Jesus Christ, the one you sent to earth.*

*John 6:68 ...Peter said to Him, "Lord, to whom shall we go? You have the words of **eternal life**."*

*1 John 5:20 ...We also know that the Son of God has come and has **given us understanding** so that we may **know the true God**.*

***We are in union with the one who is true**, in his Son Jesus Christ. He is the true God and is **eternal life**.*

*John 4:13- Everyone who drinks of this water will thirst again; but whoever drinks of the water that I will give him shall never thirst; but the water that I will give him will become in him a well of water springing up to **eternal life**."*

John 7:38 ...Whoever believes in me, as Scripture has said, rivers of living water will flow from within them."

John 3:5-8 ...Very truly I tell you, no one can enter the kingdom of God unless they are born of water and the Spirit. Flesh gives birth to flesh, but the Spirit gives birth to spirit. You should not be surprised at my saying, 'You must be born again.'

Bridegroom and Bride

Judaic mystics saw mankind, or Malkuth as the Bride and Tifereth as the Bridegroom.

*Revelation 22:17 ...The **Spirit and the bride** say, "Come!" And let the one who hears say, "Come!" Let the one who is thirsty come; and let the one who wishes take the free gift of **the water of life**.*

*Revelation 19:7 ...Let us rejoice and be glad and give him glory! For the wedding of the Lamb has come, and his **bride** has made herself ready.*

*Revelation 21:9...Come, I will show you the **bride, the wife of the Lamb."***

*Revelation 21:2...I saw the Holy City, the new Jerusalem, coming down out of heaven from God, prepared as a **bride** beautifully dressed for her husband.*

221

The source of these verses in Revelation come from Isaiah:

*Isaiah 62:4-5 ...Never again will you be called "The Forsaken City" or "The Desolate Land." Your **new name** will be "The City of God's Delight" and "The Bride of God," for the Lord delights in you and will **claim you as his bride**.*

*As a young man marries a young woman, so will your Builder marry you; as a bridegroom rejoices over his **bride,** so will your God rejoice over you.*

By Their Fruits

Matthew 7:15-20 ...Beware of false prophets, which come to you in sheep's clothing, but inwardly they are ravening wolves.

Ye shall know them by their fruits. Do men gather grapes of thorns, or figs of thistles? Even so every good tree brings forth good fruit; but a corrupt tree brings forth evil fruit.

A good tree cannot bring forth evil fruit, neither can a corrupt tree bring forth good fruit. Every tree that brings not forth good fruit is hewn down, and cast into the fire.

*Wherefore **by their fruits ye shall know them**.*

Other Mystic Similarities

Moses' Snake and the Cross

In the practice known as Gematria, Messiah and the Hebrew word for snake as in the serpent that Moses lifted up on a pole in the wilderness, both add up to 358.

Numbers 21:8...The Lord said to Moses, "Make a snake and lift it up as a banner. Anyone who is bitten can look at it and live.

John 3:14 ...Just as Moses lifted up the snake in the wilderness, so the Son of Man must be lifted up, that everyone who believes may have eternal life in him."

Cock Crow

Cock crows three times – in the Zohar the cock crowing three times means an omen of death (Stewart, pg. 102).

John 13:38 ...The cock shall not crow, till you have denied me three times.

In Isaiah we see a prophecy that has strong similarities to the death of Jesus and the one of the few references of a rooster of cock in the Bible outside of the story

*Isaiah 22:17 ...For thou hast hewed thee out a **sepulcher** here, thou hast hewed out a monument carefully in a high place, a dwelling for thyself in a rock.*

*Behold the Lord will cause thee to be carried away, as a **cock** is carried away, and he will lift thee up as a garment.*

*He will **crown thee with a crown of tribulation**,*

Jesus and the Ten Sefiroth

King

Kether - "Crown", "Authority" or "King" The crown also represents Ein-Sof, the Almighty unknowable God and spiritual Abba, the **Father** of creation. This is the highest level where the Throne of God resides and is above comprehension.

*Matthew 28:18 ...And Jesus came up and spoke to them, saying, "**All authority** has been **given to Me** in heaven and on earth.*

*Mark 15:2 ...Pilate asked Jesus, "Are you the **king of the Jews**?" Jesus replied, "You have said it."*

*Acts 13:23 ...And it is one of **King David's descendants,** Jesus, who is **God's promised Savior** of Israel!*

Wisdom

Hokhmah – "*Wisdom* comes from nothingness." Proverbs says that Wisdom was from the beginning before anything was made, as the "first of His works."

Wisdom is the first manifestation of awareness and intellect. Wisdom with Understanding is Knowledge.

*Matthew 13:54 ...Coming to his hometown, he began teaching the people in their synagogue, and they were amazed. **"Where did this man get this wisdom** and these miraculous powers?" they asked.*

Understanding

Binah – "Understanding" or "Discernment" is the feminine Sefiroth of the Spiritual World – white dove at Jesus Baptism. She is also seen as the Spiritual Mother, the womb from which creation is born, giving shape to the "**Spirit**" of God, the giver of life.

*John 1:32 ...I saw the **Spirit** come down from heaven **as a dove** and remain on him.*

*Luke 4:1 ....Jesus, **full of the Holy Spirit**, left the Jordan and was led by the Spirit into the wilderness*

*Luke 2:47 ...And all who heard Jesus were astonished at his **understanding***

225

John 1:3 ...Through him all things were **created***;*

Luke 10:27 ...And Jesus said to him, 'Thou shalt love the Lord thy God with all thy heart, and with all thy soul, and with all your **understanding.**

Knowledge

Da'at - "Knowledge" or "Reason" represents the upper triad of Kether, Hokhmah and Binah as the "revealed" light of God. The door to higher knowledge. It can be said that all ten Sefiroth are united as one and seen as Da'at, the "Light of the World."

Matthew 7:7 ... Ask and it will be given to you; seek and you will find; **Knock at the door***, I will answer.*

Da'at who is manifested through Sefiroth Tifereth, that humans, if they are humble, can see the light of God. This is the "Divine Light" or the "Hidden Light," that is shining down to Malkuth, the earthly kingdom, through Him.

Mark 4:22 ...For nothing is **concealed** *except to* **be revealed***, and nothing* **hidden** *except to* **come to light.**

*John 12:46 ...I have come as **Light into the world**, so that everyone who believes in Me will not remain in darkness.*

Da'at can be seen as the manifestation of the "knowledge of God" embedded in humankind, the light that separates us from the animal world, the divine knowledge within us that helps discern good from evil. This is the figure of Ze`ir Anpin and Da'at (Lesser YHWH) as seen through the six lower Sefiroth.

To the mystic, this was secret knowledge reviled through the Torah, the revelation of God to Moses, the Word of God.

*Matthew 13:11 ...Jesus answered, Knowledge **about the mysteries of the kingdom of heaven** has been given to you.*

*Luke 18:34 ...The disciples did not understand any of this. Its **meaning was hidden from them**, and they did not know what he was talking about.*

Strength

Gevurah – "Power," "Strength" or "Justice." This is the power of God seen in creation and in His judgment of evil in the world.

*Luke 4:14 ...And Jesus returned in the **power of the Spirit** to Galilee*

*Luke 8:46 ...Someone has touched me, Jesus replied, for I feel that **power** has gone out from me.*

*Luke 9:1 ...Jesus called the Twelve together and **gave them power** and authority over all the demons and to heal diseases.*

Mercy

Hesed – "Kindness" or "Loving Kindness" is the source of restoration. Grace, Mercy and Compassion are components of this attribute.

*Luke 18:38 He called out, Jesus, Son of David, **have mercy on me**!*

*John 9:3 ...Jesus answered, He was born blind in order that **God's mercy** might be openly shown in him.*

John 1:17 ...but God's unfailing love and faithfulness came through Jesus Christ.

Beauty

Tifereth – "Beauty," "Compassion" or "Glory" mediates between Hesed and Gevurah; also a balance of Justice and Mercy.

*Matthew 20:34 ....**Jesus had compassion** on them and touched their eyes.*

*Luke 9:32 ...When they woke up, **they saw Jesus' glory** and the two men standing with him.*

*John 2:11 ...This miraculous sign at Cana in Galilee was the first time Jesus **revealed his glory.***

*John 8:54 ...Jesus replied, "If I glorify myself, my glory means nothing. My Father, whom you claim as your **God, is the one who glorifies me**.*

This also represents the Son of the Father. The Son is the Lesser Countenance, the revealed image of God as the bridegroom, the Messiah with Shekinah and Malkuth as the bride.

*John 20:31 ...But these are written that you may believe that Jesus is the Messiah, the **Son of God**, and that by believing you may have life in his name.*

*Matthew 27:54 ...seeing the earthquake and the things that took place, feared greatly, saying, Truly this man was **Son of God**.*

*Matthew 16:16 ...Simon Peter answered, You are the Messiah, the **Son of the living God**.*

*Revelation 19:7 ...Let us rejoice and be glad and give him **glory**! For the wedding of the Lamb has come, and his **bride** has made herself ready.*

Foundation

Yesod – "Cornerstone" the channel in which God and the Shekinah strive to reunited with each other. Jesus quotes Psalm 118:22 and refers to himself as the cornerstone that was rejected.

> *Matthew 21:42 ...Jesus said to them, Have you never read in the Scriptures: 'The **stone the builders rejected** has become the **cornerstone**; the Lord has done this, and it is marvelous in our eyes'?*

> *Zechariah 10:4 ...From Judah will come the **cornerstone**...*

> *Isaiah 28:16 ...I lay a stone in Zion, a tested stone, a precious cornerstone for a sure **foundation**;*

> *Ephesians 2:20 ...We are his house, built on the foundation of the apostles and the prophets. And the **cornerstone is Christ Jesus** himself.*

Majesty

Hod – "Splendor," "Majesty," "Humility," "Gratitude." An acknowledgment of the Divine splendor; recognizing God's presence and influence in the world.

> *Matthew 9:28 ... in the regeneration, when the Son of man shall sit on the seat of his **majesty***

*Matthew 23:12 ...For those who exalt themselves will be humbled, and those who humble themselves will be **exalted**.*

*Luke 9:31 ...They appeared in glorious **splendor** and spoke about his departure that he was about to carry out at Jerusalem.*

Patience

Netsah – "Eternity," "Firmness," "Sincerity" "Victory" a means to an end, making choices in one's day-to-day life. It also implies Truth, Patience and Confidence.

*John 17:3 ...And this is **eternal** life, that they know you the only true God, and Jesus Christ whom you have sent.*

*Mark 9:19 ...O unbelieving generation! replied Jesus; how long must I be with you? How long must I have **patience** with you?*

*John 14:6 ...I am the way and the **truth** and the life.*

Earthly Kingdom

Malkuth – "Earthly Kingdom" is not an attribute of God but a reflection of God through His creation.

*John 18:36 ...Jesus answered, "My **Kingdom** is not an earthly kingdom.*

*Revelation 11:15 ...The **kingdom of the world** has become the kingdom of our Lord...*

231

Jesus as a Merkabah Rider

*Acts 1:9...After saying this, he was **taken up into a cloud** while they were watching, and they could no longer see him.*

*Psalm 104:3 ...**You make the clouds Your chariot**: You walk upon the wings of the wind*

*Isaiah 19:1 ...Behold, the **Lord rides upon a swift cloud.***

*Exodus 34:5 And the Lord **descended in the cloud**...*

*Daniel 7:13 ...In my vision at night I looked, and there before me was **one like a son of man, coming with the clouds** of heaven. He approached the Ancient of Days and was led into his presence.*

*Luke 21:27 And then shall they **see the Son of man coming in a cloud** with power ...*

*Revelation 1:7 Behold, **he comes with clouds**; and every eye shall see him, and they ...*

Mysticism in the Book of Hebrews

Hebrews 1:1-6 ...Long ago God spoke many times and in many ways to our ancestors through the prophets.

*And now in these final days, **he has spoken** to us **through his Son**.*

*God promised everything to the Son as an inheritance, and **through the Son he created** the universe.*

*The **Son radiates God's own glory** and expresses the very character of God, and **he sustains everything** by the mighty power of his command.*

*When he had cleansed us from our sins, **he sat down** in the **place of honor** at the **right hand** of **the majestic God** in heaven.*

*This shows that the **Son is far greater than the angels,** just as **the name God gave him is greater than their names.***

The Son is Greater than the angels for God never said to any angel what he said to Jesus: "You are my Son. Today I have become your Father."

*God also said, "I will be his Father, and **he will be my Son.**"*

*And when he brought his supreme Son into the world, God said, "**Let all of God's angels worship him.**"*

Veil of the Temple

When Christ was crucified, the six inch thick inner veil of the temple was torn from top to bottom. The veil was meant to obscure the mysteries of God from the everyday person and keep out that which was sinful.

*Mark 15:38 ...The curtain of the temple was **torn in two from top to bottom.***

It symbolized the Abyss, the separation that existed between man and God. The symbolization of the veil being torn indicated that man now could "know" God and have a relationship with Him; here the hidden things of God are revealed. Now there was a mediator between man and God; the Son of God, Jesus Christ.

*1 Timothy 2:5 ...For there is one God and one **mediator between God and mankind**, the man Christ Jesus*

A similar image is given at the baptism of Jesus when the heavens were opened and the Spirit of God descended as a dove upon him. Here again, the veil that separated man from God is symbolically opened and God's Spirit crosses that great Abyss and reveals Himself (Gurtner, pg. 172). This was the Kingdom of God being manifested here on earth.

234

*Mark 1:10 ...Just as Jesus was coming up out of the water, he saw heaven **being torn open** and the Spirit descending on him like a dove.*

The Death of Christ

The book of Hebrews teaches that the sacrifice of animals was an attempt to cleans one's own **consciousness** from sin that did not do the job; simply an illustration of what was necessary. It would be the death of Jesus that would bridge that Abyss, making Jesus the way, the path to God's forgiveness – something the ancient ceremonies could not do.

*Hebrews 9:8-15 ...The Holy Spirit was showing by this that **the way** into the **Most Holy Place** (Hekhalot) had **not yet been disclosed** as long as the first tabernacle was still functioning.*

*This is an illustration for the present time, indicating that the gifts and sacrifices being offered **were not able to clear the conscience** of the **worshiper**.*

*But when Christ came as **high priest** of the good things that are now already here, a he went through the greater and more **perfect tabernacle** that is not made with human hands, that is to say, is **not a part of this creation**.*

*He did not enter by means of the blood of goats and calves; but **he entered the Most Holy Place** (Hekhalot) **once for all by his own blood**, thus **obtaining eternal redemption**.*

*The blood of goats and bulls and the ashes of a heifer sprinkled on those who **are ceremonially unclean** sanctify them so that they are **outwardly clean.***

*How much more, then, will the blood of Christ, who **through the eternal Spirit** offered himself **unblemished** to God, **cleanse our consciences from acts that lead to death**, so that we may serve the living God!*

*For this reason **Christ is the mediator** of a new covenant, that those who are called may receive the promised eternal inheritance—now that he has died as a **ransom to set them free** from the sins committed under the first covenant.*

*John 1:51 ...And He said to him, "Truly, truly, I say to you, you will **see the heavens opened** and the angels of God **ascending** and **descending** on the **Son of Man**."*

*Romans 5:17 ...For the sin of this one man, Adam, caused **death to rule** over many. But even greater is God's wonderful grace and **his gift of righteousness**, for all who receive it will **live in triumph over sin and death** through this one man, Jesus Christ.*

*Romans 8:29 ...For those God foreknew he also predestined to be **conformed to the image of his Son,** that **he might be the firstborn** among many brothers and sisters.*

The Suffering Servant

Christianity takes refuge in the "prophecy" of Isaiah 53 and Zechariah 12, the Suffering Servant, as the prophecy of Jesus Christ and his suffering on the cross.

Isaiah 53:5 ...But **He was pierced** *through for our transgressions. He was crushed for our iniquities; the chastening for our well-being fell upon Him, and by His* **scourging we are healed.**

Jewish interpretation of these passages explain that this servant in the nation of Israel, as stated in the verse of Isaiah 43:10 just prior, "My Servant whom I have chosen." To the Jews of that time of Isaiah, the human image of God as His servant was seen as Israel who had suffering under the bondage of Egypt, Assyria and Babylon; these were all from the past just as the Song of the Suffering Servant is sung in pass tense.

A similar passage in Zechariah 12:10 is interpreted in a future tense as the Jews mourning over their war dead in context of the previous verse, "On that day I will set out to destroy all the nations that attack Jerusalem."

Zechariah 12:10 ...they will **look onto Me** *'concerning'* **whom they have pierced** *and they will* **mourn for him.**

Biblical Extra

1 John 5:7-8 has now been universally accepted as an addition to the original texts by a medieval scribe to strengthen the teaching of the trinity. Accurate translation says: For there are three that testify:

*John 5:7 ...For there are three **that bear record in heaven, the Father, the Word, and the Holy Ghost:** and these three are one.*

Kingdom of Heaven

Historical Jewish View

The historical Jewish view concerning the Kingdom of God was at times in reference to the future restoration of the nation of Israel and the rebuilding of the temple. It also was in reference to the religion of Judaism and "taking on the yoke of God's Kingdom." This focus is on God's sovereignty which opposes earthly kingdoms and powers and holds on to the anticipation of God's reign as King over the whole earth when evil is eradicated. It is also taken in the context of the "World to come" in a spiritual manner.

> *"The future world is not like this world. In the future world there is no eating nor drinking nor propagation nor business nor jealousy nor hatred nor competition, but the righteous will sit with their crowns on their heads feasting on the brightness of the divine presence of God"*
> *Babylonian Talmud*
> *(Neusner, pg. 37).*

John the Baptist taught his followers during the Roman occupation of Israel, to *"Repent, for the Kingdom of Heaven is at hand"* (Matthew 3:1). Many Jews of his day were praying for the day when Rome would weaken enough for the Kingdom of God to appear and destroy it. From a more mystical or spiritual approach, Jesus also made many references to the Kingdom of God or Kingdom of Heaven at this time. Christ would teach that the Kingdom of God was "*within you*" or "*among you*" (Luke 17:21) but would also indicate that his kingdom is not of his world; evidently not condoning rebellion or use of force against Rome.

> *John 18:36 ...My kingdom is not of this world: if my kingdom were of this world, then my servants would fight so that I should not be delivered to the Jews; but now is my kingdom not from here.*

Many parables were spoken by Jesus comparing the Kingdom of Heaven to the mustard seed or to treasure or to a vineyard and that we are to "*seek the Kingdom of Heaven.*" Luke would continue using these terms in the book of Acts where the phrases "*preaching the Kingdom of Heaven*" or "*concerning the Kingdom of Heaven*" and "*enter the Kingdom of Heaven*" where commonly used. Paul also would maintain this message in his letters or Epistles to the Christian Churches, preaching that Jesus was the Son of God and preaching the "Kingdom of God".

Freedom from Rome

But was this kingdom that Jesus, Luke and Paul preached, this future "physical kingdom" that the Jews longed for? Was this the freedom from the Romans and centuries of oppression and foreign rule that they had longed for, for all these years? Or was this the salvation promised to the righteous after the resurrection? Or could it be purely a spiritual after death salvation of eternal life in the presence of God in spiritual bodies? Jesus taught a mystical teaching that one would have to be *"Born Again"* to enter the Kingdom of Heaven, for salvation or eternal life; a salvation that the rich or pious religious leaders would not be able to attain and enter into this Kingdom of God. Or was it a "kingdom" that was in one's heart, a change that could come over a community or nation?

Jesus, of whom both Luke and Paul would proclaim to be the Son of God, would teach that *this was a state of mind and heart*.

> *Philippians 2:5 ...Let this mind be in you, which was also in Christ Jesus.*

Jesus said,

> *Luke 17:21 ...The Kingdom of God will not come through physical observation; neither will they say, 'it is here!' or 'it is over there!' The Kingdom of God is here all around you.*

It would be the children, the humble and the meek that would inherit the Kingdom of Heaven. The communal aspects of his teaching were to love those that hate us and to turn the other cheek as well as to love or respect your neighbor, meaning everyone. He taught to nourish the sick, to give to the poor and to take care of the widows and the elderly. His emphasis was on the children and the Beatitudes focus on those in need and poor of heart.

Beatitudes Matthew 5:3-10

Blessed are the poor in spirit, for theirs is the **kingdom** *of heaven.*

Blessed are those who mourn, for they will be **comforted**.

Blessed are the meek, for they will **inherit the earth**.

Blessed are those who hunger and **thirst for righteousness**, *for they will be filled.*

Blessed are the **merciful**, *for they will be shown mercy.*

Blessed are the **pure in heart**, *for they will see God.*

Blessed are the **peacemakers**, *for they will be called children of God.*

Blessed are those who are persecuted because of **righteousness**, *for theirs is the* **kingdom of heaven**.

Message of Hope

Jesus called the Pharisees, the religious leaders of his day, vipers and disregarded all the legalism of "do's and don'ts" that they pressured on the people as oppressive. These teachings alone in this militarily oppressive and religiously legalistic society gave hope to the poor, the sick and the elderly. This was also the teachings of the early Christian church where believers lived in communal environments, selling all that they had and dividing up the money and goods to the needy. Paul himself on return to Jerusalem brought money from the believers in Europe and Asia back to the Church in Jerusalem to be distributed to the needy. This in its self was the Kingdom of Heaven at work, just as Christ had taught his disciples during his ministry.

Salvation in this Life or After?

The Christian Church today seems to have several of these overlapping views of what the Kingdom of Heaven is. One is the spiritual state of salvation, of one after death and entering into the Kingdom of Heaven. This was the place where Jesus was going to prepare mansions for his followers; where the streets were paved with gold.

2 Cor. 5:8 ...to be absent from the body is to be present with the Lord.

Another perspective is an apocalyptic view of Christ's second coming and judgment, the resurrection of the believers and his reign on earth in the future, and another as viewing the Christian Church as the Kingdom of God, the Body of Christ, a "communal organism" if you will.

There is no direct text referring to "The Kingdom of God" or "The Kingdom of Heaven" in the Qur'an. Islamic teachings and tradition which began some five-hundred years after Christ do however echo these same traditions passed down from both Jewish and Christian influences. This perspective however is slightly different in that the Kingdom of God most commonly is in reference to Gods creation and his "dominion" or power over all things. It is of greatest importance that we as Allah's creation follow his laws or "Sharia Law". Similar to Christianity, concepts of a "Spiritual Kingdom" after the Day of Judgment, the coming of the Mahdi (prophesied redeemer) and Christ's return to earth are also prevalent in Islam referring to the beginning of a Kingdom without end.

What is the Kingdom of God?

What is the Kingdom of God or the Kingdom of Heaven referred to in the Jewish, Christian and Islamic Scriptures and tradition? Where did the term originate and what were the various orators talking about when they spoke about these things? Was this to be a true Kingdom of God on the earth that was to be physically ruled by God or was it this "communal organism," a chosen people of God?

History of Israel

After their enslavement for four hundred years by the Egyptians, the Children of Israel, also known as the Israelites, as a nation, would continue to endure many hardships over the centuries including two captivities. The first captivity was by the Assyrians in 740 B.C., which devastated the Northern Ten Tribes, dispersing them, many of them never to return, also known as the

Ten Lost Tribes of Israel. Later on around 597 B.C., came the Babylonian Captivity of southern Israel. During this time over several years, the remaining Jewish people were exported out of Israel into the land of Babylon, ironically the same area in which Abraham their forefather had come from, and destroyed the Temple and the city of Jerusalem.

The exile ended about 538 B.C. some sixty years later, with the conquest of Babylon by the Persian Empire and Cyrus the Great. Cyrus, being a monotheist, was quite tolerant of the Jewish faith and allowed the Jews to return to Israel and assisted them in the rebuilding of both Jerusalem and the temple. During this time (586 B.C.), Solomon's temple had been robbed, looted and then destroyed, leaving only rubble. All the gold and significant religious artifacts, including the Ark of the Covenant, had been either hidden by the Jews or taken away by the Babylonians and never recovered even to this day.

After the exile ended, a new temple was then constructed under the direction and leadership of Zerubbabel around 520 B.C. and stood in Jerusalem until at the time of Christ. It was during Christ's lifetime that the temple built by Zerubbabel was rebuilt again by King Herod in 18 A.D. Consequently, not long after its completion in 68 A.D., Herod's temple was again destroyed in 70 A.D. by fire during the siege of Jerusalem by Titus and the First Jewish-Roman War and never rebuilt (Comfort, pg. 614).

The Ark of the Covenant and its contents, including the Ten Commandments, had been lost and the Babylonian and Persian influences began changing the Jewish ways of thinking, transforming their culture (Boren, 2000, pg. 17). It was at this time under Ezekiel and Jeremiah during the rebuilding of Israel that the Jewish religion matured and a new religious process and priesthood was developed. It was during this time of change that that the synagogue was most likely established where prayer and Scripture reading were performed on the Sabbath. It was also during this period that the two Jewish religious sects of the Pharisees and Sadducees were formed.

Persian rule had been controlled at a distance by governors in Syria with many Jews dispersed throughout the Persian Empire; Persia eventually would fall to the armies of Alexander the Great in 334 B.C., and for the next 200 years, various entities would rule over Israel including Egypt and Syria as the Greek Empire was broken up leading to Roman rule. Israel would then finally rule itself for a short period of time, for about 100 years, after freeing itself from the Greek Seleucid Empire.

When the Seleucid king Antiochus IV in 168 B.C sacrificed a pig in the Temple to the Greek god Zeus, the Jews revolted. After some twenty-five years of rebellion under the Maccabees, the Jews finally freed themselves from Greek rule, resulting in the Jewish Hasmonean dynasty that ruled from 140 to 37 B.C. just before the birth of Christ. Then during a civil war in 64

B.C. that started between the Jewish king and High Priest Hyrcanus, who was a Pharisee and his younger brother Aristobulus, who was a Sadducee, the Roman general Pompeius Magnus (also known as Pompey) decided to intervene and stop the war. After a battle with Aristobulus for Jerusalem, Pompey took the city and returned Hyrcanus his former position as High Priest but not as king, his former position. In 40 B.C., however, Hyrcanus' brother Aristobulus' son Antigonus took the dynasty back from him and exiled Hyrcanus to Babylon, pronouncing himself as king and High Priest of Israel (Feldman, pg. 209).

The Idumean (Edomites, descendants of Esau who converted to Judaism), King Herod the Great, who had been elected as "King of the Jews" (Richardson, pg. 265) by the Roman Senate then overthrew Antigonus, executing him and returned Hyrcanus back to the High Priesthood; Herod later killed Hyrcanus for plotting against him. Herod then took over the Hasmonean dynasty; instituting the Herodian dynasty for Rome in 36 B.C. (Feldman, 1988, pg. 378). Herod later, in an attempt to win the hearts of the Jewish People would refortify the second temple built under Zerubbabel hundreds of years before. Rome would stay in Israel giving the Jews relative protection until the Jewish revolt in 66 A.D., and later resulting in the destruction of Jerusalem and Herod's temple in 70 A.D. by the Romans. It was during this time of Roman occupation that Jesus was born.

King of the Jews

The Jews had either been occupied or held captive by various foreign empires for over five-hundred years and the Jews longed for self-rule and freedom. It was a Jewish king that the Jews now wanted, an "Anointed One" or Messiah. The Tanakh or Hebrew Scriptures had referred to many different historical persons as Messiah, such as many Jewish kings, priests and even Cyrus the Great, a Persian, who had freed the captive people of Israel from bondage in Babylon. It was Cyrus who had said in II Chronicles 36:23, *"The Lord, the God of heaven, has given me (Cyrus) all the Kingdoms of the earth and he has appointed me to build a temple for him at Jerusalem in Judah."*

King Herod the Great, who was a Jew, had been elected as "King of the Jews" by the Romans to pacify the Jews and keep them under control; a Messiah if you will. It was under Herod the Great's rule that Jesus was born and to whom the Three Wise Men (Magi) had come asking where the "King of the Jews" had been born. This would then anger Herod, for he was the "King of the Jews" by Roman appointment. Herod then decreed that all the Jewish male children under the age of two be put to death, prompting Mary and Joseph to flee Israel for Egypt where they would stay until Herod the Great's death in 4 B.C. Herod Antipas, his son, would participate in both John the Baptists and Christ's death.

The Messiah

The Messiah that the Jews of Jesus day now yearned for would however be sent by God to bring peace, not only to Israel, but to the whole world. This Messiah would gather all the Jews from around the world back to Israel as foretold by the prophets and rid Israel of its oppressors and usher in the Kingdom of God or the Messianic Age and would not be Herod. In fact, John the Baptist who Herod had beheaded preached this message, *"Repent, for the Kingdom of Heaven is at hand,"* a message that ultimately was the reason for the death of Jesus.

It was Jesus who the disciples of John had said, *"We have found the Messiah,"* which is, being interpreted in Greek, the Christ. It was John who said,

John 1:26-28 ...I baptize with water; but there stands one among you, whom you do not know; he it is, who comes after me, is preferred before me, whose shoe's latchet I am not worthy to unloose.

He will baptize you with the Holy Ghost and with fire. Whose winnowing fork is in his hand, and he will thoroughly purge his floor and gather his wheat into the garner; but he will burn up the chaff with unquenchable fire.

See Malachi 4:1

249

During his life, Jesus would claim to be "of God", the "Son of God" and "one with God". It was these claims that were considered to be blasphemy, deserving of death by the Jewish High Priests; it was they who brought Jesus to the Romans saying that He claimed to be the "King of the Jews", which had been Herod the Greats title. It was for this that He was crucified by the Romans; challenging their authority, proclaiming to be "king". It was on the cross that Pilate wrote the title, JESUS OF NAZARETH, THE KING OF THE JEWS, written in Hebrew, Greek and Latin for the whole world to see.

Perspectives

The Jewish point of view of what the Kingdom of Heaven is can be found in the book of I Chronicles, most likely written during the Babylonian captivity in the 5th Century B.C. Now, because the religious Jews avoided the use of the word "God", Lord or Heaven were used instead. Here we see the first indirect reference to the Kingdom of the Lord or of YHWY where David says *"For all that is in the heaven and in the earth is yours. Yours is the Kingdom"*(Psalm 89:11), a saying repeated by Christ in "the Lord's Prayer."

God says in Exodus 19: 5 that *"all the earth is mine"* and promises Moses that He will "create from his people a Kingdom of Priests." The Davidic covenant spoke to David through the prophet Samuel speaks of an Eternal Kingdom out of David's lineage.

The Kingdom of Heaven

II Samuel 7:12, 13 ...He is the one who will build a house for my Name, and I will establish the throne of his kingdom forever.

It is evident throughout all of the Jewish texts that God is king of all (Psalm 22:28 and Psalm 103:19). Isaiah would however prophesy of a physical rule, a human king with a Kingdom with no end (Isaiah 9:6-7; 11:1-10). Ezekiel continues to prophesy of when David again becomes King and God's sanctuary will be with his people forever (Ezekiel 37:21-28). Then Daniel prophesies of the coming of the "Messiah" (Daniel 9:25). Later on in the book of Daniel, King Nebuchadnezzar of Babylon, after Daniel friends Shadrach, Meshach and Abednego had survived the fiery furnace, says this of the Jewish "High God".

Daniel 4:3 ...How great are his signs and how mighty his wonders are! His Kingdom is an everlasting Kingdom and his dominion is from generation to generation?

Author Dr. David H. Stern in his book, "Jewish New Testament Commentary", pages 16 and 17, states this.

The word 'Heaven' was used in pious avoidance of the word "God"; and to this day Hebrew 'Malkuth - haShammayim' (Kingdom of Heaven on earth) substitutes in Jewish religious literature for "Kingdom of God", an expression found frequently in the New Testament..."

251

"In both Yochanan's (John the Baptist') and Yeshua's (Jesus') preaching (Matthew 4:17) the reason for urgency to repent is that the Kingdom of Heaven is near.

The concept of the Kingdom of God is crucial to understanding the Bible. It refers neither to a place nor to a time, but to a condition in which the ruler-ship of God **is acknowledged** *by humankind, a condition in which God's promise of a restored universe free from sin and death are, or begin to be, fulfilled."*

The Jewish people of Jesus day had grown up with these "mystical" teachings and it was with this vision of Israel's future that the people listened intently to his teachings. Jesus continually taught about the Kingdom of Heaven throughout his ministry; this message was a message that the people yearned to hear, a message that stirred hope in a freedom from foreign oppression.

Not long before Christ, the Maccabees had overthrown the Greek Seleucid rule and briefly established a Jewish ruled Hasmonean dynasty. But now although King Herod was "Jewish," the nation was being occupied by Rome and clearly noted with Roman soldiers everywhere present. Although Jesus clearly taught that this Kingdom of Heaven would **not be made of hands** and was **not of this world**, it still was this teaching that attracts the crowds and also leads him to his death at the hands of the Romans.

(See Mark Dennis – Kingdom of Heaven)

The Last Merkabah Rider

Mohammed's Night Journey

In the Qur'an there is a story of Mohammed's Merkabah experience, who flies through the night on a horse from Mecca to Jerusalem. The story continues with two men lifting him up to the seventh heaven like Enoch, where he saw a very great light and fiery troops of angels. This story seems to have been influenced by other religions besides just Judaism and Christianity. The Qur'an and Hadith story of Mohammed's night journey into heaven where he then ascends to heaven and speaks to God and the prophets strongly resembles the Zoroastrian story of Arta Viraf (Warraq, pg. 279).

> *Glory to (Allah) Who did take His servant for a Journey by night from the Sacred Mosque to the farthest Mosque, whose precincts We did bless,- in order that We might show him some of Our Signs: for He is the One Who hears and sees (all things).*

> *Surah 17.1*

As stated before, the ancient Persian book of Arta Viraf describes the night journey of Viraf, the "*upright one*", who was guided in flight by an angel and crosses the great gulf on the Chinvat Bridge into the next world. Here Viraf meets God, Ahura Mazda, who shows him heaven and those who are righteous and have entered after death.

253

It was Mohammed's flight that established the *ablution*, which is the washing before prayer as well as the Islamic custom of praying five times each day. It is his steed, Buraq that flew Mohammed to heaven where he meets with Abraham, Moses, Jesus (Isa) and John the Baptist. Here Allah requests that Mohammed tell his people to pray to Him fifty time a day; Mohammed goes on to persuade Allah to reduce the prayers to five times a day.

Some scholars say that the ritual of praying five times a day and the *ablution* comes from the ancient 2nd Century Sabaean religious cult of Mohammed's day (originating from Seba, son of Cush). Many of Mohammed's relatives were believed to be of the Sabaean faith; even Mohammed was called "*the Sabaean*" in some texts which is interpreted as "*convert*" in Islamic texts.

> *Those who believe and those who follow the Jewish Scriptures and the Christians and the Sabaeans, any who believe in Allah and the Last Day and leads a righteous life, will receive their recompense from their Lord. They have nothing to fear, nor will they grieve.*
>
> *Surah 2:62*

Knowing God

The teaching that humans can become "one with God" and be able to "know God," was the foundation of the Christian Gnostics teachings and embraced by

254

many in the Arabian wilderness. These teachings are also somewhat similar to the teachings of Buddhism in the east which flourished some five hundred years earlier. The idea of Jesus that "the kingdom of God is within you" is also seemingly Gnostic as well; where one can "know truth beyond words." This is "finding the Dao," the right path is also often referenced in the Qur'an.

Many of these Gnostics believed that Jesus, although human, may have reached a kind of "divinity" through this "knowledge" and that "the kingdom of God within you" implies that man can "know God" or "become one with God." This Gnostic belief most likely would not have diminished the oneness and power of God in Muslim faith, simply expressing ones level of "spiritual maturity;" being "one with God" is not the same as being "Equal" with God. This type of teaching however was against the teachings of most Christians of that day, who believed that Jesus was God in the flesh.

Teachings

Muhammad taught that first and foremost, God was one God and that faith in God alone was sufficient for salvation in the afterlife. Second, that one must live a life pleasing to God, being obedient to His commandments. These commandments were revealed in the Scriptures that were given to Moses at Sinai, a covenant or commitment to God that was written down in the Torah. He also taught that one must believe in the prophets of God and obey their teachings; these prophets were Abraham, Isaac, Ishmael, Jacob, Moses and Jesus, as well as many more not even listen in the Qur'an. Muhammad would be the most important and the last of God's prophets and obedience to his teachings were of utmost importance.

These teachings are also the foundations of both Judaism and Christianity, that there is only one God, the God of Abraham and that one should live a life pleasing to Him. That one should obey the commandments of God given to Moses at Sinai; to love God and not to serve any god but God; to be good to ones parents and close family, to care for the orphans, widows, the needy and the elderly. Not to kill, cheat or steal; to be kind to speak good words to each other, to continue in prayer and to give to the poor.

Who was Jesus?

Islam clearly teaches that Jesus (Isa) was not divine, but only human; that the similarities of Jesus with God are the same as the similarities of Adam with God (who was created in God's image), and that God created Jesus from the dust of the earth. Jesus was the son of Mary, and was only but a prophet of God. He was the fulfillment of God's promises which God had conveyed to Mary; a soul that was created by God. In fact, when Jesus is asked by God if he told the people, "Take me and my mother as two gods alongside God," Jesus says to Him, "I would never say what I had no right to say."

256

Although Jesus is referred to as the Word of God and the Messiah in the Qur'an and that Islam teaches that Jesus will return in the Second Coming on the Day of Judgment to restore the earth. In Islam as in Judaism, there is only one God and Jesus, although he is the Messiah, was not God. It is taught that after his return to earth, Jesus will rule the earth for a short period of time, eradicating evil, and then he will die.

The Qur'an teaches that if anyone makes others equal with God, God will prohibit him from the Garden, and hell will be his home. Those people who say that God is the third of three are defying the truth; there is only One God. If they persist in what they are saying, a painful punishment will distress those of them who persist. Believe, then in God and His apostles, and do not say, "God is a trinity." Cease from this declaration for your own good. God is but One God; it is far from His magnificence that He should have a son.

Docetism

Some Gnostic Gospels and the Qur'an teach that the Jews did not truly kill Jesus however, nor did they crucify him, but it only appeared so to them.

> *Qur'an Sura 4:158 ..."Those who argue about it are in suspicion regarding it and have no real knowledge about it, only speculation; no one is certain that they killed him! No! God took him up to Himself."*

257

To secular scholars, this clearly comes from the Gnostic teachings of Docetism (Ehrman, pg. 181), meaning "*to seem*" or "*appear as*." It was believed by many in the early days of Christianity, that if Jesus was divine and could not die; whoever was on the cross was a substitute for Jesus and only appeared to be Jesus.

Others believed in the "*swoon hypothesis*," that he merely fell unconscious and later was revived. This Islamic teaching possibly was influenced by the Gnostic Gospel of *The Apocalypse of Peter;* that Jesus did not die on the cross but was caught up to heaven and that he only seemed to die. The teaching is that either his body on the cross was a complete illusion or someone else such as Judas was substituted for him. Either way, Jesus was not killed; it only seemed so to the Jews.

*But this one into whose hands and feet they drive the nails is his fleshly part, which is the **substitute** being put to shame, the one who came into being **in his likeness**.*

The Apocalypse of Peter

Some of the Gnostic Gospels are the *Infancy Gospel of James*, the *Infancy Gospel of Thomas*, the books of *Enoch* and the *Apocalypse of Peter*. Most were destroyed under the Roman Church yet are believed to have influenced Islam; many are in the Gnostic Nag Hammadi library of Egypt.

(See Mark Dennis – Visions in the Desert)

Creation

Spiritual Kingdom

In respect to the Spiritual Kingdom this analogy is used in mystic teaching. At the time of creation, in the beginning, through God's divine will, the union of Wisdom (Father) with the Understanding (Mother) produces Revealed Knowledge (Son) which is "Logos," or "Reason," the creation of *Adam Kadmon*, the spiritual Adam. When the vessels that contained the light of God shattered, evil and good were created along with the Earthly Kingdom of mankind.

Proverbs 3:19-20 ...By **wisdom** *the Lord laid the earth's foundations, by* **understanding** *he set the heavens in place; by his* **knowledge** *the deeps were divided.*

Proverbs 24:3-4 *...By* **wisdom** *a house is built, and through* **understanding** *it is established; through* **knowledge** *its rooms are filled with rare and beautiful treasures.*

Daniel 2:21-22 *...Praise be to the name of God for ever and ever;* **wisdom** *and* **power** *are his. He changes times and seasons; he deposes kings and raises up others.*

He gives **wisdom** *to the wise and* **knowledge** *to the* **discerning**. *He* **reveals deep and hidden things**; *he knows what lies in* **darkness**, *and* **light dwells with him**.

Proverbs 9:10 ...*The fear of the Lord is the beginning of* **wisdom**, *and* **knowledge** *of the* <u>Holy One</u> *is* **understanding**

Exodus 31:3 ...*I've filled him with the* <u>Spirit of God</u>, *with* **wisdom,** **understanding** *and* **knowledge.**

Proverbs 2:6 ...*For the Lord gives* **wisdom**; *from his mouth come* **knowledge** *and* **understanding**.

Wisdom, Knowledge and Understanding

Knowledge - the range of one's **understanding**; the state of being **aware** of something; it is information, awareness of what is real and true. This awareness give the ability to know right from wrong; the Knowledge of Good and Evil. Many believe that it is this **discernment** that sets man apart from the animal kingdom.

Understanding - the **knowledge** and ability to judge a particular situation or subject; the power of comprehending. It is the ability to gain meaning from the important aspects of your knowledge.

Wisdom - the ability to understand things that other's cannot **understand**; knowledge of what is proper or reasonable. It is knowing what to do with or how to apply this important information that you now know. It is wisdom that gives life and meaning to what you know and understand. *Ecclesiastes 7:12* says, "**wisdom** gives **life** to those who have **knowledge**."

Understanding is a bridge between Wisdom and Knowledge. Proverbs chapter 1 shows this relationship between Knowledge, Understanding and Wisdom. In Proverbs 1, we see the simple and young need instruction in order to **gain knowledge**. Through knowledge, one **gains understanding** and with understanding over time one **gains wisdom**.

Gaining Wisdom and Knowledge:

*For gaining **wisdom** and **knowledge**;*

*For **understanding** words of awareness;*

*For receiving **knowledge** in discreet behavior, doing **what is right**, just and fair;*

*For giving care to those who are simple, **knowledge** and maturity to the young.*

*Let the **wise** listen and add to their **knowledge**, and let those who **understand** get guidance, so that they may have **understanding** for these proverbs and parables, the sayings and riddles of the **wise**.*

*Having awe and respect for the Lord is the beginning of this **knowledge**, but **fools despise wisdom and instruction**.*

Proverbs 1

Earthly Kingdom

In respect to the Earthly Kingdom, to the mystics, this came about from the fall of man when he lost his Divine light, the Shekinah light of God; the union with God's feminine Shekinah was lost. To the mystic, mankind could no longer walk in the Garden with God; humanity is pictured as a forlorn lover in exile, eager to return to Ein-Sof, the Eternal One. The Bride and the Bridegroom are separated because of Adam and Eve's disobedience. The light of God which once enlightened all of creation no longer shone down; the soul of man became dark, separated from God, as in exile.

Mankind was in a state of disrepair, in need of mending and out of touch with God. A deep longing, a need to reunite, like the forlorn lover is in all of man. The need to "know" the Creator and have shelter from the calamity and chaos in the world.

In order to know an incomprehensible God, attributes of humankind, who was made in the likeness of God, were assigned to God. Although these attributes have been corrupted by many and made into demigods with limited powers over time, these attributes became the tool, through understanding, that humankind could "know" God in a personal way. The mystic Jews of ancient history were strongly monotheistic in their teaching, that there was only one God and this must not be misunderstood. The corruption of this teaching has led to modern day mysticism that has created "gods" from the divine

262

attributes of God. The path to restoration only comes with prayer and meditation on God, His revelations and His names. An attempt by man to come back in harmony with God. This is a way that mankind in making steps toward God, brings God's Kingdom closer to man; redeeming and restoring man to God.

The exiled soul of mankind, through the knowledge of God, could be redeemed; a salvation that was based in "knowing God" rather than in faith alone. It was in understanding the ten Sefiroth, the ten attributes of God, that one came to "know" God. In knowing the "limited" God, man could reunite with the "limitless" and "unknowable" God. Having this knowledge brings man to God, fools despise this wisdom and instruction. Rejection of this knowledge only brings hardship.

Redemption

Redemption or salvation is the process of being "bought back" to the mystics was a process of the soul. Here the soul was viewed as a field that needed to be cultivated; a healing of the soul through the knowledge of God. It was in sleep while dreaming and in meditation that one's soul began to mend; in the state of the unconscious, man could commune with God. To the mystic, redemption was solely man's responsibility.

It was through incessant prayer and meditation that the mystic would enter into a trance, a visionary state in which they could enter into the palaces of the seven heavens and come to the throne-chariot of God. This was the goal of the Merkabah Riders, a way to re-unite with God, to heal and nourish the soul and be redeemed by God. Prophets throughout the Scriptures attained this goal and their stories written down for us to read.

Wisdom's Rebuke:

> *Out in the open wisdom calls aloud, she raises her voice in the public square; on top of the wall she cries out, at the city gate she makes her speech:*

> *"How long will you who are simple love your simple ways? How long will mockers delight in mockery and fools hate knowledge?*

> *Repent at my rebuke! Then I will pour out my thoughts to you, I will make known to you my knowledge.*

> *But since you refuse to listen when I call and no one pays attention, when I stretch out my hand, since you disregard all my advice and do not accept my rebuke,*

> *I in turn will laugh when disaster strikes you; I will mock when calamity overtakes you.*

> *When calamity overtakes you like a storm, when disaster sweeps over you like a whirlwind, when distress and trouble overwhelm you.*

Then they will call to me but I will not answer; they will look for me but will not find me, since they hated knowledge and did not choose to fear the Lord.

Since they would not accept my advice and spurned my rebuke, they will eat the fruit of their ways and be filled with the fruit of their schemes.

For the waywardness of the simple will kill them, and the complacency of fools will destroy them; but whoever listens to me (Wisdom) will live in safety and be at ease, without fear of harm."

Proverbs 1

Visions of the Merkabah Riders

Mysticism and the Fall

Fall of Man

When the vessels that contained the light of God where shattered, good and evil were created along with the world in which we inhabit. The point at which this happened was when Adam and Eve listened to the deceptive whispers of the "Shiny One," the serpent and ate of the fruit that they were forbidden to eat.

In reading the context of the Garden of Eden from any version of any religion, we see that trees bore fruit which were to be eaten.

Genesis reads:

*Genesis 3:6 ... And when the woman saw that the tree was **good for food**, and that it was pleasant to the eyes, and a tree to be desired to make one wise, she took of the fruit thereof, and did eat"*

The fruit of all trees was therefore created by God to be eaten as food and nourishment, digested and returned to the soil. The death of the fruit then clearly was designed into creation; the Creator created the *cycle of life*. Fruits bear the seeds of the plant that grew it; therefore new life springs forth through the death of the fruit and presumably the death of the plant that bore it. If plants would continue to live and produce new plant life through seedlings, all nutrients would eventually be removed from the soil and the forest floor would become over grown.

It seems therefore that here in Malkuth, the "Earthly Kingdom," **death was in the Creator's design** - the *cycle of life*. If the death of the leaf, the death of the fruit that was eaten and the eventual death of the plant that grew the fruit was designed into the life cycle, then also will not the microorganisms that break down the fruit also die and go through their own cycle of life? Consider also insects and mammals in this cycle of life. Was death really a result of the "curse" or part of the design? Consider also this that the Tree of Life was to **give Eternal Life**; therefore even the death of man must have been designed into creation even before the "curse". If man were not designed to die, why would he need to gain "eternal life" and live forever?

Human beings, therefore, according to these writings in Genesis, are like God and created in His image. The text indicates that the only thing keeping mankind from being "gods" is man's mortality, which seems to be already designed into creation. Eating of the "Tree of Life" would therefore make mankind into "gods," living forever.

*Genesis 3:22 ...Behold, the man is **become as one of us**, to knowing good and evil. (Let us prevent him now) from putting forth his hand, and taking also of the tree of life, and eating, lest they **live forever**.*

So He drove out the man and he placed at the east of the Garden of Eden Cherubim's and a flaming sword, which turned every way, to keep the way of the tree of life

The knowledge of Good and Evil was clearly not intended for mankind, at least in the beginning. Although man could never become like God, as God is omnipotent (all-powerful), omniscient (all-knowing) and omnipresent (everywhere present), man could both know good and evil and become "like" God. Man was not driven out of the Garden as punishment for attaining the knowledge of Good and Evil, he was driven out of the Garden to prevent him from eating of the Tree of Life and living forever (See Mark Dennis – World of the Forsaken).

Fall of Lucifer

In a parallel story, the angel Lucifer, one of the highest angels and an angel of Light, decided to be "like" God as well and raise his throne to the level of God's throne.

Isaiah 14:12-13 ... How you have fallen from heaven, O morning star, son of the dawn! You have been cast down to the earth, you who once laid low the nations!

For you said to yourself, 'I will ascend to heaven and set my throne above God's stars.

Although the book of Isaiah was clearly referring to Nebuchadnezzar of Babylon in the text, its origin is from the book of 2 Enoch:

2 Enoch 29:2 ... and their raiment a burning flame, and I commanded that each one should stand in his order.

*Here Satanail with his angels was thrown down from the height. And one from out the order of angels, having turned away with the order that was under him, conceived an impossible thought, to place his throne higher than the clouds above the earth, **that he might become equal in rank to my power.***

*And **I threw him out** from the height with his angels, and he was flying in the air continuously above the bottomless.*

Fall of Man

Both Adam Kadmon and Lucifer were created as pure creatures in the beginning, without sin. Both however attempted to become "like" God and were thrown out of the Garden and from the heavenly realm. In Jewish mystic teaching, the realm of this Higher Garden of Eden is Beri'ah, the second world, the Moral **world**. This is the world of the throne of judgment; a **world** where one can discern right from wrong and good from evil. A world through which the light of God in the Spiritual world emanates down into the Created world (Ponce', pg. 66).

This Garden was the first of God's creation where self-awareness first took place. After the vessels of light were broken, the third world of Yetzirah was formed, known as the Formed World. This is the world of the senses, desire and of emotion; also called the Lower Garden of Eden. It is here that Malkuth, the "Earthly Kingdom," resides with the Abyss separating us from the spiritual world of God; it is because of man's separation from God, that the desire to "know" God arises.

Similar to Lucifer being thrown from the heaven heights, man was also thrown out of this heavenly Garden. Again, at the tower of Babel, mankind tries to reach up to the heavens into the realm of God. God again disrupts this attempt and scatters mankind by confusing their language.

Visions of the Merkabah Riders

Conclusion

In the Beginning

The Jewish mystics firmly believed that there is only one Almighty God. This God was omnipotent, omniscient and omnipresent; that is to say, all-powerful, all-knowing and everywhere present. Before creation, there was nothing to relate Him to, nothing to know him by, therefore this Almighty God could not be known. It was in the act of creation that God revealed Himself; man could see His awesome glory, authority and power, and he could realize His mighty wisdom, gain understanding and knowledge through the incredible beauty of His creation. The story of God's creation was revealed to these believers through the Torah, the story of God. The Torah revealed His Law by which His judgment on sin commenced as well as by which His unending mercy, forgiveness, compassion and loving kindness was also shown. The Torah was the foundation of their faith, the way to live one's life in this physical world.

All of these characteristics or attributes that were attributed to God were man's own "good" attributes; these were to be nourished and developed in one's self as characteristics of God within man. In this way, man was created in the image of God, in His own likeness. As man lived out these attributes in himself, the light of God would shine forth and help bring light to others who lived in the darkness of fear, anger, hate and selfishness. This darkness was an attribute that

273

mankind had inherited from Adam under the "fall" when man became separated from God through disobedience. Now, between man and God was a great Abyss, a vast chasm by which only a small amount of God's light would cross. The mysteries of God were hidden from man, God's will and plan for man was unknown. In man's ignorance and finiteness, man struggled with the evil that was in him, becoming deceitful and wicked, destroying God's creation as well as himself and others, living in the darkness of pain and fear.

Only a few would strive to nourish the small amount of light that could be kindled within them, that small flicker of God's light from the dawn of creation that still remained. These mystics found that in dwelling on God's revelation, the revelation of Himself given in the Torah, in creation and within man's own finite heart, that this light could be rekindled and bring hope, happiness, contentment and a longer more prosperous life. This light was contagious and spread within one's family, tribe and nation, as long as it was nurtured.

The attributes of God within man were the image of God in man. Adam was a perfect man in the beginning, and although human, was perfect in every way, yet locked into space and time. He was the image of God, yet not divine. He was perfect, yet could not transcend space and time as God could, neither was Adam perfect in knowledge or power as God is. These mystics longed for this impossible lost human "perfection."

274

The Bride

This mysticism grew and prospered in ancient Judaism; much wisdom and knowledge was gained by those who studied the Torah and meditated on God's holy name. They strove to "know" God and to become "one" with Him and have a personal relationship with Him. They used the illustration of being God's bride, a forlorn bride who longed to be back in the arms of the One she loved, to be one with Him; she is the Shekinah.

It was believed that power was found in this relationship with God. It was in this ancient wisdom that a power was gained that had to be protected from those who would abuse it for their own selfish gain. It is said that it was in the names of God that one could attain this power; it had to be harnessed and the secrets of this power could only be passed on to those who were spiritually mature. According to Hagigah 2:1, a warning is given to mystic teachers and Rabbi's to only teach the mystical doctrines of creation to one student at a time. Traditionally this hidden knowledge was only passed from teacher to student, father to son; only after the age of forty and only if they had proven their moral and spiritual maturity.

The Merkabah Riders

Many of these mystics could also attain visions of God and his Holy celestial temple through meditation, prayer, the singing of hymns and through fasting. In these visions, the glory of God could be seen on many celestial levels or heavens of which each level became more challenging and dangerous. These were the Merkabah Riders, the riders of the Throne Chariot, the mystics who attained these visionary secrets of God. Visions of the seven heavens and the seven palaces or temples, known as *Hekhalot*, through which the Merkabah mystic such as Enoch, Ezekiel, Daniel and Isaiah traveled as seen in their writings. Many believe that Jesus and his Apostles also experiences these visions as we see in the Mount of Transfiguration, Paul's vision of Christ on the road to Damascus and most notably in John's vision in the book of Revelation.

The Messiah

It was also in the person of Jesus Christ as the Son of Man that we see the teachings of these ancient mystic beliefs. The mystics had long taught, centuries before Christ, that a deliverer was to come, a human in the likeness of Adam, perfect in every way, yet not divine and subject to death as all mankind was. Enoch, Ezekiel and Daniel all pictured this man as the "Son of Man" (meaning human), who was chosen before time and was with God before creation. He was the "firstborn" of creation and associated with the Torah as the "Word of God" that existed with God; in some text it is he who would be the one to initiate creation through the power of God Almighty. It would be this Deliverer, this Savior that would come as the Messiah and overcome Israel's enemies, judge the world and rule over the world for a period of time, then die. Paul describes Jesus as this second Adam.

Son of God

The mystics also taught that these attributes of God would shine brightest in this human Messiah and was referred to as the Lesser YHWH, the perfect image of **God** in human form. All men in a way were sons of **God** in that they were His creation and had a flicker of His divineness within them.

This coming Messiah however was this chosen one, God's Elect, who would come as the Deliverer, the Son of God, the firstborn of God's creation, the Light of God for the world. To his disciples, Jesus was this Light, the one who would lead the world out of darkness into the Kingdom of Light. Jesus was the one who these prophets had prophesied, the coming Deliverer who would free them from the hands of the Romans and issue in God's Kingdom on earth.

Jesus taught them that he was "one with the Father" and that the "way" to the Father was through him. Jesus claimed to be the Light of the World but also told his disciples that they too were the light of the world. In the Gospels, Jesus is called both the Son of Man, linking him directly to this prophecy of the Messiah, as well as the Son of God, the Lesser YHWH, the perfect image of God, the perfect reflection of God in a perfect yet mortal human being. This to the mystic was an anthropomorphic description of the divinity, appearing as the first primal man, Adam Kadmon. This Lesser YHWH is seen in the lower seven Sefiroth and acts as a mediator between God and man.

Ten Sefiroth

The attributes of God referred to in the beginning of this section were shown as actually "good" attributes man as a way to describe God and to know Him in a limited way. The basic structure was given as ten attributes or Ten Sefiroth; each of these ten however, although assigned ten names, are also expressed more liberally with many more attributes; the mystic explains this as Ten Sefiroth within Ten Sefiroth and ten more inside them and so on with innumerable good attributes ascribed to Him, as God is Good!

Knowledge of Good and Evil

This good is the power that conquers evil, that vanquishes darkness. Man, at the "fall" when he fell from God's grace, took on the evil attributes, the "knowledge of evil" that we all have inherited from Adam. It was only through the "knowledge good," the "knowledge of God," that we can attain His good attributes and this light to overcome the darkness.

Tree of Life

These Ten Sefiroth are illustrated in the diagram of a tree. This Tree of Life is drawn in four levels; the spiritual level, the moral level, the sensual or emotional level and the physical level. This tree also branches off into three branches or pillars; the Pillar of Strength, the Pillar of Mercy and the Middle Pillar or the Pillar of Compassion.

Conclusion

These three pillars are paths for God's light that gives us life, to shine down to man across the great Abyss, and are also the paths for man's ascension to God through prayer and meditation in a "spiritual" way. Some mystics also picture the Tree of Life to have a darker side; although the light of God may shine through it and mediate His light through the Middle Pillar (Eye of the Needle), the two left and right branches of this tree represent the trees of "good" and "evil."

Mother and Father

These three pillars are also illustrated as masculine and feminine in much the same way that languages around the world have masculine and feminine words. The right pillar contains the masculine attributes and the left, the feminine attributes; the center attributes are neutral. The spiritual world connected with mankind forms a spiritual trinity, father (God), mother (Creation) and son (mankind) pointing down; the physical trinity of man, woman and God points up; a symbol of unity, the "Sacred Union". This star to many represents the relationship between God and humanity but also of Good and Evil. The two triangles put together creates the Star of David or Solomon's Seal as seen in the Israeli flag today.

> *Numbers 24:17 ...I shall see him, but not now: I shall behold him, but not nigh: there shall come a **Star out of Jacob**...*

279

This is also seen in the two way covenant that God made with Moses and the people of Israel on Mount Sinai where they promised to obey Him and be His people; man to God and God to man. The people of Israel agreed to this covenant when they said,

Exodus 19:8 ...All that the Lord has spoken we will do!"

In this way there is also a masculine and feminine link in the Ten Sefiroth vertically where God is the Bridegroom and Israel was the Bride.

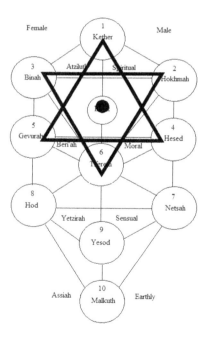

Conclusion

In the ancient world, during the captivity and the Jewish dispersion or Jewish diaspora throughout the world, Israel was symbolized in the city of Jerusalem, the city they loved so much. Isaiah portrays her as awaiting for the coming of the Messiah and the book of Revelation envisions the Bridegroom, the slain Lamb, the Messiah as Jesus and the "New Jerusalem" as the Bride. Many Christians today portray the Bride in this context as the "Christian Church" although its source is clearly from Isaiah in reference to the New Jerusalem.

The Message

The message of the Jewish mystics at first was simple; a desire to "know" their creator. Over the centuries this simple mystic belief blossomed into a complex religion and evolved into the several more religions with thousands of sects, cults and denominations today. The original desire to now God became obsessive to some, dedicating their whole lives to this search for God, locked up away from mankind in constant meditation, prayer and fasting. It was these prophets and monks who were the first Merkabah Riders, who saw these vision of the Almighty. Most orthodox believers of these various religious groups today sincerely believe that these visions were truly revelations given to them by God and written so in inspired Scripture as truth. Many believe that these visions were merely induced as trances brought on by chanting, meditation, the lack of sugar in their systems from days of fasting and various pharmaceuticals that they may have breathed in or ingested.

These things may never be known but the message of their original search still lives on today as many of us too desire the same thing; having the same emptiness in our hearts, the desire to know God. It was this very message that Jesus Christ taught those who followed him, that we can become "one with God," having a personal relationship with the Father and be able to know Him.

Salvation

Salvation over the centuries and to various believers in countless places have had numerous concepts. These concepts can be divided into two categories; salvation in this life and salvation in the life to come. These two categories can also be broken into separate subsets of salvation of what it meant to different societies in different times.

In this World for the Nation - To the ancient Jew, especially in the time of bondage, persecution and captivity, salvation was for the here and now, for the nation of Israel to be freed from bondage and to be saved from captivity. The belief in mystical things was amplified greatly under the captivity with their beloved city and temple in ruins. They longed for the return to this city and for a Messiah that would save them from captivity and rebuild their city and temple.

It was Cyrus the Great who became the Anointed One when he freed the Israelites from captivity and financed the rebuilding of the Temple and the walls of Jerusalem. This salvation was only temporary as they were soon under the rule of the Greeks, the Seleucid rule of Antioch and then the Romans. It was again in 70 AD that the temple was again destroyed and the wall of Jerusalem torn down. The Jews today long as their ancestors once did for the rebuilding of the temple and the coming of the Messiah to rid them forever from those who oppress them – a salvation for Israel, for the Jewish people here in this life.

*Isaiah 46:13 ...I will **grant salvation to Zion**, my splendor to Israel.*

*Jeremiah 3:23 ...Our worship of idols on the hills and our religious orgies on the mountains are a delusion. Only in the Lord our **God will Israel ever find salvation.***

It was through the suffering of Israel as the "Suffering Servant" that Israel will one day be redeemed. The descendants of this ancient Israel will someday see this salvation and will live long prosperous lives.

*Isaiah 53:10 ...Yet it was the Lord's will to crush him and **cause him (Israel) to suffer**, and though the Lord makes his life an offering for sin,*

*__He will see his offspring__ and **prolong his days**, and the will of the Lord will prosper in his hand.*

283

In this World for the Individual - There also was not only a salvation for the people of Israel as a whole but a personal salvation that would bring the individual peace, contentment, happiness, prosperity and long life. This salvation was attained through ones devotion to God and in fact would result in the nations own salvation as a whole if they as a society would only maintain their focus on God.

*Psalm 91:16 ...I will reward them **with a long life** and give them **my salvation.**"*

*Deuteronomy 6:2 ...fear the Lord your God as long as you live **by keeping all his decrees and commands** that I give you, and **so that you may enjoy long life.***

*Proverbs 3:2 ...My son, **do not forget my teaching,** but **keep my commands in your heart**, for they will **prolong your life** many years and **bring you peace and prosperity**.*

*Isaiah 12:2 ...Surely **God is my salvation**; I will trust and not be afraid. The Lord, the Lord himself, **is my strength and my defense**; he has **become my salvation.**"*

*Isaiah 33:2 ...Be our strength every morning, our **salvation in time of distress**.*

*Isaiah 33:6 ...He will be the **sure foundation for your life**, a **rich store of salvation** and **wisdom** and **knowledge**; the fear of the Lord is the key to this treasure.*

Conclusion

It was the prophets of ancient Israel that continually warned them to repent; if they would repent, then God would bless them. The people many times resorted to their own evil selfish ways and killed these prophets which brought God's wrath on the nation as a whole. Most salvation that is spoken of in the Hebrew Bible makes reference to both this personal and national salvation for this life and in the world. Even the few references to *eternal salvation* simply are interpreted as a salvation that it will continue indefinitely in this physical world for the nation.

*Isaiah 45:17 ...But **Israel will be saved** by the Lord with an **everlasting salvation**; you will **never be put to shame** or disgraced, **to ages everlasting**.*

Day of Judgment - The next type of salvation spoken of is in reference to the Day of Judgment and salvation from God's wrath. Even then, many of the references in the Hebrew Bible still refer to this life and to this world, not the world to come. This Day to them was not a spiritual judgment in the next life but the destruction of those who lived sinfully within the House of Israel or were enemies of Israel.

*Proverbs 11:4 ...Riches won't help on the **Day of Judgment**, but **right living** can **save you** from mortal danger.*

Zephaniah 2:3 ...Seek the Lord, all you humble of the land, you who do what he commands.

Seek righteousness, *seek* **humility***; perhaps you will be* **saved on the day of the Lord's anger.**

Eternal Life - The concept of eternal salvation, a salvation in the next life, seems to be more of a Christian concept written in the Gospels and the other writings of the Apostles.

Matthew 25:46 ...Then they will go away to **eternal punishment***, but the righteous* **to eternal life."**

1 John 1:2 ...we **proclaim to you the eternal life***, which* **was with the Father** *and has* **appeared to us***.*

1 John 2:23-25 ... No one who denies the Son has the Father; **whoever acknowledges the Son has the Father also.**

As for you, see that what you have **heard from the beginning remains in you***.*

If it does, **you also will remain in the Son** *and* **in the Father***. And this is what* **he promised us eternal life.**

1 John 5:11 ...And this is the testimony: God has **given us eternal life***, and this life is in his* **Son***.*

Conclusion

*1 Timothy 4:8 ...godliness has value for all things, holding promise for **both** the **present life** and the **life to come**.*

*Titus 1:1-2 ...to further the faith of God's elect and their **knowledge of the truth** that **leads to godliness**, in the **hope of eternal life**, which God, who does not lie, **promised before the beginning of time.***

*John 17:3 ...Now **this is eternal life**: that they **know you**, the **only true God**, **and Jesus Christ**, **whom you have sent.***

*John 3:36 ...Whoever **believes in the Son has eternal life,** but **whoever rejects the Son** will **not see life***, for God's wrath remains on them.

Role of Religions

National governments throughout the world for centuries have had the role of protecting their people from the destructive nature of themselves and others. Over time, laws were developed according to traditions and needs. The governments became as it were the legal shepherds of their flocks, herding them, hemming them in and protecting them legally.

Religious organizations also developed over the centuries and created moral standards and in some cases laws for which their people were to live by; rules that would protect them socially from the destructive nature

287

of themselves and others. These religious organizations as temples, synagogues, churches and mosques all had the responsibility of moral shepherds of their flocks, herding and hemming them in and protecting them morally. In some cases such as in Jewish and Islamic societies, these government institutions and religious organizations were one in the same; to the ancient Jew, this was the Mosaic Law; today we see this in Islamic Sharia Law which developed out of Mosaic Law.

Following a religion or religious creed however does not save anyone, in this world or the world to come. Religion may be the path or the portal to which one may become closer to God and receive salvation but religion on its own does nothing; salvation is a gift from God and God alone. Religions focus is on doing what is expected of society and what they believe God expects out of them. Religion in many cases burdens one's self with fear, worry, guilt and shame; the very darkness that mankind longs to be delivered or saved from. Religion can even stir up hatred and anger, bigotry and disgust of others, shedding darkness and suffering on people and increasing the need for man's salvation. Religion begins as a path to knowing God but in the end can become the very reason for ones need of salvation.

Personal Salvation

To the Jewish mystic even before the time of Jesus, it was the Light of God, that one receives through knowing God, that brought forth salvation in one's life.

Knowing the Almighty was impossible but knowing the "limited" God in the human likeness of Adam Kadmon, as the human reflection or manifestation of God was possible. The representation of God's attributes in human form was seen as the "face of God."

*Psalm 80:3 ...Restore us, O God; let your **face shine**, that we **may be saved**!*

The face of God was seen as the Extended **Countenance** through the ten Sefiroth. The Lesser **Countenance** through the lower seven Sefiroth was the illustration of the Lesser YHWH, God's attributes in man; the perfect man as the Son of God, what man strived to become but could not become in this world.

*2 Corinthians 4:6 ...God said, "Let **light shine out of darkness**," He made his **light shine in our hearts** to give us the **light of the knowledge** of God's glory **displayed in the face of Christ**.*

These devoted believers who longed to know God and desired to be more like God, wanted to become who they were meant to be in the very beginning, like the first Adam. It was through this devotion, spending time in prayer with God, spending time in Scripture and meditating on the goodness and mercy of God that their hearts were changed.

It wasn't in the **doing** of religious mandates through social pressure or of selfish desire that one received this salvation, it was in **being** changed from within; having the **heart and mind of God**, letting the Spirit of God shine His light through them. It was in **being** and **not in doing** that one gained this personal salvation. This is that peace that passes all understanding, this is that mind that is Christ Jesus; in this salvation joy, love, contentment and kindness all shine forth and from this salvation comes the fruit of the Spirit.

*Philippians 2:5 ...Let this **mind be in you**, which **was also in Christ Jesus**.*

*Philippians 4:7 ...And the **peace of God, which passes all understanding**, shall keep your **hearts and minds** through Christ Jesus.*

*Galatians 5:22 ...But the **fruit of the Spirit** is **love, joy, peace, forbearance, kindness, goodness, faithfulness, gentleness** and **self-control**. Against such things there is no law.*

Religion has a tendency to make people believe that they can gain salvation from doing good, seemingly promoting the idea that if you try hard enough that you can somehow gain God's approval. Many seek salvation merely through fear of God's wrath and do good to others to gain Gods mercy, not in love for others but for one's own selfish gain and in fear for one's self-preservation.

Conclusion

In spending ones time in devotion, prayer and meditation on with God and on the good attributes of God, one becomes over time more like God. Through this renewal and rebirth, one also becomes the Light of the Word for others to see God's light and they themselves become lights to the world as well.

*Psalm 119:105 ...**Your word is a lamp** for my feet, a **light on my path**.*

*Ephesians 6:18P...**Pray in the Spirit at all times** and on every occasion. Stay alert and **be persistent in your prayers** for all believers everywhere.*

*Psalm 119:99 ...I have more understanding than all my teachers, for **your words** are **my meditation**.*

*Psalm 119:174 ...I long for **Your salvation**, O Lord; **Your instruction is my delight**.*

*James 4:8 ...**Come near to God** and **he will come near to you**.*

*Ephesians 2:8 ...For it is by **grace you have been saved**, through faith, and this is **not from yourselves**, it is the **gift of God***

*Matthew 5:14 "**You** are the **light of the world**."*

For the Apostles, this ancient belief rang true. It was Jesus who was the Son of God and Jesus who was the mediating High Priest who was without sin.

> *Hebrews 4:14 ...Therefore, since we have a* **great high priest** *who has* **ascended into heaven,** *Jesus the* **Son of God,** *let us hold firmly to the faith we profess.*
>
> *For we do not have a* **high priest** *who is unable to empathize with our weaknesses, but we have one who has been* **tempted in every way,** *just as we are—***yet he did not sin.**
>
> *Let us then* **approach God's throne** *of grace with confidence, so that* **we may receive mercy and find grace** *to help us* **in our time of need.**

Mankind's fall from grace put him under the curse of darkness, enveloped in the dark attributes of man that leads to guilt, fear and hatred, in dire need for God's Light and Salvation. It is when man turned to God and put his faith in Him rather than in what he did or tried to do, that God gives him rebirth with the hope of salvation not only in this life but in the life to come.

> *Tutus 3: 3-7 ...At* **one time we too were foolish,** **disobedient, deceived** *and* **enslaved** *by all kinds of passions and pleasures.*
>
> **We lived in malice and envy, being hated** *and* **hating one another.**

292

Conclusion

*But when the kindness and **love of God** our Savior appeared, **he saved us**, **not because of righteous things we had done**, but **because of his mercy**.*

He saved us through the washing of rebirth *and **renewal by the Holy Spirit**, whom he **poured out on us generously** through Jesus Christ our Savior,*

*So that, having been **justified by his grace**, we **might become heirs** having the **hope of eternal life.***

A Universal Truth

This truth is universal; just as the Apostle Paul taught that salvation was not only for the Jew but also for the Gentile, let it also be known that **this salvation is for all mankind** and **not just the Christian**. We may argue over what our interpretation of these ancient beliefs mean, whether or not Jesus was fully God or the reflection of God. Mankind, in his ignorance may never know in this life the meaning of all of this, but one thing we do know is that division, strife, hate and anger only stir up guilt, fear, anxiety, grief and hostility. These are not the fruit of the Spirit nor are they the attributes of the sons of God. As children of God we need to be the Light of the World, encouraging each other, loving each other and giving to each other so that we can live in peace, contentment and happiness; living long and prosperous lives in the Light of His salvation.

Visions of the Merkabah Riders

Conclusion

Galatians 4:6 ...Because you are his sons, God sent the Spirit of his Son into our hearts, the Spirit who calls out, "Abba, Father."

Conclusion

Psalms 23

The Lord is my shepherd; I shall not want. He maketh me to lie down in green pastures: he leadeth me beside the still waters.

He restoreth my soul: he leadeth me in the paths of righteousness for his name's sake.

Yea, though I walk through the valley of the shadow of death, I will fear no evil: for thou art with me; thy rod and thy staff they comfort me.

Thou preparest a table before me in the presence of mine enemies: thou anointest my head with oil; my cup runneth over.

Surely goodness and mercy shall follow me all the days of my life: and I will dwell in the house of the Lord forever.

Visions of the Merkabah Riders

References

Alter, Michael J. (1998), Why the Torah Begins with the Letter Beit, f Jason Aronson, Incorporated, Northvale NJ

Appleton, E.R. (2005) An Outline Of Religion, Kessinger Publishing Company, PO Box 1404 Whitefish MT

Aristophanes, Birds, lines 690–699. (Translation by Eugene O'Neill, Jr., Perseus Digital Library; translation modified.)

Assmann, Jan (1998) Moses the Egyptian: The Memory of Egypt in Western Monotheism, First Harvard University Press, Cambridge, MA

Assmann, Jan (2008) Of God and gods, University of Wisconsin Press, Madison WI

Assmann, Jan (2001) The Search for God in Ancient Egypt, Cornell University Press, Ithaca New York

Barnard, Jody A (2012), The mysticism of Hebrews: Exploring the Role of Jewish Apocalyptic Mysticism, Mohr Siebeck, Tubingen, Germany

Boren, Kerry Ross (2000) Following the Ark of the Covenant, Cedar Fort, Inc., Springville, UT

Bohak, Gideon (2008), Ancient Jewish Magic: A History Cambridge University Press, New York, NY

Buddhadasa Bhikku (1989), Me and Mine: Selected Essays of Bhikkhu Buddhadasa, SUNY Press, State University of New York, Albany NY

Budge, E. A. Wallis (2009) Tutankhamen, Amenism, Atenism and Egyptian Monotheism, With Hieroglyphic Texts of Hymns To Amen and Aten, BiblioBazaar, P.O. Box 21206

Bulgakov, Sergiĭ (2012), Unfading Light: Contemplations and Speculations. Eerdmans Publishing, Grand Rapids, Michigan

Cardin, Nina Beth (1999), Tears of Sorrow, Seeds of Hope: A Jewish Spiritual Companion for Infertility, Jewish Lights Publishing, Woodstock, VT

Collins, John Joseph (2001), Seers, Sibyls, and Sages in Hellenistic-Roman Judaism, Brill Academic Publishers, Danvers, MA

Comfort, Philip (2004) The Complete book of Who's Who in the Bible, Tyndale House Publishing, Wheaton Ill.

Dan, Joseph (1999) The "Unique Cherub" Circle A School of Mystics and Esoterics in Medieval Germany Pg. 260 Mohr Siebeck Publishing, Tübingen, Germany

Dennis, Mark (2012) The Kingdom of Heaven, Perspectives, CreateSpace Independent Publishing, On-Demand Publishing, LLC.

References

Dennis, Mark (2013), Visions I The Apocalypse of Enoch, CreateSpace Independent Publishing, On-Demand Publishing, LLC.

Dennis, Mark (2013), Visions II The Revelation of Daniel, CreateSpace Independent Publishing, On-Demand Publishing, LLC.

Dennis, Mark (2013), Visions III The Revelation of John, CreateSpace Independent Publishing, On-Demand Publishing, LLC.

Dennis, Mark (2013), Visions IV Visions in the Desert - Part I, CreateSpace Independent Publishing, On-Demand Publishing, LLC.

Dennis, Mark (2012) World of the Forsaken, The Human Condition, CreateSpace Independent Publishing, On-Demand Publishing, LLC.

Douglas, James (1987), Zondervan Illustrated Bible Dictionary, Zondervan, Grand Rapids, Michigan

Ehrman, Bart D. (1996), The Orthodox Corruption of Scripture: The Effect of Early Christological, Oxford University Press, Oxford University Press, Great Clarendon St, Oxford, United Kingdom

Feather, Robert (1999), The Mystery of the Copper Scroll of Qumran: The Essene Record of the Treasure of Akhenaten, Bear & Company, Rochester VT

Feldman, Louis H. (1988) Josephus, The Bible, and History, Yamamoto Shoten Publishing, Tokyo, Japan

Flood, Finbarr (2000), The Great Mosque of Damascus: Studies on the Makings of an Ummayyad Visual Culture, Brill Publishing, Danvers, MA

Frankfurter, David (1998), Pilgrimage and Holy Space in Late Antique Egypt, Koninklijke Brill, Plantijnstraat 2, Leiden, 2321 JC, Netherlands

Freud, Sigmund. (1939) Moses and Monotheism, Random House Publishing 1745 Broadway, New York, NY

Gauding, Madonna (2009), The Signs and Symbols Bible: The Definitive Guide to Mysterious Markings, Sterling Publishing Company, Inc., New York, NY

Gurtner, Daniel M. (2007), The Torn Veil: Matthew's Exposition of the Death of Jesus, Cambridge University Press, Cambridge UK

Halperin, David Joel (1988), The Faces of the Chariot: Early Jewish Responses to Ezekiel's Vision, Mohr Siebeck Publishing, Tübingen, Germany

Jacobs, Steven Leonard (2010), The Jewish Experience: An Introduction to Jewish History and Jewish Life, Fortress Press, Minneapolis, MN

Kaplan, Aryeh (1995), Meditation and Kabbalah, Rowman & Littlefield Publishers, Lanham, MD 20706

Kline, Morris (1972), Mathematical Thought From Ancient to Modern Times: Volume 1, Volume 1, Oxford University Press, New York, NY

References

Leet, Leonora (2003), The Kabbalah of the Soul: The Transformative Psychology and Practices of Jewish Mysticism, Inner Traditions, Bear & Company, One Park Street, Rochester, VT

Leet, Leonora (2004), The Universal Kabbalah, Inner Traditions, Bear & Company, One Park Street, Rochester, VT

MacKendrick, Paul (1981), The Greek Stones Speak: The Story of Archaeology in Greek Lands, W. W. Norton & Company, New York, NY

Margolies, Morris B. (2000), A Gathering of Angels, Jason Aronson, Northvale, NJ

Martínez, Florentino García (1992), The Dead Sea Scrolls Translated: The Qumran Texts in English, Brill Publishing, Danvers, MA

Mead, George R. S. (2012), The Corpus Hermeticum Jazzybee Verlag, Germany

Meineck, Peter (1998), Aristophanes 1: Clouds, Wasps, Birds, Hackett Publishing Company, Indianapolis, IND

Mendenhall, George E. (2001) Ancient Israel's Faith and History, Westminster John Knox Press, Louisville KT

Neusner Jacob (1976), Talmudic Judaism in Sasanian Babylonia: Essays and Studies, Volume 1, Brill Publishing, Leiden, Netherlands

Paulsen, David (2007), Mormonism in Dialogue with Contemporary Christian Theologies, Mercer university Press, Macon GA

Ponce', Charles (1973), Kabbalah, An Introduction and Illumination for the World Today, Weaton Ill., Theosophical Publishing House

Pritchard, James B. (1969) Ancient Near Eastern Tests Relating to the Old Testament, Third Edition with Supplement Publication, Princeton: Princeton University Press, Princeton, NJ

Prophet, Elizabeth Clare (1992), Inner Faces of God, Kabbalah, Volume 1, Summit University Press, Livingston MT

Richardson, Peter (1999) Herod: King of the Jews and Friend of the Romans, First Fortress Press, Edinburgh, Scotland

Ruck, Carl A. P. (2006), Sacred Mushrooms: Secrets of Eleusis, Ronin Publishing, Oakland CA

Scholem, Gershom (1990), Origins of the Kabbalah, Princeton University Press, Princeton, NJ

Sherman, R. Edwin (2005), Bible Code Bombshell: Compelling Scientific Evidence that God Authored the Bible, New Leaf Press, Green Forest AR

Sherwin, Byron L. (2006), Kabbalah: An Introduction to Jewish Mysticism, Rowman & Littlefield Publishers, Lanham MD 20706

References

Smetham, Graham (), The Grand Designer: Discovering the Quantum Mind Matrix of the Universe, Shunyata Press, Brighton, England

Stern, David H. (1992), Jewish New Testament Commentary Jewish New Testament Publications, Incorporated, Clarksville, MD

Stewart, William (1998), Dictionary of Images and Symbols in Counseling, Jessica Kingsley Limited, Bristol PA

Waite, Arthur Edward (2007), The Holy Kabbalah Cosimo, Inc., Chelsea Station, New York, NY

Warraq Ibn (1998), The Origins of the Koran: Classic Essays on Islam's Holy book, Prometheus Publications, Amherst NY

Wright, J. Edward (2000), The Early History of Heaven, Oxford University Press, New York, NY

Yohai, Shim'on ben (1999), The Zohar, Press of the Yeshivat Kol Yehuda, Tel-Aviv, Israel

Visions of the Merkabah Riders

Index

Aaron, 82, 112, 115, 116, 121, 122, 123, 124, 140, 152

Abba, Xxxiv, Xxxvii, 14, 16, 28, 111, 147, 212, 224, 295

Abel, 106, 205

Abijah, 81, 123, 124

Abomination, 74, 87

Abraham, Xxxi, 1, 37, 38, 39, 49, 51, 121, 135, 136, 137, 138, 245, 254, 256

Abram, 38, 50, 51, 137

Abyss, 14, 17, 19, 104, 107, 146, 187, 212, 234, 235, 274, 279

Acts, 105, 151, 224, 232, 240

Adam, Xxx, Xxxiv, 2, 24, 26, 41, 47, 48, 86, 102, 108, 109, 111, 113, 127, 145, 149, 194, 195, 205, 215, 236, 256, 259, 262, 274, 276, 277, 278, 289

Adam Elyon, 86

Adam Kadmon, Xxx, Xxxiv, 26, 86, 127, 149, 259, 277, 289

Adonai, 5, 11, 83, 143

Afraid, 103, 119, 139, 284

Agape, Xxxvi

Ahasuerus, 82

Ahura Mazda, 204, 253

Akhenaten, 114, 115, 133, 301

Aleph, 32, 163

Aletheia, 185, 186

Alexander, 65, 176, 177, 246

Alexandria, 71, 145

Allah, 139, 202, 244, 253, 254

Almighty, Xxix, Xxxi, Xxxiv, Xl, 1, 4, 12,

15, 25, 26, 29, 55, 56, 57, 69, 95, 103, 120, 125, 127, 139, 149, 192, 204, 205, 212, 224, 273, 276, 281, 289

Alpha, Xxix, 1, 15

Altar, 61, 62, 81, 87, 123, 178

Amara, 130

Amen, Xxxv, Xl, 115, 116, 129, 130

Amenhotep, 128, 129, 133

Amenism, 114, 115, 128, 129, 142

Ammon, 173

Amorite, 112, 121, 122, 123, 124, 136

Amun, 115, 128, 129, 130, 132

Anathema, 74

Ancestor, 122, 233, 283

Ancient, Xxix, Xxxi, 2, 4, 12, 35, 36, 47, 50, 56, 57, 64, 71, 72, 73, 77, 79, 84, 85, 91, 100, 101, 112, 115, 127, 129, 130, 131, 133, 135, 136, 139, 142, 174, 181, 184, 185, 186, 190, 195, 203, 205, 213, 215, 216, 232, 235, 253, 254, 262, 275, 276, 281, 282, 283, 285, 288, 292, 293, 299, 302, 303, 304

Angel, 19, 22, 35, 39, 40, 44, 59, 70, 78, 79, 81, 90, 93, 97, 110, 111, 113, 123, 204, 233, 253

Anger, 10, 43, 47, 153, 248, 273, 286, 288, 293

Animal, 49, 64, 72, 227, 235, 260

Anointed, 90, 91, 101, 176, 248, 282

Anthropomorphic, Xxxii, 277

Antioch, 72, 178, 283

Antiochus, 65, 87, 153, 177, 178, 246

Antiochus IV Epiphanes, 87, 177, 178

Apocalypse, 37, 39, 51, 206, 258

Apostate, 117, 119

Apostle, 58, 114, 150, 201, 206, 293

Arabia, 140, 141, 142

Aramaic, 99, 139

Archaeology, 303

Archangel, 50, 111, 114, 119, 120

Arche, 146, 185, 186, 187

Arich Anpin, 26, 27, 28, 57, 195, 197

Aristophanes, 146, 299, 303

Ark, 62, 245, 246, 299

Armageddon, 174

Armies, 44, 143, 175, 246

Artemis, 71

Artifacts, 121, 245

Ascend, Xliv, 9, 33, 35, 95, 96, 113

Ascended, 22, 57, 106, 109, 112, 141, 292

Ascending, 45, 236

Ascension, Xliv, 1, 109, 112, 279

Ascent, 22, 33

Ascetic, 152, 181

Asher, 4, 5, 12, 140

Asia, 71, 90, 177, 243

Assiah, Xxxii, Xxxiii, Xxxviii, 2, 8, 23, 25, 26

Assyrian, 136, 139, 173

Astrology, 37

Aten, 128, 129, 130, 132, 133, 139

Atenism, 114, 115, 128, 133

Athravan, 38

Aton, 129, 131, 139, 143

Attributes, Xxx, Xxxi, Xxxii, Xxxiii, Xxxiv, Xxxv, Xxxvi, Xxxviii, Xxxix, Xliv, 2, 4, 7, 8, 10, 11, 12, 13, 16, 25, 29, 32, 45, 50, 57, 113, 116, 135, 147, 164, 190, 193, 197, 198, 212, 228, 231, 262, 263, 273, 274, 277, 278, 279, 289, 291, 292, 293

Atziluth, Xxxii, Xxxiii, Xxxiv, 2, 8, 11, 14, 17, 197

Authority, Xxxiv, Xxxv, 92, 107, 192, 213, 224, 228, 250, 273

Awareness, Xxxv, Xxxvi, Xlviii, 17, 23, 225, 260, 261

Awe, Xxx, Xl, 261, 273

Babylon, 30, 35, 36, 37, 38, 48, 63, 65, 68, 69, 80, 84, 96, 173, 174, 175, 176, 177, 237, 245, 247, 248, 251

Babylonia, 4, 303

Badr, 141

Balaam, 136

Balance, Xxxvii, 12, 18, 75, 92, 228

Baptism, 101, 152, 225, 234, 249

Barnabas, 114, 192

Bath, 72, 87

Battle, 81, 126, 137, 141, 152, 173, 174, 202, 247

Beasts, 92, 130, 131

Beatitudes, 5, 106, 241, 242

Beauty, Xxxiii, Xxxvii, 2, 5, 7, 10, 17, 18, 24, 28, 66, 198, 228, 259, 273

Beginning, Xxix, Xxx, Xxxv, Xlvii, 1, 13, 15, 49, 50, 132, 135, 146, 148, 150, 177, 186, 187, 189, 205, 207, 213, 225, 244, 259, 260, 261, 273, 274, 278, 286, 287, 289

Begotten, 186, 187, 188, 192

Beings, 55, 79, 80, 85, 138

Belief, Xxv, Xxxi, Xli, 42, 91, 101, 116, 129, 133, 137, 181, 211, 255, 281, 282, 292

Believe, 1, 22, 35, 36, 42, 61, 71, 72, 74, 80, 91, 111, 114, 116, 121, 124, 125, 127, 128, 133, 135, 136, 140, 151, 152, 153, 175, 176, 202, 203, 206, 207, 217, 219, 229, 254, 255, 257, 260, 276, 281, 288, 290

Belshazzar, 91, 175

Belteshazzar, 37

Bible, 2, 41, 50, 53, 74, 77, 107, 139, 141, 142, 146, 201, 202, 223, 252, 285, 300, 301, 302, 304

Binah, Xxx, Xxxv, Xxxvii, 2, 5, 7, 11, 13, 14, 15, 28, 32, 147, 197, 212, 225, 226

Birth, 39, 50, 105, 124, 149, 178, 188, 190, 201, 202, 205, 219, 221, 246

Blasphemy, Xliii, 74, 215, 250

Bless, Xl, 31, 38, 41, 87, 106, 112, 113, 137, 242, 253, 285

Blood, 71, 87, 103, 125, 174, 182, 235, 236

Body, 22, 23, 56, 114, 129, 145, 189, 193, 206, 243, 258

Bondage, 237, 248, 282

Born, 13, 106, 119, 123, 183, 188, 221, 225, 228, 241, 247, 248

Bottomless, 107

Bowl, 61, 64, 71, 89, 90, 91

Brass, 56, 59, 70, 84

Bread, 38, 137

Bride, Xxxiii, Xxxiv, Xxxvii, Xxxix, 14, 16, 19, 25, 28, 30, 31, 32, 81, 182, 191, 212, 221, 222, 229, 262, 275, 280, 281

Bridegroom, Xxxiv, Xxxvii, Xxxix, 2, 14, 19, 28, 212, 221, 222, 229, 262, 280, 281

Bridge, 19, 204, 235, 253, 261

Bright, 49, 67, 68, 97, 117

Bronze, 61, 62, 63, 174

Buddhism, 202, 213, 215, 255

Build, Xl, 106, 248, 251

Built, 61, 62, 66, 67, 72, 75, 76, 230, 245, 247, 259

Burning Bush, 30, 138, 140

Cain, 205

Calamity, 262, 264

Calendar, 153

Calf, 65, 85

Canaan, 129, 132, 135, 136

Canaanite, 137, 139, 143

Candles, 62, 70, 71, 89, 90, 91

Cannabinoids, 73

Canon, 36

Captivity, 32, 35, 37, 54, 69, 71, 82, 90, 91, 108, 135, 173, 174, 192, 244, 248, 250, 281, 282

Carchemish, 173

Care, 241, 256, 261

Catholic, Xxxi, 3, 185, 203

Celestial, 22, 39, 40, 51, 75, 111, 112, 127, 275

Celibacy, 152, 193

Chanting, 115, 130, 281

Chaos, 146, 179, 187, 262

Chariot, I, Xxvii, Xxx, Xliv, 1, 9, 20, 35, 40, 41, 51, 52, 53, 54, 92, 120, 232, 263, 276, 302

Cherubim, 20, 41, 48, 59, 61, 62, 66, 67, 68, 69, 76, 119

Child, 124, 206, 210, 217

Chinvat, 204, 253

Chosen, 36, 110, 122, 123, 149, 150, 175, 205, 212, 237, 244, 276, 277

Christ, 23, 26, 30, 35, 39, 51, 58, 59, 73, 85, 99, 104, 111, 114, 116, 127, 145, 146, 164, 178, 183, 184, 186, 190, 192, 193, 196, 197, 198, 201, 202, 203, 206, 211, 212, 215, 220, 228, 230, 231, 234, 235, 236, 237, 239, 241, 243, 244, 245, 246, 248, 249, 250, 252, 276, 282, 287, 289, 290, 293

Christian, 1, 3, 30, 74, 89, 99, 100, 102, 103, 133, 145, 181,

190, 192, 201, 202, 204, 206, 211, 212, 214, 217, 240, 242, 243, 244, 254, 281, 286, 293

Christianity, 80, 100, 115, 130, 196, 201, 202, 203, 206, 214, 237, 244, 253, 256, 258

Church, Xxxi, Xxxix, 3, 30, 91, 100, 102, 103, 145, 189, 190, 192, 203, 213, 242, 243, 258, 281

City, Xxxiii, 38, 69, 70, 81, 82, 96, 115, 125, 127, 136, 141, 175, 176, 179, 221, 222, 245, 247, 264, 281, 282

Clergy, 1, 194

Cloud, 30, 41, 44, 69, 77, 110, 141, 232

Cock, 223, 224

Code, Xlvi, Xlvii, Xlviii, Xlix, 163, 164, 165, 167, 168, 171, 172, 304

Cohen, 122, 152

Coincidence, Xlvi, 62, 129

Colossians, 10, 149, 189, 192, 193

Comfort, 245, 297, 300

Commandment, Xxxvi, 209, 210

Committed, 102, 236

Commune, 5, 9, 263

Community, 125, 152, 178, 213, 241

Compassion, Xxxvi, Xxxvii, 8, 9, 10, 18, 24, 217, 228, 273, 278

Complete, 31, 258, 300

Comprehend, Xxxiv, 29, 30, 147, 224

Conceal, 226

Conceived, 20, 107

Concept, 146, 190, 193, 212, 213, 252, 286

Confidence, Xxxvii, 231, 292

Conformed, 184, 236

Conquest, 92, 176, 245

Contentment, 274, 284, 290, 293

Control, 18, 177, 178, 248, 290

Corinthians, Xxxvi, 23, 32, 86, 116, 145, 193, 194, 195, 196, 197, 199

Cornerstone, 8, 214, 230

Corpus, 184, 187, 303

Correlation, 62, 105, 184

Corruption, 117, 153, 205, 222, 262, 301

Countenance, Xxxvii, 19, 26, 27, 28, 57, 195, 212, 229, 289

Court, 37, 69, 70, 115, 129, 142

Covenant, Xxxvi, 5, 53, 121, 141, 152, 236, 245, 246, 250, 255, 280, 299

Creation, Xxix, Xxx, Xxxi, Xxxiii, Xxxiv, Xxxv, Xxxvi, Xxxvii, Xxxviii, Xlii, 4, 5, 7, 11, 13, 14, 15, 16, 17, 18, 22, 23, 24, 25, 27, 28, 29, 30, 31, 42, 71, 90, 100, 108, 116, 131, 132, 146, 148, 149, 150, 171, 179, 189, 190, 212, 224, 225, 227, 231, 235, 244, 250, 259, 262, 273, 274, 275, 276, 277, 279

Creative, 3, 4

Creator, 2, 38, 128, 143, 214, 262, 281

Creatures, 13, 52, 55, 59, 65, 76, 77, 78,

83, 85, 102, 103, 104

Cross, 164, 204, 206, 223, 237, 250, 258, 274

Crown, Xxxiii, Xxxiv, 2, 5, 7, 11, 24, 27, 31, 112, 195, 197, 224

Crucify, 215, 234, 250, 257

Crystal, 20, 48, 58, 59, 66, 67, 76, 85

Cube, 170

Cult, 128, 133, 139, 254

Culture, 36, 37, 80, 135, 246

Cup, 62, 63, 214, 297

Curse, 292

Cyrus, 65, 175, 176, 245, 248, 282

Damascus, 142, 193, 276

Daniel, Xliv, 12, 20, 27, 32, 36, 37, 45, 48, 49, 54, 56, 57, 58, 59, 61, 72, 77, 80, 84, 85, 86, 92, 103, 104, 108, 111, 116, 171, 175, 186, 232, 251, 259, 276, 302

Dao, 213, 255

Darius, 65, 89, 91, 175, 176

Darkness, 8, 10, 18, 23, 44, 104, 117, 146, 147, 152, 153, 174, 185, 187, 218, 227, 259, 273, 277, 278, 279, 288, 289, 292

Daughter, 28, 121, 124

David, Xxxi, Xl, 15, 40, 82, 97, 115, 122, 123, 124, 126, 129, 130, 135, 173, 224, 228, 250, 251, 279, 302, 305

Death, Xli, 8, 39, 40, 65, 99, 103, 105, 111, 114, 116, 125,

126, 129, 133, 152, 174, 177, 179, 194, 201, 203, 204, 206, 207, 211, 213, 215, 223, 235, 236, 237, 241, 243, 248, 249, 250, 252, 253, 276, 297, 302, 303

Dedicating, 39, 281

Deeds, 13, 119, 148

Defiled, 178, 196

Deity, 127, 136, 176, 213

Delight, Xxxiii, 222, 264, 291

Deliverance, 151, 240, 276, 277, 288

Descend, 9, 33, 41, 42, 45, 52, 104, 113, 121, 124, 141, 184, 232, 234, 235, 236

Descendant, 48, 123, 124, 126

Describe, 48, 64, 67, 116, 118, 119, 278

Desecrated, 178

Desert, 111, 115, 116, 125, 132, 152, 153, 175, 181

Desire, Xxix, Xxxiii, Xli, Xlii, Xliii, 1, 13, 125, 131, 281, 282, 290

Despise, 261, 263

Destined, 39

Destroy, 50, 62, 69, 70, 71, 82, 90, 100, 102, 142, 174, 178, 203, 213, 237, 239, 245, 258, 265, 274, 283

Destruction, Xliv, 36, 63, 89, 99, 103, 104, 106, 142, 151, 174, 247, 285, 287

Deuteronomy, 41, 53, 103, 110, 284

Devil, 104, 152

Devoted, Xliii, 32, 220, 289

Devotion, Xli, 284, 289, 291

Devout, Xxxi, 125, 204

Diaspora, 82, 281

Die, 49, 87, 176, 206, 257, 258, 276

Discernment, Xxxiii, Xxxv, 49, 147, 148, 225, 227, 259, 260

Discovered, 80, 179

Diseases, 78, 228

Disobey, Xxxiv, 8, 149, 190, 262, 274, 292

Disperse, 82, 244, 246, 281

Distress, 132, 142, 257, 264, 284

Divinity, Xxx, Xxxii, Xxxvi, Xxxviii, Xli, Xliii, 1, 4, 12, 16, 23, 31, 33, 41, 49, 51, 101, 109, 113, 125, 127, 145, 147, 185, 195, 197, 198, 211, 226, 227, 230, 239, 255, 256, 258, 259, 262, 274, 276, 277

Docetism, 206, 257, 258

Doctrine, Xli, 4, 14, 35, 105, 145, 194, 197, 199, 206, 211, 216

Door, 67, 72, 75, 85, 109, 112, 226

Dove, 13, 225, 234, 235

Dynasty, 128, 177, 178, 246, 247, 252

Eagle, Xxxii, 52, 65, 72, 78, 85

East, 44, 62, 63, 70, 79, 213, 255

Eden, Xxxiii, 17, 117, 205

Edomites, 173, 247

Egypt, 44, 114, 115, 128, 129, 130, 131, 132, 133, 135, 142, 145, 152, 173, 174, 177, 178, 186, 213, 237, 246, 248, 258, 299, 302

Ehyeh Asher Ehyeh, 4, 5, 12, 140

Ein-Sof, Xxix, Xxxiii, Xxxiv, 1, 2, 4, 12, 15, 18, 29, 30, 144, 195, 224, 262

El, 5, 38, 136, 137, 138, 139, 143

Elders, 65, 77, 80, 81, 83, 85, 104, 117

Eleazar, 83, 122

Elect, 1, 75, 103, 150, 182, 183, 277, 287

El-Elyon, 38, 137, 139

Elijah, Xliv, 53, 54

Elizabeth, 123, 304

Elohim, 5, 13, 40, 138, 139, 143

Emanate, Xxxiii, 4, 18, 29

Embedded, 16, 227

Embraced, 212, 254

Empire, 38, 82, 89, 128, 153, 173, 175, 176, 177, 178, 192, 245, 246

Empty, 17, 187, 189, 282

Emulate, Xliii, 199

Endless, Xxix, Xxxiv, 1, 144

Endure, 30, 244

Energy, 29, 33, 185

Enlightenment, 147, 262

Enoch, Xliv, 1, 2, 12, 19, 20, 22, 23, 27, 28, 35, 36, 38, 39, 41, 47, 48, 50, 51, 53, 55, 57, 58, 59, 66, 72, 75, 77, 78, 79, 85, 86, 92, 95, 96, 99, 100, 101, 102, 103, 104, 105, 106, 107, 108, 109, 110, 111, 112, 113, 114, 116, 117, 118, 119, 120, 127, 149, 150, 153, 181, 182, 183, 204, 205, 258, 276

Envy, 199, 292

Ephesians, 105, 189, 190, 194, 230, 291

Epiphanes, 65, 87, 153

Epistles, 190, 192, 201, 240

Equilibrium, 8, 18

Erebus, 146, 187

Ergonovine, 73

Ergot, 73

Eros, 146, 187

Esau, 247

Essene, 153, 301

Esther, 30, 64, 82

Eternity, Xxxiii, Xxxv, Xxxvii, 2, 7, 10, 24, 30, 38, 78, 106, 120, 143, 151, 182, 192, 198, 206, 214, 220, 223, 231, 235, 236, 241, 250, 262, 285, 286, 287, 293

Eve, 24, 205, 215

Everlasting, 139, 251, 285

Evil, Xxxiii, Xxxiv, Xxxvi, 3, 8, 9, 10, 23, 49, 57, 102, 103, 147, 150, 222, 227, 239, 257, 259, 260, 274, 278, 279, 285, 297

Exile, 30, 125, 245, 262

Exodus, Xxxvi, Xlv, Xlvi, 22, 41, 44, 53, 110, 115, 121, 129, 130, 133, 135, 136, 138, 140, 141, 152, 169, 170, 232, 250, 260, 280

Eye, 9, 25, 133, 232, 279

Eye Of The Needle, 9, 25, 279

Ezekiel, Xxxii, Xliv, 32, 35, 36, 37, 48, 49, 53, 54, 56, 57, 58, 59, 61, 62, 68, 69, 70, 72, 76, 77, 79, 80, 81, 85, 101,

104, 108, 116, 174, 246, 251, 276, 302

Ezra, Vii, Xlii, 35, 36, 37, 72, 77, 82, 108, 135, 176

Face, Xxx, 19, 30, 31, 32, 49, 56, 57, 66, 67, 75, 78, 116, 119, 120, 129, 130, 150, 197, 289

Faith, Xxv, Xxxi, 3, 35, 38, 91, 121, 178, 190, 194, 199, 206, 211, 213, 245, 254, 255, 263, 273, 287, 291, 292, 303

Faithful, 74, 116

Fall, Xxxii, Xxxiv, 2, 10, 11, 29, 38, 89, 95, 96, 100, 103, 106, 107, 108, 149, 173, 177, 178, 179, 183, 192, 246, 262, 274, 278, 292

Family, 122, 124, 151, 256, 274

Famine, 92, 132, 179

Fasting, Xliii, 22, 33, 275, 281

Father, Xxxiv, Xxxvii, Xlvi, 13, 14, 15, 27, 28, 49, 76, 81, 99, 111, 112, 122, 123, 127, 136, 137, 138, 140, 142, 146, 147, 152, 173, 183, 185, 187, 188, 191, 195, 196, 207, 210, 211, 212, 213, 214, 215, 216, 217, 219, 224, 229, 233, 238, 245, 259, 275, 277, 279, 282, 286, 295

Fear, 10, 66, 75, 103, 120, 150, 254, 260, 265, 273, 284, 288, 290, 292, 293, 297

Female, 9, 14, 24

Feminine, Xxxii, Xxxv, 8, 11, 13, 18, 24, 25, 27, 28, 30, 32, 146, 225, 262, 279, 280

Fiery, 23, 52, 61, 62, 66, 84, 102, 118,

119, 186, 204, 251, 253

Fight, 173, 175, 240

Figurative, 30, 212

Finiteness, 4, 10, 274

Fire, I, Xxvii, Xxix, Xxxii, Xliii, 15, 32, 35, 38, 42, 47, 48, 51, 52, 53, 54, 56, 58, 59, 61, 66, 67, 68, 71, 75, 77, 92, 104, 105, 120, 141, 184, 222, 245, 249

Firstborn, 148, 149, 183, 184, 189, 236, 276, 277

Flesh, Ix, 49, 67, 187, 199, 211, 212, 217, 221, 255

Flight, 204, 253, 254

Flood, 65, 100, 108, 205

Flow, 8, 29, 56, 59, 92, 198

Focus, 37, 89, 128, 151, 183, 196, 239, 241, 284, 288

Follow, 9, 40, 141, 194, 218, 220, 244, 254, 297

Followers, 38, 106, 116, 133, 201, 239, 243

Food, 73, 131, 179, 196

Foolish, Xxxix, 261, 263, 264, 265, 292

Foot, 72, 81

Footstool, 119, 126

Foreign, 131, 240, 248, 252

Foreknew, 184, 236

Foretell, 206, 249

Forever, 5, 150, 183

Forgive, 22, 110, 235, 273

Forlorn, Xxxix, 30, 262, 275

Form, Xxix, Xxx, Xxxii, Xxxiii, Xxxv, Xxxvii, Xlii, 3, 8, 13, 17, 23, 24, 25, 26, 28, 42, 57, 118, 127, 138, 146, 148, 187, 192, 195, 212, 246, 277, 289

Former, 67, 75, 247

Foundation, Xxxi, Xxxiii, Xxxviii, 2, 5, 7, 8, 10, 24, 25, 28, 35, 66, 102, 133, 198, 212, 214, 230, 254, 273, 284

Fountain, 182

Fragments, 99, 104

Frankincense, Xliii, 73

Freedom, 240, 246, 248, 252

Freemasonry, 133

Friend, 192, 304

Fruit, 117, 199, 222, 265, 290, 293

Frustration, 10, 153, 178

Fulfill, 101, 252, 256

Fullness, 189

Fundamentals, Xxxi, 91, 206, 217

Fungi, 73

Future, 58, 85, 126, 237, 239, 240, 243, 252

Gabriel, 50, 78, 81, 119, 123

Galatians, 199, 290, 295

Galilee, 217, 227, 229

Gamaliel, 192

Garden, Xxx, Xxxiii, 2, 5, 17, 117, 205, 214, 257, 262

Gateway, 25, 70, 264

Gematria, Xlviii, 164, 223

Genealogy, 49, 123, 124

General, 176, 247

Generated, 71, 73

Generation, 37, 51, 108, 231, 251

Genesis, Xxx, Xlvii, 22, 38, 39, 45, 47, 48, 50, 99, 105, 107, 108, 119, 136, 137, 138, 187

Gentile, 196, 293

Gentle, 43, 120, 199, 290

Gevurah, Xxx, Xxxvi, Xxxvii, 2, 5, 7, 17, 18, 27, 32, 198, 227, 228

Giant, 63, 81

Gideon, 143

Gilgamesh, 79

Gimmel, 163, 164

Glory, Xxxii, Xxxv, Xxxvii, Xxxix, Xl, 11, 12, 17, 30, 31, 35, 41, 49, 53, 55, 57, 59, 67, 69, 70, 81, 95, 96, 116, 120, 127, 142, 150, 181, 183, 184, 186, 187, 199, 207, 215, 219, 221, 229, 231, 233, 273, 275, 289

Gnosis, 4

Gnostic, 49, 100, 114, 181, 183, 185, 186, 190, 191, 192, 194, 196, 203, 206, 211, 212, 213, 254, 255, 257, 258

Gnostikos, 181

Goddess, 72, 136

Godlike, 40

Godliness, 287

Gods, 72, 113, 129, 132, 136, 137, 138, 139, 196, 216, 256, 262, 299

Gold, Xliii, 56, 62, 64, 72, 84, 89, 243, 245

Golden, Vii, 64, 90, 146, 174

Good, Xxxiii, Xxxiv, Xliv, Xlv, 8, 9, 10, 23, 25, 49, 106, 119, 147, 183, 185, 188, 214, 222, 227, 235,

256, 257, 259, 260, 273, 278, 279, 290, 291

Goodness, 199, 289, 290, 297

Gospel, 39, 76, 183, 190, 191, 201, 203, 205, 206, 258

Government, 287, 288

Governor, 82, 91, 176

Grace, Xxxi, Xxxvi, 40, 183, 186, 189, 190, 193, 194, 228, 236, 278, 291, 292, 293

Graciousness, Xxxvii, 18, 201

Gratitude, Xxxviii, 230

Greece, 72, 177

Greek, Xxxvi, 14, 72, 73, 99, 113, 114, 145, 146, 147, 153, 178, 181, 183, 184, 185, 186, 187, 189, 190, 192, 203, 246, 250, 252, 303

Grief, 254, 293

Grigori, 118

Guard, 3, 22, 35, 110, 176

Guide, 23, 142, 147, 204, 253, 261, 302

Guilt, Xlv, 288

Gulf, 105, 204

Hadith, 253

Haggadah, 205

Hagigah, 275

Hair, 12, 27, 28, 56, 59, 68, 84, 85, 205

Halls, Xliv, 112

Hallucinations, 73

Hammadi, 186, 213, 258

Hammurabi, 79

Hand, 5, 40, 41, 44, 53, 68, 70, 71, 72, 81, 87, 90, 103, 113, 126, 127, 198, 233, 239, 249, 264, 283

Happiness, 274, 284, 293

Haran, 136, 137

Harim, 82

Harm, 92, 263, 265

Harmony, 202, 263

Harrat, 141

Hasmonean, 177, 178, 246, 247, 252

Hatred, 10, 199, 239, 241, 264, 265, 273, 288, 292, 293

Head, Xxix, Xl, 12, 19, 27, 28, 51, 68, 84, 85, 118, 149, 181, 189, 205, 297

Healing, 30, 143, 151, 190, 209, 228, 237, 263, 264

Hear, 43, 110, 202, 218, 219, 252

Heart, Xxxvi, 10, 18, 38, 95, 146, 187, 196, 207, 209, 210, 212, 226, 241, 242, 274, 284, 290

Heaven, Xxxvii, Xxxix, Xl, Xliv, 13, 22, 23, 33, 38, 40, 45, 48, 52, 54, 57, 66, 68, 84, 85, 87, 93, 95, 96, 103, 106, 107, 108, 112, 113, 117, 118, 119, 120, 145, 146, 150, 181, 187, 193, 195, 196, 204, 205, 218, 221, 224, 225, 227, 232, 233, 235, 238, 239, 240, 241, 242, 243, 244, 248, 249, 250, 251, 252, 253, 254, 258, 292, 305

Heavenly, Xxx, 22, 31, 35, 51, 57, 75, 76, 79, 109, 110, 111, 120, 145, 195

Heavens, Xl, Xliv, 1, 2, 14, 18, 22, 23, 33, 35, 40, 47, 58, 75, 85, 86, 109, 113, 116, 117, 118, 120, 142, 174, 187, 204, 234, 236, 259, 263, 275

Hebrew, Xxix, Xli, Xlii, Xlv, Xlvii, Xlviii, 9, 11, 12, 15, 30, 32, 36, 44, 57, 105, 109, 111, 120, 135, 136, 139, 142, 152, 153, 163, 164, 170, 174, 223, 248, 250, 251, 285

Heights, 40, 63, 95, 107, 184, 192

Hekhalot, 35, 47, 57, 75, 276

Hell, 153, 184, 190, 204, 257

Hellenistic, 145, 178, 181, 198, 203, 300

Hellenized, 153, 184, 192

Heracles, 72

Herding, 287, 288

Heresy, 3, 4, 100, 192, 199, 203, 217

Hermetism, 113, 114, 184, 187, 188, 190, 196, 303

Herod Antipas, 245, 247, 248, 249, 250, 252, 304

Hesed, Xxx, Xxxvi, Xxxvii, 2, 5, 7, 17, 27, 198, 228

Hesiod, 186, 187

Hezekiah, 124

Hidden, Xxxiii, Xxxiv, Xlvii, 11, 16, 19, 27, 28, 30, 36, 57, 78, 79, 116, 129, 130, 150, 179, 195, 199, 205, 216, 218, 226, 227, 234, 245, 259, 274, 275

High, Xxxiii, Xxxiv, Xxxvii, Xliv, Xlvi, 8, 11, 12, 13, 14, 17, 20, 22, 38, 39, 40, 42, 49, 50, 51, 52, 55, 58, 70, 72, 73, 82, 91, 96, 100, 105, 109, 111, 112, 120, 123, 127, 128, 131, 137, 139, 146, 150, 153, 189, 223, 224,

235, 247, 250, 251, 292

Highest, Xxxiii, Xxxiv, Xxxvii, Xliv, 8, 11, 12, 13, 14, 17, 22, 40, 52, 120, 224

Hinduism, 181, 202, 213

Hiram, Xl, 61, 62

History, 79, 89, 99, 100, 121, 132, 135, 173, 175, 178, 239, 244, 248, 262, 301, 302, 303, 305

Hod, Xxx, Xxxviii, 2, 5, 7, 24, 28, 32, 198, 230

Hokhmah, Xxx, Xxxv, 2, 5, 7, 11, 12, 13, 14, 15, 147, 197, 225, 226

Holies, 53

Holy, Xlv, 19, 31, 40, 41, 43, 47, 49, 53, 55, 56, 68, 70, 86, 87, 95, 102, 103, 104, 112, 113, 120,

126, 142, 143, 150, 182, 184, 202, 206, 216, 217, 221, 225, 235, 238, 249, 260, 275, 293, 302, 305

Honor, Xxxv, 210, 233

Hope, Xliii, 78, 101, 242, 252, 274, 287, 292, 293, 300

Horse, 92, 103, 204, 253

Horus, 128, 133

Hostility, 119, 293

House, Xxxviii, Xl, 9, 66, 67, 76, 82, 105, 117, 138, 173, 230, 251, 259, 285, 297, 300, 302, 304

Household, 110, 115, 151

Huge, 64, 65, 81, 118

Human, Xxxi, Xxxii, 1, 10, 19, 25, 26, 57, 78, 101, 118, 127, 147, 149, 191, 192, 207, 211, 219, 235,

237, 251, 255, 256, 274, 276, 277, 289

Humanity, 101, 212, 262, 279

Humankind, 16, 227, 252, 262

Humans, 16, 212, 226, 254

Humility, 16, 201, 226, 231, 241, 285, 286

Husband, Xxxix, 221

Hyksos, 132

Hymn, 115, 130

Hyrcanus, 247

Idolatry, 137, 196, 199, 283

Ignorance, 10, 274, 293

Ignore, 62, 65, 185

Illness, 73, 175, 178

Illumination, 72, 304

Illustration, 9, 65, 71, 85, 127, 235, 275, 278, 279, 289

Image, Xxix, Xxx, Xxxii, Xxxvii, 5, 9, 19, 26, 28, 41, 62, 70, 76, 77, 79, 80, 84, 86, 90, 92, 95, 127, 128, 138, 145, 149, 184, 195, 212, 213, 229, 234, 236, 237, 256, 273, 274, 277, 305

Imma, Xxxv, Xxxvii, 14, 16, 28, 31, 147, 212

Immediately, Xliv, 81, 114, 211

Important, Xxxvi, 137, 209, 210, 244, 256, 260

Impossible, Xlii, 20, 107, 118, 274, 289

Incense, 61, 62

Incessant, 117, 118, 263

Incomprehensible, Xxix, 2, 4, 5, 11, 192, 197, 262

Indescribable, Xxix, Xxxi, 52, 120

India, 176, 177, 202

Indiana Jones, 135

Indwell, 30, 31

Ineffable, Xxix, 31

Inexpressible, 192, 193

Infancy, 177, 205, 206, 213, 258

Infertility, 300

Infinite, Xxix, 4, 144, 146, 187

Influence, Xxxviii, 41, 105, 115, 142, 145, 190, 203, 230

Inherit, 78, 106, 199, 214, 220, 233, 236, 241, 242, 274, 278

Initiate, 194, 276

Innumerable, 130, 192, 278

Insight, 51, 183

Inspired, Xlii, 74, 100, 281

Instance, 41, 53

Instruction, 261, 263, 291

Intelligence, Xxxv, 1, 13, 184, 225

Intention, Xlvii, 125

Intercessor, 1, 113, 194

Interesting, 18, 108, 122, 183

Interpretation, Xliii, Xliv, Xlv, 37, 111, 135, 137, 139, 186, 237, 249, 254, 285, 293

Intoxicants, 73

Invisible, Xxxv, 149, 192

Invoke, Xliv, 3, 216

Iraq, 80

Irenaeus, 185

Iron, 84, 120

Ironically, 133, 245

Isaac, 121, 137, 256

Isaiah, Xxx, Xxxii, Xxxiii, Xxxix, Xl, Xliv, Xlvii, 17, 20, 23, 32, 35, 37, 47, 54, 55, 81, 89, 95, 96, 97, 100, 108, 111, 222, 223, 230, 232, 237, 251, 276, 281, 283, 284, 285

Ishmael, 112, 256

Islam, 115, 130, 203, 206, 213, 244, 256, 257, 258, 305

Islamic, 122, 133, 204, 214, 243, 244, 254, 258, 288

Isolating, Xliii

Israel, Xxxvi, Xxxix, Xl, 30, 31, 32, 35, 42, 43, 44, 62, 64, 65, 70, 81, 82, 91, 100, 108, 110, 111, 115, 121, 122, 129, 133, 136, 139, 141, 143, 152, 173, 174, 177, 179, 213, 224, 237, 239, 244, 245, 246, 247, 248, 249, 252, 276, 280, 281, 282, 283, 284, 285, 303, 304

Israelites, 44, 82, 114, 129, 133, 135, 136, 141, 142, 174, 244, 279, 282

Ithamar, 83, 122

Ivory, 64, 65, 72

Jacob, Xlvi, 45, 121, 132, 137, 143, 256, 279, 303

James, 194, 201, 205, 258, 291, 304

Jedaiah, 82

Jehovah, Xl, Xlv, 11, 135, 139, 141

Jeremiah, 89, 104, 174, 179, 246, 283

Jerusalem, Xxxix, 36, 38, 50, 62, 63, 68, 69, 71, 81, 82, 87, 89, 90, 91, 99, 104, 108, 122, 125, 127, 137, 153, 174, 176, 178, 179, 204, 221, 231, 237, 243, 245,

247, 248, 253, 281, 282

Jeshua, 82, 91

Jesse, 97

Jesus, Xxxvi, Xliv, 8, 10, 26, 38, 39, 42, 50, 53, 54, 76, 86, 87, 97, 100, 101, 102, 105, 106, 107, 110, 111, 113, 116, 122, 123, 124, 125, 126, 127, 128, 145, 149, 151, 152, 153, 169, 181, 183, 186, 189, 190, 191, 193, 194, 195, 196, 197, 201, 202, 203, 204, 205, 206, 207, 209, 210, 211, 212, 213, 214, 215, 216, 217, 218, 220, 223, 224, 225, 226, 227, 228, 229, 230, 231, 232, 233, 234, 235, 236, 237, 239, 240, 241, 243, 247, 248, 249, 250, 252, 254, 255, 256, 257, 258, 276, 277, 281, 282, 287, 288, 290, 292, 293, 302

Jethro, 115, 121, 140, 142

Job, Xxxv, 104, 108

Joel, Ix, 32, 37, 104, 302

John, Xxxi, Xxxvi, Xliv, 13, 28, 39, 50, 54, 58, 59, 61, 62, 65, 73, 76, 80, 81, 85, 89, 90, 91, 103, 104, 105, 110, 111, 116, 122, 123, 125, 127, 146, 147, 152, 153, 164, 182, 183, 184, 185, 186, 187, 189, 190, 191, 195, 201, 203, 205, 206, 207, 210, 211, 212, 213, 218, 219, 220, 221, 223, 225, 226, 227, 228, 229, 231, 236, 238, 239, 240, 248, 249, 252, 254, 286, 287, 300, 303

John The Baptist, 39, 50, 81, 105, 110,

123, 125, 152, 183, 205, 219, 239, 248, 249, 252, 254

Joseph, 115, 123, 132, 248, 300

Josephus, 178, 301

Joshua, 133

Journey, Xliii, 125, 141, 173, 204, 253

Joy, 113, 182, 199, 290

Judah, 97, 123, 152, 173, 230, 248

Judaic, Xxxi, Xxxix, 1, 8, 91, 142, 221

Judaism, Xliii, 1, 4, 100, 115, 129, 130, 145, 181, 193, 198, 206, 239, 247, 253, 256, 275, 300, 303

Judas, 178, 258

Jude, Xxxv, 41, 53, 102, 107, 108, 111, 201

Judea, 91, 125

Judeo, 133

Judge, Xxxiii, Xxxvi, 5, 18, 40, 89, 101, 102, 114, 117, 118, 143, 149, 151, 183, 205, 227, 243, 244, 257, 260, 273, 276, 285

Jumbled, Xlii, 42

Jupiter, 59, 72, 246

Justice, Xxxvi, Xxxvii, 17, 18, 117, 227, 228

Justified, 184, 293

Kabbalah, 1, 35, 37, 181, 302, 303, 304, 305

Kavod, 30

Kenites, 140, 142

Kether, Xxx, Xxxiv, Xxxv, Xxxvii, 2, 5, 7, 11, 12, 13, 14, 15, 16, 27, 28, 195, 197, 212, 224, 226

Kethuvim, 36, 80, 135

Khaos, 146, 187

Kill, 175, 256, 257, 265

Kindness, Xxxiii, Xxxvi, Xli, Xliii, 2, 7, 9, 10, 17, 24, 198, 228, 273, 290, 293

King, Xxxv, Xl, 7, 20, 25, 37, 38, 49, 50, 51, 53, 54, 55, 61, 62, 63, 64, 65, 71, 79, 82, 84, 89, 91, 96, 100, 102, 111, 112, 114, 115, 121, 123, 124, 126, 127, 129, 130, 135, 137, 138, 153, 173, 174, 175, 176, 177, 189, 224, 239, 245, 246, 247, 248, 250, 251, 252, 259, 304

Kingdom, Xxxiii, Xxxviii, Xxxix, Xl, 2, 5, 8, 10, 23, 25, 27, 31, 32, 40, 75, 101, 173, 175, 176, 177, 190, 191, 199, 213, 217, 218, 221, 226, 227, 231, 234, 239, 240, 241, 242, 243, 244, 249, 250, 251, 252, 255, 259, 260, 262, 263, 277, 301

Know, Xxx, Xxxii, Xxxiii, Xli, Xliii, Xlv, 1, 23, 32, 36, 96, 125, 132, 151, 181, 185, 186, 188, 190, 191, 193, 196, 197, 201, 202, 210, 211, 212, 213, 216, 217, 220, 222, 227, 231, 234, 249, 254, 255, 260, 262, 263, 273, 275, 278, 281, 282, 287, 289, 293

Knowable, Xxx, Xxxi, 2, 5, 8, 29, 147, 190, 197, 198

Knowing, Xl, Xli, Xlii, Xliv, 101, 191, 210, 212, 254, 260, 263, 273, 288, 289

Knowledge, Xxx, Xxxiii, Xxxiv, Xxxv, Xxxvi, Xl, Xli, Xliv, Xlv, 1, 3, 4, 7, 9, 10, 14, 16,

42, 49, 125, 147, 148, 150, 171, 181, 189, 190, 191, 195, 196, 197, 198, 211, 216, 225, 226, 227, 255, 257, 259, 260, 261, 263, 264, 265, 273, 274, 275, 278, 284, 287, 289

Known, Xxxi, Xliv, Xlv, Xlvi, Xlviii, 4, 8, 12, 15, 17, 23, 26, 32, 35, 37, 57, 64, 65, 79, 81, 82, 84, 91, 99, 108, 113, 114, 121, 122, 125, 128, 132, 135, 136, 139, 140, 147, 149, 151, 152, 164, 169, 170, 173, 184, 186, 191, 197, 203, 204, 211, 223, 244, 247,264, 273, 276, 282, 293

Laban, 137

Ladder, Xlvi, 45

Lamb, Xxxix, 59, 83, 206, 221, 229, 281

Lamech, 50

Lamp, 62, 64, 65, 71, 89, 91, 218, 291

Land, 18, 44, 70, 80, 115, 121, 131, 133, 135, 136, 140, 141, 142, 173, 222, 245, 285

Language, Xlv, 99, 139, 201

Lapis, 58, 68

Latin, 135, 189, 250

Laver, 63

Law, Vii, Xxxvi, Xliii, 1, 42, 135, 140, 142, 175, 183, 190, 193, 194, 196, 199, 209, 210, 216, 220, 244, 273, 288, 290

Laws, 124, 198, 244, 287

Lazarus, 105, 204

Lazuli, 58, 68

Leadership, 10, 143, 153, 214, 220, 245

Legal, 124, 209, 242, 287

Lesser, Xxxvii, 19, 26, 27, 28, 57, 110, 111, 127, 137, 195, 198, 212, 227, 229, 277, 289

Letter, Xlv, Xlvi, Xlvii, 15, 32, 43, 44, 45, 110, 163, 169, 170, 299

Levant, 173, 181

Levi, 50, 121, 152

Levite, 114, 121, 122, 123, 124, 125, 152, 192

Life, Xxxi, Xxxii, Xxxiii, Xxxiv, Xxxv, Xxxvii, Xli, Xlii, 4, 8, 9, 13, 16, 24, 26, 28, 29, 31, 32, 33, 42, 43, 49, 50, 59, 66, 75, 78, 86, 104, 106, 109, 117, 119, 125, 131, 137, 145, 147, 149, 151, 152, 178, 179, 181, 182, 185, 186, 192, 195, 198, 203, 205, 206, 211, 214, 215, 216, 218, 220, 221, 223, 225, 229, 231, 241, 243, 250, 254, 255, 256, 260, 273, 274, 278, 279, 282, 283, 284, 285, 286, 287, 288, 292, 293, 297, 302

Lifespan, 108, 245

Light, Xxv, Xxx, Xxxi, Xxxiii, Xxxiv, Xxxv, Xxxvi, Xliii, 8, 9, 10, 11, 15, 16, 18, 23, 24, 28, 29, 30, 33, 44, 49, 52, 58, 72, 77, 109, 113, 118, 119, 127, 128, 143, 145, 146, 147, 152, 153, 182, 184, 185, 186, 191, 195, 198, 203, 204, 211, 212, 217, 218, 219, 226, 227, 253, 259, 262, 273, 274, 277, 278, 279, 288, 289, 290, 291, 292, 293, 300

Lightning, 41, 48, 53, 56, 58, 65, 66, 67, 77, 103, 107, 141

Likeness, Xxxvii, 5, 68, 127, 138, 258, 262, 273, 276, 289

Limitations, Xxix

Limited, Xxx, 1, 2, 18, 26, 262, 263, 278, 289, 305

Lineage, 82, 124, 136, 250

Lion, Xxxii, 52, 64, 65, 72, 78, 85, 97, 118

Lips, 5, 120

Listen, Vii, 22, 110, 217, 218, 219, 256, 261, 264

Literature, 30, 32, 35, 59, 100, 114, 184, 251

Liturgy, 1, 40, 194

Live, 30, 104, 164, 183, 202, 223, 236, 255, 256, 265, 273, 283, 284, 287, 293

Locust, 174, 179

Logic, 145

Logos, 14, 145, 146, 147, 184, 185, 186, 190, 259

Longsuffering, 199

Lord, Xxx, Xxxvi, Xxxvii, Xxxviii, Xl, Xlv, 11, 20, 41, 43, 44, 52, 54, 55, 56, 57, 68, 69, 70, 78, 79, 87, 90, 92, 93, 95, 96, 100, 102, 103, 106, 111, 112, 117, 118, 119, 120, 123, 126, 127, 129, 131, 132, 137, 139, 143, 148, 149, 150, 151, 174, 176, 182, 183, 185, 193, 196, 199, 207, 209, 215, 220, 224, 226, 230, 231, 243, 250, 254, 259, 261, 265, 280

Lost, Xlv, 10, 109, 175, 245, 246, 262, 274

Love, Xxxvi, Xxxvii, Xli, 5, 17, 146, 148,

191, 199, 207, 209, 210, 216, 217, 219, 226, 228, 241, 256, 264, 290, 293

Loved, 275, 281

Lover, 30, 112, 262

Luke, Xxxviii, 39, 50, 53, 80, 81, 100, 110, 123, 124, 190, 201, 204, 209, 225, 226, 227, 228, 229, 231, 232, 240, 241

Luther, Xxxi

Lying, 10, 183

Maccabees, 177, 178, 246, 252

Macedonia, 177

Macroprosopus, 12, 19, 26, 27, 28, 57

Magi, 37, 38

Magic, Xxxi, Xliv, 3, 4, 35, 37, 71, 83, 84, 114, 155, 157, 158, 159, 160, 161, 170, 216

Magic Cube, 170

Magnificence, 48, 49, 67, 72, 257

Mahatma Gandhi, 202

Majesty, Xxxv, Xxxviii, Xl, 24, 32, 40, 131, 144, 230, 233

Male, 9, 14, 24, 25, 26, 124, 248

Malkuth, Xxx, Xxxiii, Xxxiv, Xxxvi, Xxxvii, Xxxviii, 2, 5, 7, 9, 14, 16, 19, 23, 25, 27, 31, 32, 212, 221, 226, 229, 231

Man, Xxix, Xxx, Xxxi, Xxxii, Xxxiii, Xxxiv, Xxxviii, 1, 2, 4, 5, 7, 8, 9, 10, 11, 19, 23, 26, 28, 30, 33, 52, 56, 57, 58, 59, 68, 69, 70, 72, 81, 84, 85, 86, 87, 100, 101, 103, 105, 106, 116, 117, 125, 127, 130, 131, 138, 145, 149, 150,

164, 181, 188, 193, 195, 197, 198, 202, 204, 205, 211, 212, 218, 219, 222, 223, 225, 229, 230, 232, 234, 236, 255, 260, 262, 263, 273, 274, 276, 277, 278, 279, 280, 288, 289, 292

Manifest, Xxxv, 12, 16, 27, 28, 30, 101, 195, 198, 199, 225, 226, 227, 234

Manifold, 116, 130

Mankind, Xxxiii, Xxxiv, Xxxvi, Xxxviii, Xli, Xlii, 5, 8, 9, 11, 19, 23, 28, 29, 30, 31, 32, 113, 119, 147, 181, 186, 190, 191, 195, 197, 213, 221, 234, 259, 262, 263, 274, 276, 279, 281, 288, 292, 293

Mansion, 75, 76, 106, 243

Manuscripts, 4, 35, 176

Mara, 215

Mark, I, 80, 190, 201, 209, 212, 218, 224, 226, 231, 234, 235

Marvelous, 118, 119, 120, 230

Mary, 122, 123, 124, 205, 248, 256

Masada, 179

Masculine, Xxxii, Xxxv, 8, 13, 17, 24, 27, 28, 146, 279, 280

Masonic, 133

Masons, 133

Matthew, Xxxvi, Xxxix, Xl, 10, 54, 80, 123, 124, 190, 201, 209, 217, 222, 224, 225, 226, 227, 228, 229, 230, 231, 239, 242, 252, 286, 291, 302

Maturity, 211, 246, 255, 261, 275

Meaning, Vii, Xlii, Xliii, 1, 11, 12, 13, 14, 17, 18, 25, 111, 136, 142, 147, 169, 174, 184, 186, 189, 227, 241, 258, 260, 276, 293

Measure, 63, 70, 118, 119

Mecca, 142, 253

Mechanical, 65, 71

Medes, 38, 96, 175

Mediator, Xxxvii, 18, 19, 28, 197, 198, 212, 228, 234, 236, 277, 279, 292

Medieval, 1, 3, 238

Medina, 141

Meditate, Xli, Xlii, Xliv, 9, 33, 44, 83, 125, 181, 190, 212, 263, 275, 279, 281, 289, 291, 302

Meekness, 106, 199, 241, 242

Megiddo, 174

Melchizedek, 38, 39, 40, 42, 49, 50, 51, 100, 104, 109, 111, 112, 113, 115, 116, 126, 127, 128, 137, 186

Memorize, Xliii, 35, 36

Men, Vii, Ix, 23, 37, 40, 43, 50, 53, 75, 78, 83, 86, 103, 107, 109, 119, 125, 126, 131, 138, 184, 196, 204, 222, 229, 248, 253, 277

Menorah, 62, 64, 70, 71, 90, 91, 92

Mephorash, Xlvi, 44, 169, 170

Mercy, Xxxvi, Xxxvii, Xl, 5, 8, 10, 17, 18, 24, 27, 28, 31, 52, 78, 117, 228, 242, 273, 278, 289, 290, 292, 293, 297

Merkabah, I, Xxvii, Xliii, Xliv, 1, 9, 20, 33, 35, 37, 47, 73, 85, 112, 116, 193,

204, 232, 253, 264, 275, 276, 281

Merkabah Rider, Xxvii, Xliii, Xliv, 9, 33, 35, 47, 53, 73, 85, 116, 232, 253, 264, 275, 276, 281

Mesopotamia, 79, 136

Message, 39, 106, 126, 183, 210, 240, 242, 249, 252, 281, 282

Messenger, 110, 113, 184, 190

Messiah, Xxx, Xxxvii, Xxxix, Xl, 19, 100, 101, 126, 127, 164, 176, 190, 201, 205, 212, 223, 229, 248, 249, 251, 257, 276, 277, 281, 282, 283

Messianic, Xxxiv, 126, 249

Metatron, 22, 109, 110, 111, 112, 113, 114

Methuselah, 50, 99

Mezuzot, 109

Michael, 45, 78, 111, 113, 114, 120, 299

Microprosopus, 19, 26, 27, 28, 57, 84

Midian, 115, 121, 140, 141, 142

Midrash, 64

Mildness, 8, 27, 31

Mind, Xxxvi, 11, 73, 105, 118, 126, 175, 185, 209, 212, 241, 290, 305

Mingled, 107, 185

Ministry, 56, 124, 243, 252

Miracle, Xlv, 39, 105, 217, 225, 229

Mohammed, 141, 253, 254

Money, 153, 243

Monogenes, 183, 185, 186

Monotheism, 38, 91, 114, 115, 128, 131,

133, 142, 245, 262, 302

Moon, 18, 24, 104, 118, 119, 153

Moral, Xxxii, Xxxiii, Xxxviii, 2, 8, 17, 23, 191, 196, 198, 275, 278, 287

Morning, Xli, 81, 95, 97, 98, 108, 122, 126, 284

Mortal, 277, 285

Mosaic, 133, 194, 196, 288

Moses, Xxxvi, Xlii, Xliv, 1, 30, 38, 41, 42, 44, 52, 53, 59, 80, 82, 110, 114, 115, 121, 123, 128, 129, 133, 135, 138, 140, 141, 142, 152, 164, 174, 183, 190, 193, 194, 198, 209, 223, 227, 250, 254, 255, 256, 280, 302

Mosque, 253

Mother, Xxxv, Xxxvii, 13, 14, 15, 28, 31, 32, 49, 106, 122, 123, 124, 136, 146, 147, 212, 225, 256, 259, 279

Mount, 1, 30, 41, 42, 53, 95, 103, 110, 112, 140, 141, 142, 202, 276, 280

Mountain, 42, 70, 95, 140, 141, 142, 174, 179, 185, 187

Mourn, 237, 242

Mushrooms, 73, 304

Muslim, 211, 213, 255

Myriads, 118

Mystery, Xlvi, 47, 115, 183, 199, 227, 234, 274, 301, 302

Mystic, Xxxi, Xxxii, Xlii, Xliii, Xliv, 1, 35, 72, 75, 77, 95, 102, 110, 145, 181, 193, 197, 198, 199, 213, 214, 216, 223, 227, 239, 241, 252,

262, 263, 275, 276, 277, 278, 281, 282, 288

Mysticism, Xxvii, Xxxi, Xxxii, Xxxix, Xli, 1, 3, 4, 20, 22, 32, 35, 37, 38, 41, 44, 71, 83, 84, 86, 91, 116, 133, 147, 181, 190, 192, 194, 196, 198, 203, 209, 211, 216, 217, 233, 262, 275, 299, 303, 304

Mystics, Xxxix, Xli, Xliv, Xlvi, 22, 30, 32, 37, 42, 57, 147, 153, 190, 191, 212, 221, 262, 263, 273, 274, 275, 276, 277, 279, 281

Mythology, 184, 186, 203

Nabonidus, 175

Nabopolassar, 173

Nag, 186, 213, 258

Name, Xxix, Xxx, Xxxii, Xxxiii, Xlii, Xlv, Xlvi, Xlvii, 3, 4, 13, 19, 22, 27, 31, 39, 41, 43, 44, 49, 83, 84, 96, 104, 107, 109, 110, 111, 114, 121, 124, 129, 135, 136, 137, 138, 139, 140, 142, 143, 149, 150, 152, 169, 170, 189, 202, 222, 229, 233, 251, 259, 275, 297

Names, Xlii, Xliv, Xlv, Xlvi, Xlvii, 3, 4, 22, 45, 78, 79, 82, 84, 107, 109, 113, 123, 133, 135, 143, 149, 150, 185, 216, 233, 263, 275, 278

Narrow, 9, 25

Nation, 82, 133, 151, 201, 237, 239, 241, 244, 252, 274, 282, 285, 287

Nature, Xxix, Xxxii, Xliii, 13, 18, 24, 25, 73, 116, 128, 133, 145, 184, 185, 195, 198, 287

Nazarenes, 116

Nebuchadnezzar, 37, 65, 82, 84, 173, 174, 175, 176, 179, 189, 251

Necessary, 131, 235

Necho, 173

Needy, 243, 256

Negative, 8, 10

Nehemiah, Vii, Xlii, 36

Nehu, 189

Neighbor, 210, 241

Neither, 14, 44, 191, 196, 222, 241, 252, 274

Netsah, Xxx, Xxxvii, 2, 5, 7, 24, 28, 198, 231

Neutral, Xxxii, 8, 18, 279

New Testament, 30, 37, 38, 39, 51, 55, 86, 100, 101, 102, 103, 104, 107, 116,
127, 201, 203, 204, 207, 251, 305

Night, 44, 49, 55, 56, 57, 68, 84, 95, 118, 141, 146, 175, 187, 203, 204, 232, 253

Nike, 72

Nile, 131

Nineveh, 173

Noah, 50, 85, 99

Nonexistent, 146, 187

North, 62, 63, 77, 79, 133, 136, 142

Nothing, Xxix, 123, 146, 187, 193, 214, 215, 216, 218, 226, 229, 254, 273, 288

Nothingness, Xxix, Xxxv, 225

Nourish, 241, 264, 273, 274

Number, Xlvi, Xlviii, 11, 15, 81, 86, 109, 122, 136, 163, 164, 169, 170, 171, 182, 223, 279, 282

Nurtured, 146, 274

Obey, 38, 117, 220, 255, 256, 280

Observation, 118, 241

Occult, Xxxi

Occupy, 125, 132, 152, 239, 247, 248, 252

Offering, 185, 283

Offspring, 97, 283

Oil, Xxxix, 61, 64, 71, 72, 91, 92, 117, 297

Old Testament, 36, 39, 80, 89, 100, 101, 104, 106, 107, 108, 176, 304

Olive, 61, 64, 71, 72, 90, 91, 92, 117

Olympia, 72

Omega, Xxix, 1, 15

Omnipotent, 273

Omnipresent, 144, 273

Omniscient, 273

Oneness, 4, 211, 214, 255

Open, Xli, 56, 117, 175, 181, 186, 234, 236

Opposite, 18, 109

Oppression, 87, 114, 240, 242, 249, 252, 283

Oral, Xlii, Xliii, 35, 37, 42, 77, 112, 176, 244

Order, Xli, 20, 38, 40, 42, 50, 65, 72, 124, 126, 128, 228, 253, 261, 262

Organism, Xlii, 42, 243, 244

Origin, Xxxii, 11, 29, 35, 62, 71, 82, 89, 90, 95, 96, 103, 129, 133, 135, 136, 185, 205, 238, 244, 254, 281, 282, 304, 305

Orthodox, Xxxi, 42, 206, 281, 301

Outside, Xxxi, 29, 81, 82, 122, 141, 223

Overcame, 147, 175, 276, 278

Overlaid, 64, 113, 243

Overthrew, 247

Overthrown, 174, 252

Oxen, Xxxii, 52, 59, 61, 62, 63, 64, 78, 80

Pacify, 235, 248

Paganism, Xxxi, 114, 190

Pain, 8, 10, 257, 274

Palace, 48, 75, 112, 176

Palestine, 177, 181

Parable, 106, 204

Paradise, 117, 193, 204

Paradox, 214

Parallel, Xxxii, 103

Participate, 81, 122, 248

Parts, 36, 63, 84, 99, 104, 109, 117

Partzufim, 27

Pass, Ix, Xlvi, 1, 35, 37, 42, 57, 77, 108, 138, 150, 173, 216, 237, 244, 275, 290

Passage, 35, 36, 101, 196, 237

Passionate, 209

Passover, 81, 122

Past, 118, 146, 181, 191, 199, 237

Path, Xxxiii, 25, 48, 66, 67, 147, 151, 201, 213, 235, 255, 263, 288, 291

Patience, Xxxvii, 78, 231

Patriarchs, 64

Paul, Xxxvi, Xliv, 10, 23, 32, 102, 103, 105, 114, 117, 145, 149, 150, 183, 189, 190, 192, 193, 194, 195, 196, 197, 198, 199, 201, 204, 206, 240, 241, 243, 276, 293, 303

Peace, 12, 23, 49, 92, 112, 127, 132, 143, 199, 242, 249, 284, 290, 293

Pentateuch, 135

Pentecost, 81, 105, 122

People, Xxxvi, Xxxvii, Xlii, 3, 54, 56, 62, 87, 102, 131, 132, 136, 137, 153, 181, 193, 194, 209, 212, 217, 218, 219, 225, 242, 244, 245, 247, 248, 250, 251, 252, 254, 256, 257, 280, 283, 284, 285, 287, 288, 290

Perceived, Xliv, 20, 23, 110

Perfect, 26, 38, 127, 137, 235, 274, 276, 277, 289

Period, 3, 36, 40, 48, 81, 87, 122, 132, 141, 178, 179, 246, 257, 276

Permitted, 193, 209

Persecute, 242, 282

Persia, 37, 38, 82, 89, 91, 96, 175, 176, 177, 178, 192, 203, 245, 246, 248, 253

Persist, 257, 291

Person, 96, 147, 149, 198, 214, 234, 276

Personal, Xxxi, Xli, Xliii, 1, 262, 275, 282, 284, 285, 288, 290

Perspective, 9, 73, 124, 203, 243, 244

Peter, Xliv, 114, 206, 220, 229, 258, 303, 304

Pharaoh, 65, 114, 115, 128, 129, 133, 173

Pharisee, 105, 192, 247

Pharmaceuticals, 281

Philip, 300

Philippians, 241, 290

Philistine, 138

Philo, 145

Philosophy, 3, 4, 73, 145, 146, 184, 192

Phoenician, 136

Phoenixes, 118, 119

Phrase, Xlii, Xlvii, Xlviii, 55, 100, 101, 102, 106, 108, 164, 240

Physical, Xxxii, 31, 50, 113, 151, 191, 196, 219, 240, 241, 244, 251, 273, 278, 279, 285

Picture, Xxxii, 39, 49, 105, 111, 127, 142, 149, 279

Pig, 87, 178, 246

Pilate, 224, 250

Pilgrimage, 179, 302

Pillar, Xxxii, 8, 9, 17, 18, 24, 27, 30, 31, 32, 44, 62, 141, 174, 278, 279

Pinnacle, 204

Pious, Xxxi, 241, 251

Pit, 96, 102, 209

Place, Xliv, 12, 13, 14, 17, 20, 22, 23, 42, 55, 65, 76, 87, 107, 109, 110, 114, 117, 118, 131, 142, 149, 153, 174, 175, 182, 189, 210, 223, 229, 233, 235, 243, 252, 259

Plagues, 104, 174

Plan, 11, 13, 219, 274

Plato, 73

Pleasure, 183, 189, 199, 255, 256

Poetry, 30, 35, 186, 187

Point, Xxxiv, Xlii, Xliv, 1, 12, 15, 50, 52, 63, 107, 190, 192, 250, 279

Polytheism, 114, 133, 142

Polytheistic, 128, 132, 136

Pompey, 247

Poor, 132, 220, 241, 242, 256

Portray, Xxxix, 20, 281

Position, Xxxvii, Xlviii, 247

Positive, 10, 171

Possible, 65, 74, 77, 80, 83, 84, 85, 89, 91, 100, 101, 104, 105, 106, 108, 119, 127, 128, 129, 133, 135, 138, 141, 152, 185, 192, 203, 204, 205, 206, 258, 289

Power, Xxx, Xxxiv, Xxxv, Xxxvi, Xxxvii, Xl, Xli, Xliv, Xlv, 3, 7, 10, 11, 13, 17, 18, 20, 28, 32, 40, 50, 57, 78, 87, 91, 105, 107, 113, 128, 151, 169, 173, 185, 188, 189, 211, 215, 216, 225, 227, 228, 232, 233, 239, 244, 255, 259, 260, 262, 273, 274, 275, 276, 278

Practical, 3, 4, 35

Practice, Xlviii, 3, 4, 73, 81, 122, 152, 164, 178, 194, 198, 206, 223, 303

Praise, 5, 142, 144, 185, 201, 259

Pray, Xli, 22, 30, 112, 117, 191, 214, 239, 254, 291

Prayer, Xl, Xliii, 3, 5, 9, 30, 31, 33, 43, 112, 115, 125, 128, 129, 130, 132, 181, 182, 190, 212, 246, 250, 254, 256, 263, 275, 279, 281, 289, 291

Preach, 114, 191, 193, 201, 240, 249, 252

Precious, 58, 72, 85, 230

Predestination, 105, 184, 236

Preference, 122, 249

Prepare, 22, 76, 106,

110, 111, 210, 221, 243, 297

Presence, Xxxviii, 31, 33, 78, 79, 93, 110, 111, 113, 149, 150, 197, 230, 232, 239, 241, 297

Present, 143, 203, 235, 243, 252, 273, 287

Preserve, 72, 99, 150, 290

Press, 299, 300, 301, 302, 303, 304, 305

Pressure, 213, 242, 290

Preventative, 3

Previous, Xliv, Xlvii, 54, 84, 151, 169, 170, 174, 204, 211, 237

Priest, Vii, Xli, Xlvi, 1, 36, 38, 39, 40, 42, 49, 50, 51, 71, 72, 73, 80, 81, 82, 91, 105, 109, 111, 112, 114, 121, 122, 123, 124, 125, 126, 127, 128, 133, 136, 137,

140, 152, 153, 176, 185, 189, 192, 194, 217, 235, 247, 248, 250, 292

Priesthood, 38, 50, 112, 115, 116, 121, 123, 246, 247

Primordial, 12, 32, 277

Prince, 111, 113, 117, 119

Process, Xxxv, 246, 263

Proclaim, Xxxvii, 41, 207, 241, 250, 286

Product, 14, 17, 45, 92, 147, 259

Prolong, 283, 284

Prometheus, 305

Promise, 141, 252, 287

Pronounce, Xlii, Xlv, Xlvi, 11, 139, 247

Proper, 22, 171, 260

Prophecy, Ix, 41, 50, 101, 102, 175, 190,

206, 223, 237, 251, 277

Prophet, 9, 17, 18, 19, 25, 32, 36, 54, 62, 73, 80, 89, 104, 135, 202, 210, 222, 230, 233, 249, 250, 253, 256, 264, 277, 281, 285, 304

Prophetic, 5

Prosper, 115, 283

Prospered, 275

Prosperity, 284

Prosperous, 274, 283, 293

Protect, 3, 5, 205, 247, 275, 287, 288

Protestant, Xxxi

Proverbs, Xxxv, 12, 13, 14, 147, 148, 149, 150, 225, 259, 260, 261, 265, 284, 285

Provide, Xlii, 51, 113, 133, 151

Psalm, Xxx, Xxxvii, Xxxviii, Xli, 9, 13,

39, 40, 42, 50, 101, 105, 108, 116, 126, 130, 182, 216, 230, 232, 251, 284, 289, 291, 297

Ptolemaic, 178

Ptolemy, 177

Punishment, 18, 205, 257, 286

Pure, 61, 63, 84, 87, 92, 184, 198, 240, 242

Purpose, Xlv, Xlviii, 163

Pyramid, 133

Quaked, 66, 75, 141

Queen, 30, 82

Qumran, 39, 111, 115, 125, 126, 127, 152, 153, 179, 190, 213, 217, 301, 303

Qur'an, 122, 123, 141, 203, 204, 206, 213, 243, 253, 255, 256, 257, 305

Ra, 128, 129, 132, 133

Rabbi, 112, 201, 217, 275

Rabbinic, 153

Rachel, 137

Radiance, 30, 69, 70, 233

Rain, 120, 132

Rainbow, 58, 85, 118

Rank, 20, 107

Raven, 205

Realize, 273

Realm, Xxxiii, 13, 18, 25, 101, 117

Reason, Xxxv, 3, 11, 14, 145, 147, 150, 185, 195, 215, 226, 236, 249, 252, 259, 260, 288

Rebel, 22, 110, 173, 178, 240, 246

Rebirth, 219, 291, 292, 293

Rebuild, 36, 38, 71, 90, 176, 239, 245, 246, 282

Rebuke, 47, 264, 265

Receive, Xxxvii, 1, 76, 112, 177, 189, 191, 219, 236, 254, 261, 288, 290, 292

Recent, 62, 71, 125, 202, 213

Recite, Xliii, 43, 51, 52

Recognize, Xxxviii, 107, 219, 230

Reconstructed, Xxxiv, 153

Record, 238, 301

Recovered, 36, 245

Red, 92, 104

Redemption, 30, 151, 198, 206, 235, 263, 264, 283

Refine, Xliii, 87, 198

Reflection, Xxxvii, Xxxviii, Xli, 26, 39, 72, 127, 142, 150, 211, 213, 231, 277, 289, 293

Reformation, Xxxi

Refuge, Xli, 139, 152, 237

Regent, 175, 176, 177

Region, 73, 177

Rehoboam, 173

Reign, 82, 103, 175, 239, 243

Rejection, 119, 125, 181, 219, 230, 263, 287

Rejoice, 118, 119, 221, 222, 229

Relate, Xxx, 145, 273, 304

Relationship, Xxx, Xxxi, Xli, 1, 4, 171, 189, 211, 234, 261, 275, 279, 282

Religion, Xxxi, 4, 38, 73, 91, 100, 115, 128, 129, 133, 135, 201, 202, 210, 239, 246, 281, 288, 290, 299

Religious, Xli, 1, 73, 100, 105, 107, 114, 124, 125, 129, 135, 152, 178, 181, 192, 194, 198, 214, 220, 241, 242, 245, 246, 250, 251, 254, 281, 283, 287, 288, 290

Remain, 13, 225, 227, 286

Remember, 121, 124, 130

Renew, Xxxiv, 291, 293

Repent, 78, 89, 239, 249, 252, 264, 285

Represent, Xxxii, Xxxiii, Xxxiv, Xxxv, Xxxvii, 13, 14, 15, 16, 18, 22, 24, 25, 30, 32, 57, 61, 64, 70, 71, 79, 80, 81, 84, 90, 91, 93, 105, 117, 122, 137, 212, 213, 224, 226, 229, 279, 289

Required, Xliii, 50, 182

Rescued, 10, 151

Research, 71, 115, 142

Resembled, Xxix, 49, 62, 64, 65, 79, 253

Reside, Xxxiii, Xxxiv, 17, 20, 23, 117, 119, 191, 224

Respect, 48, 67, 125, 202, 210, 241, 259, 261, 262

Responsibility, 263, 288

Rest, Xxx, Xxxviii, Xl, 9, 15, 25, 56, 117, 118, 174, 201

Restoration, Xxxvi, 91, 228, 239, 263

Restore, Xxxiv, 252, 257, 263, 289, 297

Resulting, 4, 178, 219, 246, 247

Resurrection, 194, 240, 243

Return, Xxxix, 30, 35, 36, 38, 40, 62, 82, 91, 101, 103, 106, 108, 133, 137, 175, 176, 243, 244, 245, 257, 262, 282

Reunite, Xxxix, 31, 262, 263

Revelation, Xxix, Xxxviii, Xxxix, Xli, Xlii, Xliii, 12, 20, 27, 37, 39, 55, 56, 58, 59, 62, 65, 72, 77, 80, 81, 83, 85, 89, 90, 91, 92, 95, 96, 97, 103, 104, 111, 112, 116, 141, 147, 171, 174, 179, 182, 191, 193, 198, 204, 205, 213, 221, 222, 227, 229, 231, 232, 274, 276, 281

Revere, 139, 202

Review, Xliv, 59, 84, 184

Reviled, 198, 227

Revived, 128, 258

Revolt, 91, 178, 246, 247

Riches, 105, 106, 116, 130, 204, 214, 220, 241, 284, 285

Right, Xxxiii, 5, 8, 9, 12, 24, 25, 28, 40, 41, 44, 53, 72, 76, 78, 87, 90, 92, 103, 109, 112, 118, 126, 127, 147, 148, 151, 213, 219, 233, 255, 256, 260, 261, 279, 285

Righteous, Xxxiii, 17, 47, 75, 76, 104, 114, 150, 182, 191, 204, 239, 240, 253, 254, 286, 293

Righteousness, Xxxiii, 49, 96, 111, 143, 182, 183, 199, 236, 242, 286, 297

Ritual, 3, 254

River, 56, 59, 70, 86, 175

Road, 9, 193, 276

Roar, 41, 51, 70

Robe, 20, 49, 55, 67, 72, 103

Role, 113, 287, 299

Rolled, 109

Roman, Xxxi, Xlvi, 3, 62, 72, 105, 113, 153, 177, 178, 179, 183, 184, 207, 213, 236, 239, 240, 245, 246, 247, 248, 250, 252, 258, 277, 283, 300, 304

Rome, 72, 125, 177, 239, 240, 247, 252

Room, 33, 40, 210

Root, 97, 136

Royalty, 10, 115

Rule, 87, 101, 104, 115, 126, 129, 173, 175, 177, 178, 192, 236, 240, 244, 246, 248, 251, 252, 257, 276, 283

Ruler, 55, 85, 116, 117, 120, 128, 132, 177, 252

Rules, Xlviii, 86, 103, 123, 287

Rumble, 58, 65, 141

Sabaean, 254

Sabbath, Xxxix, 39, 40, 55, 111, 120, 127, 190, 209, 246

Sacred, Xxix, Xxx, 30, 31, 95, 121, 151, 202, 253, 279, 304

Sacrifice, 39, 40, 80, 81, 82, 87, 111, 122, 127, 178, 196, 206, 235, 246

Sad, 117, 118, 151

Sadducee, 246, 247

Safety, 179, 265

Sages, 35, 36, 300

Sake, 31, 114, 297

Salem, 38, 49, 50, 51, 112, 115, 127, 137

Salvation, Xxxi, 8, 38, 147, 150, 151, 152, 181, 190, 194, 206, 207, 220, 240, 243, 255, 263, 282, 283, 284, 285, 286, 288, 290, 291, 292, 293

Samuel, 80, 81, 250, 251

Sanctify, 52, 143, 236

Sanctuary, 51, 62, 251

Sarai, 50

Sargon, 173

Satan, Xxxi, 20, 100, 106, 107, 215

Satanic, 3

Saved, 10, 113, 132, 150, 151, 176, 190, 194, 207, 282, 285, 286, 288, 289, 291, 293

Savior, Xxxv, 111, 176, 224, 276, 293

Scatter, 69, 87

Scepter, 72, 126

Scholars, 36, 72, 74, 80, 116, 121, 124, 128, 135, 140, 142, 152, 175, 192, 254, 258

School, 3, 4

Scientific, 71, 132, 304

Scribe, 22, 36, 89, 108, 176, 238

Scripture, Xl, Xli, 12, 36, 37, 40, 55, 61, 65, 81, 96, 102, 110, 121, 216, 221, 246, 281, 289, 301

Scroll, Xli, 115, 152, 301

Sea, 24, 39, 40, 44, 51, 58, 59, 61, 62, 63, 72, 85, 99, 111, 116, 125, 126, 130, 152, 174, 179, 213, 217, 303

Seal, 71, 84, 171, 279

Sealed, 87, 171

Search, 4, 38, 70, 90, 281, 282, 299

Seasons, 119, 120, 259

Seat, 12, 40, 41, 53, 55, 57, 64, 127, 150, 181, 230

Secret, Xli, Xlii, Xlv, Xlvi, 3, 42, 43, 58, 75, 85, 113, 125, 183, 185, 187, 198, 211, 216, 218, 227, 275, 276, 304

Sect, 125, 152

Seed, 188, 240

Sefer, Xli

Sefiroth, Xxxi, Xxxii, Xxxiii, Xxxiv, Xxxv, Xxxvi, Xxxviii, Xl, Xliii, Xliv, 2, 4, 5, 7, 8, 9, 11, 12, 13, 16, 17, 18, 24, 25, 26, 27, 29, 31, 32, 61, 71, 84, 116, 195, 197, 198, 212, 224, 225, 226, 227, 263, 277, 278, 280, 289

Seleucid, 153, 177, 178, 192, 246, 252, 283

Self, Xliii, 3, 17, 23, 63, 139, 151, 243, 248, 273, 275, 285, 288, 290

Semitic, 132

Senses, Xxxiii, Xxxviii, 23, 24, 188

Sensual, Xxxii, 2, 8, 24, 198

Separate, Xxxii, Xxxix, 11, 18, 23, 29, 49, 54, 117, 131, 185, 204, 206, 212, 214, 227, 234, 262, 274, 282

Seraphim, 55, 59, 119

Sermon, 185, 187, 202

Serpent, 164, 192, 205, 223

Servant, Xxxiv, 81, 90, 113, 117, 118, 122, 123, 125, 202, 215, 236, 237, 253, 256, 283

Severity, 2, 24, 32, 198

Shaddai, 109, 136, 137, 139

Shadow, 183, 297

Shamash, 79, 80

Shamayim, 23

Shame, 258, 285, 288

Shape, 13, 17, 63, 225

Sharia, 244, 288

Shatter, Xxxiv, 259

Sheep, 100, 106, 222

Shekinah, Xxxvii, Xxxviii, Xxxix, 11, 19, 25, 28, 30, 31, 32, 33, 109, 147, 212, 229, 230, 262, 275

Shem, Xlvi, 44, 169, 170

Sheni, 64

Shepherd, 106, 143, 184, 297

Shin, 15, 32, 105, 110, 164

Shine, 8, 16, 20, 29, 41, 48, 49, 67, 147, 218, 226, 262, 273, 277, 279, 289, 290

Show, 50, 58, 85, 123, 132, 141, 190, 221, 253

Sick, 241, 242

Siddhārtha, 215

Siege, 36, 174, 178, 245

Similar, Xxxi, 20, 28, 36, 50, 56, 57, 59, 61, 73, 79, 81, 85, 92, 97, 100, 102, 103, 104, 105, 106, 107, 113, 114, 116, 127, 128, 130, 139, 143, 174, 185, 203, 204, 205, 213, 223, 234, 237, 244, 255, 256

Simply, Xxxii, 3, 4, 47, 71, 73, 80, 89, 127, 135, 136, 147, 202, 211, 219, 235, 255, 261, 264, 265, 281, 285

Sin, 101, 102, 109, 114, 206, 234, 235, 236, 252, 273, 283, 285, 292

Sinai, 1, 30, 41, 42, 52, 103, 110, 112, 140, 141, 142, 255, 256, 280

Sing, Xli, 41, 52, 55, 104, 117, 118, 119, 120, 185, 275

Single, 52, 71, 80

Sisters, 184, 236

Sitting, 20, 58, 71, 85, 119, 124, 176

Slain, 83, 281

Slaughter, 174, 179

Slavic, 99

Sleep, 78, 79

Slightly, 123, 244

Slowly, 125, 153, 213

Snake, 164, 223

Snow, 49, 67, 84, 117

Soar, 52, 146

Society, Xlv, 3, 37, 100, 242, 282, 284, 287, 288, 290

Solar, 108, 153

Soldiers, 118, 119, 252

Sole, 99, 128, 130, 263

Solid, 62, 89, 105

Solomon, Xl, Xliv, 30, 59, 61, 62, 63, 64, 65, 71, 108, 121,

126, 135, 173, 174, 176, 245, 279

Son, Ix, Xxxvii, Xl, Xlvi, 10, 15, 16, 19, 28, 40, 49, 50, 57, 59, 84, 85, 95, 99, 100, 101, 103, 108, 110, 111, 112, 113, 121, 125, 127, 129, 136, 138, 140, 147, 149, 150, 152, 153, 164, 173, 175, 177, 178, 183, 184, 185, 186, 187, 188, 189, 195, 196, 203, 205, 206, 207, 209, 211, 212, 213, 214, 217, 219, 220, 223, 228, 229, 230, 232, 233, 234, 236, 240, 241, 247, 248, 250, 254, 256, 257, 259, 275, 276, 277, 279, 284, 286, 287, 289, 292, 293, 295

Song, 30, 39, 40, 51, 52, 108, 111, 118, 127, 132, 237

Sophocles, 73

Sorcerers, 37

Sorrow, 132, 300

Sought, 4, 152, 181

Soul, Xxxvi, 4, 147, 151, 195, 209, 226, 256, 262, 263, 264, 297, 303

Sound, 69, 132

Source, Xxxi, Xxxii, Xxxiii, Xxxiv, Xxxvi, 38, 39, 77, 83, 89, 95, 97, 99, 111, 125, 127, 205, 206, 217, 222, 228, 281

South, 62, 63, 69, 70, 79, 136

Southern, 80, 173, 245

Sovereign, 143, 239

Space, 23, 127, 274, 302

Spark, 13, 76, 120

Speak, 5, 10, 11, 43, 69, 76, 86, 103, 105, 106, 110, 123, 138, 141, 145, 174, 183,

191, 193, 195, 197, 199, 206, 218, 250, 253, 256, 303

Speculative, 3, 4

Speech, 131, 184, 264

Spheres, 11, 14, 24

Spirit, Ix, Xxx, Xxxvi, Xl, Xlii, Xliii, 4, 11, 13, 14, 15, 27, 48, 55, 57, 58, 65, 68, 70, 78, 79, 85, 86, 93, 100, 103, 105, 114, 145, 147, 149, 150, 182, 183, 187, 188, 191, 195, 199, 221, 225, 227, 234, 235, 236, 242, 260, 290, 291, 293, 295

Spiritual, Xxx, Xxxii, Xxxiii, Xxxiv, Xxxv, Xxxviii, 2, 3, 4, 8, 9, 10, 11, 13, 14, 15, 17, 25, 28, 29, 31, 73, 85, 101, 110, 117, 119, 125, 128, 145, 149, 151, 190, 191, 192, 195, 197, 211, 217, 224,

225, 239, 240, 243, 244, 255, 259, 275, 278, 279, 285, 300

Splendor, Xxxiii, Xxxviii, Xl, 2, 5, 7, 10, 24, 41, 48, 53, 67, 126, 198, 230, 231, 283

Split, Xxxi, 8, 89

Spoke, 12, 22, 103, 106, 123, 136, 217, 218, 224, 231, 233, 244, 250

Square, 170, 264

Stand, Xli, 12, 29, 40, 52, 62, 64, 69, 70, 76, 79, 83, 86, 87, 92, 93, 120, 183, 205, 218, 229, 249

Star, 15, 95, 97, 108, 279

State, Xliv, 151, 241, 243, 260, 262, 263, 300

Statement, 4, 108, 109, 115, 147, 178, 215, 237, 251

Statue, 71, 72

Stellar, 85, 117

Stir, 252, 288, 293

Stolen, 65, 137

Stone, 25, 42, 80, 96, 130, 143, 230

Store, 117, 284

Story, Xlii, 35, 38, 39, 47, 50, 51, 84, 95, 100, 105, 106, 107, 108, 113, 122, 123, 146, 175, 203, 204, 205, 214, 223, 253, 264, 273, 303

Straight, 25, 76, 111

Streams, 56, 58, 59, 67

Streets, 243

Strength, Xxxiii, Xxxvi, Xli, 8, 10, 18, 24, 27, 227, 238, 278, 284

Strive, Xxxviii, 1, 4, 143, 181, 199, 230, 274, 275, 289, 293

Strong, Xli, 4, 42, 44, 50, 57, 104, 105, 143, 145, 149, 150, 216, 223, 253, 262

Structure, Xxxi, Xxxiv, Xlvii, Xlviii, 129, 278

Student, Xlvi, 89, 275

Study, 4, 125, 132, 142, 192, 275, 303

Subject, 260, 276

Suffer, 8, 175, 237, 283, 288

Sufficient, 137, 139, 255

Sufism, 181

Sun, 18, 20, 24, 48, 49, 64, 67, 79, 104, 109, 115, 118, 119, 128, 130, 150

Support, 4, 9, 38, 72

Suppressed, 128, 178

Supreme, 86, 120, 128, 133, 138, 234

Surah, 253, 254

Surrounded, 52, 58, 66, 77, 152, 179

Survived, 115, 173, 251

Swoon, 258

Symbol, Xxxiv, Xxxix, 13, 15, 17, 80, 81, 90, 92, 126, 133, 192, 234, 279, 281, 302, 305

Synagogue, 39, 124, 217, 225, 246

Synoptic, 183, 190, 203

Syria, 72, 131, 136, 142, 177, 246

Tabernacle, 30, 53, 121, 152, 235

Tablet, 42, 80, 114

Talmud, Xliii, 43, 112, 217

Talmudic, 303

Tanakh, 36, 80, 89, 135, 248

Targum, 64

Tarnished, 202

Tartarus, 146, 187

Taurus, Xxxii

Teach, Xxix, Xxx, Xxxi, 1, 2, 3, 4, 17, 39, 51, 102, 105, 106, 124, 181, 183, 189, 192, 194, 198, 201, 202, 203, 204, 206, 207, 209, 210, 211, 212, 213, 214, 217, 219, 225, 238, 239, 241, 242, 243, 252, 254, 255, 256, 257, 258, 262, 275, 276, 277, 282, 284, 293

Teacher, Xlvi, 22, 42, 80, 106, 113, 124, 194, 198, 201, 220, 256, 257, 275, 291

Tema, 175

Teman, 142

Temperance, 18, 43, 199

Temple, Xliv, 9, 20, 30, 32, 36, 37, 38,

39, 40, 48, 51, 55, 61, 62, 63, 65, 66, 68, 69, 70, 71, 72, 73, 80, 81, 82, 87, 90, 91, 99, 104, 111, 121, 122, 123, 124, 125, 126, 135, 153, 174, 176, 178, 204, 205, 217, 234, 239, 245, 246, 247, 248, 275, 276, 282, 283,288

Temporary, 176, 282

Temptation, 215, 292

Ten Commandments, 42, 138, 141, 209, 246

Terah, 136

Testimony, 183, 219, 238, 286

Tetragrammaton, Xlv, 11, 86, 139

Theology, Xxx, Xxxi, 4, 14, 113, 133, 184, 186, 192, 203, 217, 304

Thirst, 182, 220, 242

Thomas, 206, 258

Thought, Xxix, 1, 3, 4, 10, 11, 20, 99, 107, 110, 190, 264, 302

Thousands, 41, 49, 53, 56, 63, 68, 80, 102, 103, 108, 118, 281

Throne, Xxxiii, Xxxiv, Xli, Xliv, 1, 9, 12, 17, 20, 22, 32, 35, 40, 41, 48, 49, 51, 52, 54, 55, 56, 57, 58, 59, 61, 62, 64, 65, 67, 68, 71, 72, 77, 78, 79, 83, 84, 85, 91, 93, 95, 102, 103, 104, 107, 111, 112, 119, 120, 127, 149, 150, 175, 176, 181, 204, 224, 251, 263, 276, 292

Thrown, 102, 104

Thunder, 58, 65, 132, 141

Tifereth, Xxx, Xxxvii, 2, 5, 7, 16, 17, 18, 19, 27, 28, 84, 198, 212, 221, 226, 228

Tikkun, Xxxiv, Xxxvi

Time, Xxxi, Xxxix, Xli, Xlv, 1, 11, 23, 32, 35, 36, 37, 38, 39, 40, 48, 49, 51, 56, 59, 68, 73, 77, 81, 82, 87, 91, 100, 101, 102, 103, 104, 108, 117, 119, 121, 122, 126, 127, 128, 129, 131, 133, 135, 136, 137, 138, 139, 141, 145, 171, 173, 174, 175, 176, 177,179, 192, 199, 203, 217, 223, 229, 233, 235, 237, 239, 245, 246, 247, 252, 254, 257, 259, 261, 262, 274, 275, 276, 282, 284, 285, 287, 288, 289, 291, 292, 302

Timothy, Xxxv, 150, 151, 197, 234, 287

Titus, 178, 245, 287

Today, Xxix, Xxxi, Xlvi, 3, 36, 38, 50, 91, 100, 124, 129, 132, 133, 135, 136, 137, 201, 202, 205, 233, 243, 279, 281, 282, 283, 288, 304

Toes, 81, 84

Tombs, 130, 131

Tongue, 66, 105, 120, 131, 204

Torah, Xlii, Xliii, Xliv, Xlv, Xlvi, Xlvii, Xlviii, 30, 36, 37, 42, 43, 80, 103, 112, 121, 124, 135, 141, 163, 165, 166, 172, 198, 214, 217, 227, 255, 273, 274, 275, 276, 299

Torn, 234, 235, 283, 302

Torso, 27, 84

Toth, 114

Touch, 109, 262

Tradition, Xliii, 1, 30, 82, 99, 121, 122, 124, 153, 181, 184, 192, 210, 243, 244, 275, 287, 303

Traits, Xliii, 146

Trance, Xliv, 263, 281

Transcend, 35, 113, 188, 274

Transfiguration, 53, 101, 106, 276

Transform, 22, 151, 246, 303

Translate, 11, 39, 86, 99, 145, 184, 187, 238, 299, 303

Treasure, 65, 240, 284, 301

Tree, Xxxi, Xxxii, Xxxiv, Xxxv, 8, 9, 16, 24, 26, 31, 32, 104, 117, 222, 278, 279

Tremble, 66, 75, 142

Triad, Xxxiii, Xxxiv, Xxxv, Xxxvi, Xxxvii, 8, 9, 11, 14, 15, 17, 226

Triangle, 15, 279

Tribe, 50, 97, 121, 122, 123, 152, 192, 274

Tribulation, 104, 179, 224

Trinity, 14, 15, 129, 191, 217, 238, 257, 279

Triumph, 97, 236

Troops, 23, 119, 126, 204, 253

Trouble, Xxxi, Xli, 210, 264

Trust, 210, 284

Truth, Xxxvii, 28, 183, 186, 190, 191, 199, 211, 213, 216, 231, 255, 257, 281, 287, 293

Type, Xliv, 152, 193, 211, 255, 285

Tyre, 61, 62

Ugaritic, 139

Ugliness, 10

Unbelieving, 231

Unblemished, 236

Unclean, 199, 236

Unconscious, 258, 263

Uncontaminated, 121

Understanding, Vii, Xxx, Xxxii, Xxxiii, Xxxv, Xxxvi, Xl, Xli, Xliii, 1, 2, 4, 5, 7, 10, 12, 13, 14, 17, 24, 30, 31, 32, 87, 147, 148, 150, 183, 188, 191, 197, 212, 217, 218, 219, 220, 225, 226, 227, 252, 259, 260, 261, 262, 263, 273, 290, 291

Underworld, 131

Unending, Xxxvii, 273

Unexplainable, 4, 12

Unfailing, 207, 219, 228

Unfinished, 133

Ungodly, 102

Union, Xli, 1, 11, 12, 14, 24, 25, 30, 31, 147, 181, 185, 197, 220, 259, 262, 264, 279

Unique, 45

Universal, 128, 238, 293, 303

Universe, 11, 112, 186, 233, 252, 305

University, 299, 300, 301, 302, 304, 305

Unknowable, Xxix, Xxxiv, 1, 190, 197, 224, 263

Unknown, 191, 206, 274

Unloose, 249

Unquenchable, 249

Unrighteousness, 183

Untouchable, 171

Upper, Xxxiii, Xxxv, Xxxviii, 25, 197, 226

Upright, 148, 204, 253

Upward, 66, 184

Ur, 136

Uriel, 124

Usher, 249

Ushma, 43

Utterance, 12, 16

Uzziah, 20, 55

Valley, 297

Value, Xlviii, 86, 164, 287

Vanquishes, 278

Vasiariah, 45

Vault, 41, 58, 68

Vav, 31

Vehuel, 45

Vehuiah, 45

Veil, 204, 234, 302

Verlag, 303

Verse, 55, 103, 186, 187, 237

Vespasian, 178

Vessels, Xxxiv, 20, 259

Vevaliah, 45

Victory, Xxxvii, 24, 28, 72, 112, 231

Vineyard, 240

Violence, 137, 202

Vipers, 152, 242

Viraf, 203, 253

Virgin, Xxxix, 123, 124, 202

Vision, I, Ix, Xxv, Xxvii, Xliv, 9, 20, 22, 28, 32, 35, 47, 48, 51, 52, 54, 55, 56, 57, 58, 59, 66, 67, 68, 69, 70, 71, 73, 75, 76, 77, 81, 83, 84, 85, 86, 89, 90, 91, 92, 102, 112, 116, 136, 193, 204, 209, 232, 252, 275, 276, 281, 302

Visionary, Xliv, 89, 263, 276

Visual, 85

Voice, 12, 41, 51, 52, 56, 69, 70, 110, 111, 118, 119, 120, 132, 148, 264, 299

Void, 146, 187, 189, 212

Volcano, 141

Vowels, Xlv, Xlvi, Xlviii, 139, 163

Wall, 44, 66, 175, 179, 264, 283

Wander, 138

Wandering, 121

War, 3, 152, 173, 177, 178, 202, 237, 245, 246

Warn, 16, 275, 285

Washing, 254, 293

Watchers, 100

Water, Xxxii, 8, 15, 32, 44, 59, 61, 62, 63, 66, 87, 106, 149, 179, 182, 183, 204, 220, 221, 235, 249

Ways, Xxxi, Xliv, 5, 26, 31, 83, 113, 115, 116, 233, 246, 264, 265, 285

Waywardness, 265

Weakness, 10, 196

Wealth, 215

Wedding, 3, 221, 229

West, 62, 63, 79

Wheel, 52, 76, 79, 118

Whirlwind, 47, 52, 53, 54, 57, 85, 264

Wicked, 81, 87, 102, 274

Wife, Xxv

Wilderness, 30, 111, 121, 125, 140, 164, 175, 181, 212, 223, 225, 255

Windstorm, 77

Wine, 38, 117, 137

Winged, 59, 72, 117, 118, 119, 120, 146, 187

Wisdom, Xxx, Xxxiii, Xxxv, Xxxvi, Xl, 2, 5, 7, 10, 12, 13, 14, 17, 24, 31, 36, 65, 114, 116, 130, 145, 147, 148, 149, 150,

151, 181, 182, 183,
184, 188, 189, 190,
191, 197, 199, 201,
225, 259, 260, 261,
263, 264, 265, 273,
275, 284

Wise, Xxxv, Xxxix, Xl,
87, 201, 248, 259,
261

Witchcraft, Xxxi, 3,
199

Withered, 119

Witness, 91, 92, 116,
219

Wives, 119, 138

Woke, 229

Wolves, 222

Woman, 123, 222, 279

Womb, Xxxv, Xxxvii,
13, 31, 106, 123,
126, 188, 212, 225

Women, Vii, 50, 107

Wool, 12, 19, 27, 28,
56, 59, 84, 85, 205

Word, Xxix, Xxxi,
Xxxvi, Xli, Xlii,
Xliii, Xlv, Xlvii, 14,
15, 42, 57, 59, 74,
85, 102, 105, 108,
115, 129, 130, 136,
137, 138, 139, 140,
141, 145, 146, 147,
149, 150, 164, 181,
183, 184, 185, 186,
189, 190, 198, 203,
205, 207, 213, 219,
223, 227, 238, 250,
251, 257, 276, 291

Work, Xlv, 71, 149,
209, 243

Works, Xxxi, Xxxv,
13, 99, 116, 130,
148, 199, 225

World, Xxxi, Xxxii,
Xxxiii, Xxxiv,
Xxxv, Xxxvi,
Xxxvii, Xxxviii,
Xliii, 2, 3, 4, 8, 10,
11, 13, 14, 17, 20,
22, 23, 24, 25, 30,
31, 33, 49, 64, 70,
71, 72, 77, 82, 84,
90, 93, 113, 115,

119, 125, 131, 147, 148, 149, 150, 152, 173, 181, 191, 192, 196, 197, 198, 199, 201, 202, 204, 206, 212, 213, 218, 219, 225, 226, 227, 230, 231, 234, 239, 240, 249, 250, 252, 253, 262, 273, 276, 277, 279, 281, 282, 284, 285, 287, 288, 289, 291, 293, 304

Worship, Xxxi, 128, 129, 132, 136, 140, 175, 215, 217, 234, 235, 283

Worthy, 215, 249

Wrath, 151, 199, 285, 287, 290

Wreaked, 173

Wreaths, 61

Wretched, 132

Writings, Xxix, Xxxvi, Xliv, Xlviii, 30, 36, 37, 39, 40, 48, 51, 54, 61, 62, 64, 65, 77, 79, 80, 89, 101,

102, 104, 105, 107, 110, 111, 113, 114, 116, 125, 131, 135, 163, 186, 189, 201, 203, 205, 209, 215, 250, 276, 286

Xerxes, 82

Yachid, 43

Yah, 5

Yahweh, Xlv, 11, 19, 27, 121, 139

Yamamoto, 301

Yearned, 249, 252

Yehuda, 305

Yehwah, Xlv

Yemen, 142

Yeminkha, 43

Yeshivat, 305

Yeshua, Xlvii, 111, 252

Yesod, Xxx, Xxxviii, 2, 5, 7, 8, 24, 28, 198, 230

Yesterday, 132

Yetzirah, Xxxii, Xxxiii, Xxxvii, 2, 8, 23, 24, 198

Yisrael, 143

Yoḥai, 109, 305

Yohwuh, Xlv

Yoke, 239

Zadok, 124

Ze'Ir Anpin, Xxxvii, 19, 26, 27, 28, 57, 84, 110, 195, 198, 212, 227

Zealots, 179

Zechariah, 32, 37, 70, 71, 81, 89, 90, 91, 92, 93, 122, 123, 124, 125, 205, 230, 237

Zen, 213

Zephaniah, 285

Zerubbabel, 71, 82, 90, 91, 176, 245, 247

Zeus, 59, 72, 113, 114, 178, 184

Zion, 126, 230, 283

Zipporah, 121, 140

Zoe, 185, 186

Zohar, Xxx, Xlvi, 86, 109, 223, 305

Zokhrei, 43

Zoroaster, 38

Zoroastrian, 91, 203, 204, 253

Zoroastrianism, 38, 130

Zur, 143

Index